New Frontiers in Translation Studies

Series Editor

Defeng Li, Center for Studies of Translation, Interpreting and Cognition, University of Macau, Macao SAR, China

Translation Studies as a discipline has witnessed the fastest growth in the last 40 years. With translation becoming increasingly more important in today's glocalized world, some have even observed a general translational turn in humanities in recent years. The New Frontiers in Translation Studies aims to capture the newest developments in translation studies, with a focus on:

- Translation Studies research methodology, an area of growing interest amongst translation students and teachers;
- Data-based empirical translation studies, a strong point of growth for the discipline because of the scientific nature of the quantitative and/or qualitative methods adopted in the investigations; and Asian translation thoughts and theories, to complement the current Eurocentric translation studies.

Submission and Peer Review:

The editor welcomes book proposals from experienced scholars as well as young aspiring researchers. Please send a short description of 500 words to the editor Prof. Defeng Li at Springernfits@gmail.com and Springer Senior Publishing Editor Rebecca Zhu: Rebecca.zhu@springernature.com. All proposals will undergo peer review to permit an initial evaluation. If accepted, the final manuscript will be peer reviewed internally by the series editor as well as externally (single blind) by Springer ahead of acceptance and publication.

Anna Maria Cipriani • Federico Milana

AI-Powered Corpus Translation Studies at Work

Exploring Early English Translations by Aphra Behn and her Contemporaries of Fontenelle's (1686) *Entretiens sur la pluralité des mondes*

Springer

Anna Maria Cipriani
UCL Centre for Translation Studies (CenTraS)
University College London
London, UK

Federico Milana
UCL Interaction Centre
University College London
London, UK

ISSN 2197-8689 ISSN 2197-8697 (electronic)
New Frontiers in Translation Studies
ISBN 978-981-95-5932-9 ISBN 978-981-95-5933-6 (eBook)
https://doi.org/10.1007/978-981-95-5933-6

This work was supported by Anna Maria Cipriani.

This Springer imprint is published by the registered company Springer Nature Singapore Pte Ltd.
The registered company address is: 152 Beach Road, #21-01/04 Gateway East, Singapore 189721, Singapore

Preface

This book aims to explore and develop an innovative methodology for Corpus Translation Studies (CTS), which utilises Generative Artificial Intelligence to facilitate the interpretative annotation and analysis of translated literary texts. Building upon recent advancements in natural language processing and machine learning, an AI-assisted framework has been developed to support the automated annotation of stylistic and ideological features in translation corpora. Its illustration is completed with its empirical application to a case study of the three earliest English translations of Fontenelle's *Entretiens sur la pluralité des mondes* (1686). These translations, which appeared in close succession between 1687 and 1688, provide a rich dataset for examining the interplay between translation strategies and historical, political, and epistemological contexts at a pivotal moment in English and European intellectual history.

The proposed approach is based on a hybrid model of translation analysis, where AI enhances rather than replaces human expertise. Drawing on large language models (LLMs), GenAI tools can assist researchers in identifying linguistic and extra-linguistic phenomena, such as emotional tone, rhetorical stance, cultural references, and stylistic variation, across translations. By leveraging automated annotation pipelines and AI-generated interpretive commentary, the book aims to streamline the traditionally labour-intensive processes of CTS while empowering analytical rigour. The ambition is to contribute to a renewed vision of CTS that integrates digital stylistics, contextual interpretation, and scalable machine reasoning in a coherent and human-centred framework.

The motivation for this study arises from two converging needs within the field of translation research. On one hand, manual annotation, while methodologically robust, is prohibitively time-consuming, limiting the scalability and reproducibility of studies that seek to analyse large corpora of texts. On the other hand, there is a pressing demand for empirical, historically grounded studies that can offer new insights into specific translations and their ideological positioning. In this area, AI tools offer a promising solution: they reduce the annotation burden, enhance the consistency of interpretations, and provide a degree of automation that allows researchers to test hypotheses on broader evidence.

From a methodological point of view, this book is a sequel to Cipriani's *Literary Digital Stylistics in Translation Studies* (2023), where an innovative approach to using a corpus is implemented to assess stylistic features, albeit at the cost of excessive manual annotations. The automated annotations introduced in this study dramatically reduced those costs. The obtained results bring to light previously unexplored dimensions of the three earliest English translations of Fontenelle's Entretiens. While the versions by William Domville (1687) and John Glanvill (1688), now largely neglected in modern scholarship, emerge as works of considerable and historical value, Aphra Behn's (1688) translation, proposed by an author, already well-known in Restoration England as novelist, playwright, and translator, reveals newly identified and distinctive features. By deploying AI to assist with the identification and categorisation of translation choices across Behn's text and its contemporaries, the research presented here contributes to a growing body of literature concerned with authorial intervention, stylistic transformation, and ideological mediation in early modern translation. At the same time, the study demonstrates how AI can serve as a productive partner in the complexity of historically oriented analyses.

The book is organised into six chapters. It begins, in Chap. 1, by contextualising traditional corpus-based translation studies, emphasising the significant role of annotation and alignment in close textual comparison in identifying translational shifts. Chapter 2 reviews AI's role in translation studies, highlighting significant contributions and current gaps. Chapter 3 details the study's methodological framework and the design of the AI-assisted annotation system. Chapter 4 presents the illustrative case study of Fontenelle's Entretiens and its early English translations within their historical context. Chapter 5 presents and comments on the empirical results obtained using the AI-powered methodology applied to translation data, sharing insights into style, culture, and interpretation. Chapter 6 concludes with reflections on AI-powered CTS in digital humanities and future research directions.

London, UK

Anna Maria Cipriani
Federico Milana

Acknowledgements

We wish to express our sincere thanks to Prof. Defeng Li, Series Editor of New Frontiers in Translation Studies, for having accepted our book proposal. Our appreciation extends to the whole editorial team of Springer, including Emily ZY Chen and Rebecca Zhu, for their professional handling through the whole publication process, from its initial stage to the final production.

We are always grateful to the anonymous reviewers who have provided their constructive comments and good suggestions contributing so much to the quality of this research.

Our heartfelt thanks go to each and every individual who is involved in the compilation of this volume.

Competing Interests The authors have no competing interests to declare that are relevant to the content of this manuscript.

Contents

Abbreviations

AGI	Artificial General Intelligence
AI	Artificial Intelligence
ALF	Average Lexical Frequency
API	Application Programming Interface
BERT	Bidirectional Encoder Representations from Transformers
CBTS	Corpus-based Translation Studies
CDTS	Corpus-Driven Translation Studies
CSS	Cascading Style Sheets
CTS	Corpus Translation Studies
DCR	Digital Close Reading
DH	Digital Humanities
DTS	Descriptive Translation Studies
EA	Encoded Annotation
EEBO	Early English Book Online
GAI	Generative AI
GenAI	Generative Artificial Intelligence
GPT	Generalised Pre-trained Transformers
HD	Hypothetico-deductive approach
HTML	HyperText Markup Language
ICT	Information and Communication Technologies
ID	Indirect Discourse
IIM	Implicit or Indirect Manipulation
IML	Interactive Machine Learning
JSON	JavaScript Object Notation
LDS	Literary Digital Stylistic
LIME	Local Interpretable Model-Agnostic Explanation
LLMs	Large Language Models
LS	Lexical Simplification
ML	Machine Learning
NCE	Non-Conforming Expressions
NLP	Natural Language Processing

NN	Neural Network
OCR	Optical Character Recognition
RLHF	Reinforcement Learning from Human Feedback
RNNs	Recurrent Neural Networks
RW	Explicitation as Re-writing
SC	Self-Censorship
SHAP	Shapley Additive exPlanations
SLM	Small Language Models
ST	Source Text
TEI	Text Encoding Initiative
TT	Target Text
TT1	Domville's (1687) English translation of Fontenelle's *Entretiens* (1686)
TT2	Glanville's (1688) English translation of Fontenelle's *Entretiens* (1686)
TT3	Behn's (1688) English translation of Fontenelle's *Entretiens* (1686)
TTC	Type-Token Curve
TTR	Type-Token Ratio
UP	Unused Proposition
W3C	World Wide Web Consortium
XAI	Explainable Artificial Intelligence
XML	Extensible Mark-up Language

List of Figures

List of Tables

Chapter 1
Introducing AI-Powered Corpus Translation Studies

Having great culture does not mean being intelligent.

Heraclitus (535–475 BC)

1.1 A New Frontier in Corpus Translation Studies

To the best of our knowledge, no empirical applications of generative artificial intelligence (GenAI) in corpus-based translation studies have been published to date. While the academic discourse acknowledges ongoing research developments, opportunities, and challenges in this area,[1] contributions are still largely theoretical or survey-based and do not provide concrete examples of published empirical applications. These and other recent studies have raised concerns about certain limits of GenAI in the context of literary analysis. Nevertheless, scholars increasingly emphasise collaborative frameworks in which researchers are not passive recipients of AI-generated output, but rather use active agents shaping the methodological and epistemological trajectory of the field (Incelli 2025).

AI's inherent limitations in fully grasping complex humanistic inquiries have been well-documented (Chan and Wong 2025). Yet, AI-enhanced literary analysis may contribute meaningfully to academic research by supporting tasks such as literary classification and providing new interpretive perspectives (Gomathi et al. 2025). While theoretical models acknowledge that a perfect computational solution to complex intellectual tasks is unattainable, it is generally accepted that solutions which are "good enough" in practice may still yield valuable results (Sagessenmann et al. 2025). From this perspective, the future of AI lies not in replacing human scholarship but in fostering a form of "co-intelligence" wherein human and artificial reasoning mutually enhance one another (Dedema and Ma 2024). By leveraging these results, we devised a "hybrid" AI-powered corpus translation studies (CTS) approach which combines human

[1] Among recent survey articles on corpus assisted translation studies, see Wu et al. 2025. The use of generative AI in corpus translation studies is discussed in Curry and McEnery (2025), Sun et al. (2025), Tekwa (2025), Xu and Huang (2025).

A. M. Cipriani, F. Milana, *AI-Powered Corpus Translation Studies at Work*,
New Frontiers in Translation Studies,
https://doi.org/10.1007/978-981-95-5933-6_1

expertise and efficient automation under our direction and supervision and applied it empirically to the historical case study of the three early English translations of Fontenelle's *Entretiens sur la pluralité des mondes* (1686). The following sections are aimed to introduce the main concepts that have led us to carry out this research.

1.2 From AI-Versus-Human towards AI-Plus-Human

Since the inception of AI, concerns about its impact on human labour and employment have provoked debates, fostering fears of job displacement across various skills and occupations. The literature often revolves around the theme "Man versus Machine," suggesting a conflicting substitution effect where machines replace human labour. In this view, humans are seen as passive agents adapting to advancing AI by seeking new opportunities. However, as Cao et al. (2024: 2) point out, little research has focused on how workers can leverage AI technology to enhance their potential. This possibility shifts the narrative from "Man versus Machine" to "Man plus Machine." Starting with the well-known experience of chess grandmaster Garry Kasparov being defeated by IBM's Deep Blue in 1997 and followed by multiple similar contests, the interest in such outcomes has decreased. But humans have not lost interest in the game or the machine (*Ibidem*). The encounter with Deep Blue was a catalyst for people like Kasparov to pioneer Man + Machine matches, where chess players equipped with AI assistance become "centaur" players competing against AI alone, remaining unbeaten so far. The story's moral is that if AI can help humans become better chess players, it can help more of us become better at many skilled jobs.

To support their argument, the authors developed a human-AI interaction model to predict stock market trends. They selected state-of-the-art Machine learning (ML) models to build their own AI analyst. Its performance was compared with that of a "centaur analyst" made by integrating human and machine in stock analysis. They observed that combining artificial intelligence with human expertise produces the most accurate forecasts by reducing errors that either humans or machines might have committed when working alone, and also benefiting from the synergies arising from their collaboration. (*Ibid.*: 18).

Human-AI collaboration is a well-established field in the literature on human-computer interaction, dating back to the 1950s. Research in this area focuses on rethinking machine learning algorithms and their interfaces in terms of human goals, contexts, and workflows (Gillies et al. 2016). To evaluate how non-expert users interact with ML, Milana et al. (2025) developed an interactive tool that enables users to train an ML model on their own manual annotation patterns in qualitative analysis to suggest additional generated annotations. The findings of a user study with 20 non-ML-expert participants reveal that the integration of generated annotations improved critical reflection of analytical processes, enabled new thematic insights, and encouraged the adaptation of interpretative stances. Particularly valuable were instances of disagreement between the user and the model, to which participants responded by revisiting their own analytical assumptions to either consider alternative interpretations or reinforce their original reasoning through more explicit justification. In these situations, users strongly perceived the influence of their own manual analysis, a concept usually identified as "reflexivity", which is one of the pillars of critical research practices in social sciences and humanities.

Insights into human-centred ML urging a reconsideration of the dichotomy between human and machine cognition are provided by Milana (2025). They challenge the narrative of adversarial comparison between ML systems and human judgment, suggesting instead a dynamic relationship in which human analysts and ML systems iteratively interact and shape their respective contributions. Effective human-AI collaboration thrives when epistemic boundaries, particularly those involving human interpretative agency, are preserved. In this perspective, certain boundaries should still be respected, such as the researchers' desire for automation, which has only developed their own codebook, as previously observed by Marathe and Toyama (2018). Users often favour tools that extend or complement their thinking rather than replace it entirely.

In qualitative research and corpus-based translation studies, analytical validity is grounded in transparency, reflexivity, and critical engagement with multiple meanings. Machine-generated suggestions can prompt reflective inquiry, especially when they differ from human-coded themes. Participants often viewed these dissonances as valuable opportunities to reassess assumptions, provide more nuanced justifications, or revise analytical categories. Reflexivity, central to interpretive social science, involves recognising the influence of social, cultural, and institutional contexts on knowledge production. Unexpected AI interpretations highlight the human analysts' assumptions and encourage them to reassess their knowledge.

ML models are particularly valuable when they help uncover unexpected (overlooked) patterns in data. In CTS, where translated texts are complex, the model acts less as an authoritative interpreter and more as a provocateur that encourages critical inquiry by offering new viewpoints or prompting a reevaluation of the text. Integrating AI into interpretive workflows should aim to support human-centred research. Instead of fully automating processes, "interpretive augmentation" occurs when AI suggestions are evaluated and adopted through thoughtful human judgment. This aligns with the view of AI as a collaborator in context-rich and value-driven research practices.

AI also adds value to analytics by supporting manual work, and broadening the user's perspective with new data insights. This is especially true in applications where well-defined ground truths are absent, such as in CTS, because interpretive flexibility and contextual understanding remain fundamentally human abilities that AI systems can augment but not replace. The AI model serves as a cognitive tool, complementing manual analytic practices by applying the user's reasoning patterns to new data. Instead of providing objective truth or authoritative classification, the model helps scale and challenge the analyst's perspective, enabling a deeper engagement with the focused material.

The integration of AI with human work is particularly significant in areas where analytical work is interpretative, subjective, and context-sensitive, such as CTS. In these contexts, the lack of stable, externally verifiable ground truths means that analysis is seldom about distinguishing between right and wrong answers. Instead, it involves the subtle negotiation of multiple, often competing interpretations, all informed by the historical, linguistic, and cultural specificities of the texts under examination.

As Milana (2025) argues, interpretive augmentation aligns with the humanities and social sciences, where meaning is co-constructed and context-dependent. AI can enhance human insights by offering alternative perspectives and highlighting inconsistencies. However, AI should support rather than replace human judgment, serving as a tool for reflection.

In this view, it turns out that AI is just a standard technology, rather than a potential superintelligence, as stressed recently by Narayanan and Kapoor (2025), computer scientists at Princeton, in a paper that has sparked international debate. They argue that AI should be seen as a typical technology, not a superintelligence. Their widely discussed paper suggests AI will gradually reshape labour by creating new roles, much like earlier technological revolutions. We support this view of AI as a tool to enhance work, noting, however, as those authors do, that AI adoption tends to lag behind its initial innovation timing. The present study shows that adopting GenAI in CTS demands the development of a multidisciplinary approach and ongoing human oversight. As Narayanan and Kapoor stress, AI can be error-prone without proper human supervision. Our findings confirm that incorporating GenAI takes time and that human involvement is essential to guide and monitor AI errors or imprecision, which often stem from issues in external training databases rather than inconsistency or hallucinations proper.

A standard limitation of GenAI arises from its reliance on aggregating information sourced from the datasets used for machine learning training, which may result in the omission of essential flaws or the amplification of particular strengths. Without appropriate supervision, AI-generated advice or suggestions may contain these inaccuracies, reflecting challenges similar to those found in current peer-review systems within academic publishing. In fact, GenAI often amplifies strengths and overlooks flaws due to biases in its training data. Without supervision, its outputs can reflect similar issues seen in academic publications, which are assumed to be correct and reliable only because they are peer-reviewed. However, this publication system is notoriously prone to frequent judgment errors of the first or second type, which consist, respectively, in the failure to recognise valid findings or the acceptance of mistaken results. In the present study, we show how, in previous work, GenAI offered overly positive feedback on Aphra Behn's translation of Fontenelle's *Entretiens*, echoing gender-biased and apologetic literature that exaggerated her skills while ignoring her mismatches from the intended text, but also failing to appreciate her real merits in performing certain universal functions as a translator.

This episode illustrates the double mediation of GenAI: first, by the biases inherent in its training corpus, and second, by its tendency to reproduce prevailing critical trends without the corrective of historical contextualisation (Table 1.1). This also highlights how GenAI is shaped by both its biased source material and prevailing ideological distortions of critical reviews, making it crucial for researchers to approach generative tools critically and compare algorithmic results with historical context and primary evidence. It underscores the importance of maintaining a vigilant, critical stance when employing generative tools for research, ensuring that the authority of algorithmic output does not obscure the necessity of hermeneutic judgment and the triangulation of evidence across primary texts, translation practices, and the broader intellectual context under study.

1.3 Addressing the Challenges of Multiple Mediations in the Use of Generative AI

The application of GenAI to corpus translation studies offers powerful opportunities but also raises significant epistemological and methodological challenges. One of the most critical is the phenomenon of *multiple mediations*. This refers to the pathway through which GenAI mediates knowledge, interpretation, and creativity: first, through the mediation of its underlying sources—training data, scholarly publications, and cultural discourses—and second, through the mediation enacted by the system itself when it synthesises, reformulates, or elaborates upon this material. The multiple layers of mediation, while potentially generating new insights, also increase the risk of distortion, bias, and misrepresentation. Understanding the manipulation structure is crucial for ensuring that GenAI can be employed responsibly and effectively in translation studies, as well as more broadly in the humanities and sciences.

Table 1.1 Some key limitations of GenAI vs human

Concept	Description
Biases embedded in its training data	GenAI reproduces the biases embedded in its training data, often amplifying dominant critical positions while overlooking flaws or minority perspectives
Apologetic scholarly narratives	The case of Aphra Behn's translation of Fontenelle demonstrates how GenAI's feedback can mirror apologetic scholarly narratives, exaggerate strengths and neglecting textual shifts or omissions
Double mediation	Double mediation occurs through biases in the training data and a tendency to echo current critical trends without historical context
Hermeneutic judgment	Critical vigilance and hermeneutic judgment remain essential: Scholars must triangulate GenAI outputs with primary texts and historical context to prevent distortions

1.3.1 *Primary Mediation: Data, Judgement, and Scholarly Filters*

The first layer of mediation occurs in the very constitution of the datasets from which GenAI systems learn. These systems are not neutral observers of language and culture but are profoundly shaped by the corpora that train them. In the context of translation studies, such corpora include published texts (themselves being acts of mediation in their own right between the source author and target audience, *e.g.*, Bedeker and Feinauer 2006, Núñez 2012, Gosetti et al. 2025), their critical reviews, and scholarly analyses. Each of these textual sources already contains embedded assumptions, interpretative frameworks, and cultural predispositions. For example, a translation produced in the seventeenth century may reflect the political, religious, or ideological biases of its time; later critical reviews may add apologetic or polemical tones depending on the reviewer's scholarly or cultural orientations and aims. Thus, the "primary mediators" are far from impartial: they are themselves the product of layered traditions of judgement and interpretation.

This primary mediation is particularly significant in the study of historical translations such as those of Fontenelle's *Entretiens*. The earliest English translators—Domville, Glanvill, and Behn—each approached the French text with distinct intentions, ideological filters, and rhetorical strategies. Their translations, later refracted through the secondary lenses of scholarly editions and interpretations, constitute the body of evidence on which both human researchers and AI systems must rely. As such, they cannot be divorced from the cultural and intellectual histories that produced them.

1.3.2 *Secondary Mediation: Generative AI as Elaborator*

The second mediation arises when GenAI itself processes these pre-mediated sources. Unlike traditional search engines or concordance tools, GenAI does not merely retrieve information but actively synthesises, paraphrases, and recontextualises it. In doing so, it may unintentionally amplify certain voices or suppress others, depending on patterns in the training data. For instance, if the scholarly literature disproportionately highlights Behn's pioneering role as a female translator while downplaying Domville's contribution, GenAI may reproduce this imbalance and present Behn's translation as more authoritative or innovative than the evidence warrants. Conversely, if apologetic narratives dominate the training material, GenAI may provide uncritical praise of certain translations while overlooking their limitations.

This secondary mediation is both a strength and a liability. It is a strength because it allows researchers to access synthetic insights that may not be immediately evident from raw data. It is a liability because the process of elaboration introduces additional opportunities for distortion, exaggeration, or oversimplification. Thus, what the researcher receives from GenAI is never a direct reflection of the primary mediators but a refracted, reconfigured representation subject to the system's own generative logic.

1.3.3 Sources of Bias in Multiple Mediations

Bias may enter at each level of mediation. At the primary level, biases stem from ideological pre-judgements, cultural selectivity, incomplete archives, and the uneven preservation of texts. At the secondary level, biases emerge from the design of the AI model, including the selection of training data, the weight assigned to particular kinds of discourse, and the algorithms used to generate text. These two levels of bias are not independent: distortions present in the primary mediation may be magnified or transformed by the secondary mediation, leading to compounded misrepresentations.

For instance, when examining Aphra Behn's translation of Fontenelle's *Entretiens*, modern scholarship has often emphasised her role as a pioneering woman writer, sometimes interpreting her translation choices through a gendered lens. If this interpretative trend dominates the corpus on which GenAI has been trained, the system may replicate and even exaggerate this perspective, generating commentary that is disproportionately apologetic or celebratory. The danger lies not only in reproducing existing scholarly biases but also in presenting them with the persuasive authority of machine-generated synthesis, which can obscure the contingent and partial nature of the underlying evidence.

1.3.4 The Role of the Critical Human Interpreter

Given these risks, the human researcher must assume a critical mediating role. Rather than treating GenAI outputs as neutral or authoritative, scholars must scrutinise them with awareness of the mediation structure. This requires training in identifying possible sources of bias, cross-checking AI-generated claims against primary evidence, and recognising when GenAI outputs align suspiciously closely with prevailing scholarly stereotypes. The effective use of GenAI in translation studies depends on cultivating what may be termed *critical AI literacy*: the ability to distinguish between genuinely new insights and the algorithmic recycling of existing discourses.

In this sense, the human researcher becomes a *further mediator*—an arbiter who filters, evaluates, and contextualises the outputs of GenAI. To perform this role effectively, the researcher must combine domain expertise with methodological prudence. The scholar must ask: Which voices are being amplified? Which perspectives are being minimised? How do the outputs reflect the biases of both the primary and secondary mediations? Only through such vigilance can the full benefits of GenAI be realised without succumbing to the distortions of multiple mediations.

1.3.5 The Active Reader

An *additional mediator* can be found in the reader, at the end of the process of cultural and textual transmission, whose interpretative agency transforms reading into a creative act. Rather than functioning as a passive recipient of meaning, an active reader engages critically and imaginatively with the text, often producing interpretations that diverge from the author's original message (Palmer 1983; Sarocco 2023). This role has been examined historically by Benedict (1996), who showed how Restoration and eighteenth-century anthologies shaped the construction of the modern reader, defining the terms in which texts were to be consumed. Virginia Woolf (1926) further refined this notion through her celebrated concept of the "common reader." In essays such as *How Should One Read a Book?*, she argued that reading demands ethical participation and critical judgment, where the reader enters into a silent yet *collaborative* dialogue with the text.[2]

Narrative techniques, such as Woolf's stream of consciousness, interior monologue, and deliberate ambiguity, invite readers to synthesise fragmented perspectives and construct coherence from apparent discontinuity. In doing so, readers are required not only to interpret, but also to mediate cultural nuances and implicit meaning. Thus, the act of reading extends beyond lexical comprehension to include contextualization, inquiry, and interpretative bridging. A reader encountering an unfamiliar cultural reference, for instance, must reconstruct its significance within the broader narrative and cultural framework. In this sense, the active reader emerges as a cultural mediator whose engagement is indispensable, particularly in periods of intellectual transformation such as the seventeenth-century scientific, social, and cultural revolutions, where new knowledge demanded equally dynamic forms of reception. In short, the active reader serves as a cultural mediator, creatively engaging with texts to interpret, contextualise, and bridge cultural meanings that extend beyond the author's original intent.

1.3.6 A Consolidated Comparative Overview of Multi-Layer Mediation

Multi-level literary translation studies examine the following four related agents interacting with objects produced by translators who themselves serve as mediators:

1 *Training Data and Human Reviewers (First Layer).*

The original corpora and critical voices that inform AI training act as a first layer of mediation. Human reviewers, often influenced by ideological, cultural, or disciplinary perspectives, indirectly shape the knowledge that GenAI reproduces. This layer introduces both scholarly insight and the possibility of systemic distortion.

[2] See also Reynier (2009) and Wussow & Gillies (2014: *vii-xii*). Intelligent reading is a close thematic issue with a number of publications under the same title of "*How to Read a Book*" (e.g., Adler and van Doren 1972), or "*How to Read Literature*" (e.g., Eagleton 2013).

2. *Generative AI (Second Layer).*

GenAI systems act as a secondary layer of mediation by producing outputs shaped by the training corpora and algorithms that structure their responses. While they provide rapid synthesis of knowledge, their outputs are inevitably conditioned by existing discourses and biases embedded in the data, leading to a risk of amplifying biases in dominant narratives.

3. *Critical Human Researcher (Third Layer)*

The scholar plays a decisive role in filtering and contextualising GenAI outputs. Through critical AI literacy—cross-checking claims, identifying bias, and situating interpretations—the researcher acts as arbiter, ensuring that insights are not merely algorithmic recycling but grounded in evidence and rigorous analysis.

4. *Active Reader (Fourth Layer)*

Ultimately, meaning is co-constructed by the engaged reader, who interprets, contextualises, and bridges cultural nuances. Drawing on traditions from historical analyses to Woolf's notion of the "common reader," the active reader transforms texts through creative participation, ensuring the cultural transmission and ethical reception of knowledge.

Together, these layers of mediation demonstrate that meaning is not a fixed entity transmitted from author to audience, but rather the outcome of complex processes of interpretation, technological filtering, scholarly critique, and readerly engagement.

1.3.7 Towards Minimising Biases in Research Outcomes

Strategies for mitigating the risks of dual mediation include *triangulating sources, maintaining transparency in methodological design, and cultivating reflexive awareness.* Triangulation requires comparing GenAI outputs with independent sources, such as original texts, alternative translations, or different scholarly traditions. Transparency entails documenting the queries posed to GenAI, the prompts used, and the contextual conditions under which outputs were generated. Reflexive awareness requires researchers to remain conscious of their own predispositions and how these may interact with GenAI's mediations.

Moreover, it is essential to frame GenAI not as a replacement for human judgement but as a collaborator whose contributions must be critically assessed and filtered. The qualities of impartiality, responsiveness, competence, and self-determination, which are necessary for any effective mediation, must be jointly embodied by both the human researcher and the GenAI system. The researcher brings expertise, historical awareness, and ethical responsibility; the system brings computational power, pattern recognition, and generative synthesis. Only in this partnership, guided by methodological vigilance, can unbiased or at least balanced outcomes be pursued.

1.3.8 Field-Specific Considerations: Translation Studies

The implications of multi-layer mediation are especially acute in translation studies, where questions of interpretation, cultural bias, and hermeneutic nuance are central. Unlike in purely technical domains, translation analysis involves grappling with ambiguities of meaning, context, and intention. Here, the risk of bias is magnified because the very object of study—the translation—is itself a product of mediation between languages and cultures. When GenAI intervenes, it adds yet another layer of mediation, potentially compounding or complicating the interpretative task.

Yet this complexity can also be productive. By surfacing patterns of emphasis, omission, or distortion, GenAI can prompt researchers to reflect more deeply on the interpretative traditions that shape their field. In this sense, even the biases of mediation can become objects of study, revealing the contours of scholarly discourse and its transmission into computational models. Rather than simply a problem to be solved, mediation can thus serve as a heuristic lens for interrogating both the history of translation and the epistemology of digital scholarship.

1.3.9 Prudence and Insight in the Face of Multi-Level Mediation

Dealing with the challenge of various mediations requires maintaining a delicate balance between prudence and insight. On the one hand, scholars must remain cautious, recognising the risks of compounded bias and misinformation. On the other hand, they must remain open to the generative possibilities that arise when human creativity interacts with machine synthesis. The key lies in recognising the specificity of the field under study, in this case CTS , and in developing strategies to extract unbiased or balanced information from both primary and secondary mediators. Tables 1.2 and 1.3 on addressing the distortions and risks in multiple mediations.

GenAI, when used reflexively and critically, can be a powerful ally in advancing translation scholarship. But its outputs must always be contextualised within the layered mediations that produce them. By acknowledging the nature of mediation and embracing the role of the critical human interpreter, researchers can turn a potential liability into an opportunity for methodological innovation and intellectual growth.

1.4 The Descriptive Translation Studies Using Generative AI

GenAI is particularly effective when applied to descriptive approaches that are devoid of predefined theoretical conditions. This feature is discussed in a recent paper by Novy-Marx and Velikov (2025), who emphasise the primary scientific

Table 1.2 Key insights on addressing biases in multiple mediation in GenAI for CTS

Concept	Description
Four layers of biases in multiple mediations	1. *Primary mediation*: Biases embedded in training data, translations, and scholarly discourse; 2. *Secondary mediation*: Biases introduced by GenAI's synthesis, elaboration, and reformulation. 3. *Third mediation*: Biases in critical human interpreter 4. *Fourth mediation*: Biases in active reading
Biases can compound across layers	Leading to distortions that amplify prevailing scholarly stereotypes, such as overemphasising certain translators (e.g., Aphra Behn) while minimising others
The human researcher acts as a critical third mediator	Exercising AI literacy to identify distortions, cross-check claims, and contextualise GenAI outputs within historical and textual evidence
The active reader acts as a "collaborating interpreter"	Transforming reading into a creative act
Mitigation strategies	Include triangulating sources, maintaining transparencies in methods, and cultivating reflexive awareness, ensuring that GenAI becomes one of the productive collaborators rather than an uncritical authority

Table 1.3 Comparative overview of roles, risks/limitations and contributions of multiple mediators

Mediator	Role	Risks/limitations	Contribution
Training Data & Human Reviewer (first mediator)	Shapes AI outputs through curated corpora and prior scholarly commentary	May embed ideological or cultural bias; can overrepresent dominant viewpoints	Supplies scholarly insights; ensures disciplinary grounding; contributes contextual richness to AI training
Generative AI (secondary mediator)	Produces initial interpretations based on training data; synthesises and generates responses	Dependent on pre-existing corpora; reproduces biases and dominant narratives; risks of algorithmic recycling	Provides rapid synthesis; expands access to knowledge; enables new forms of textual analysis
Critical human researcher (third mediator)	Acts as arbiter; filters, evaluates, and contextualises AI outputs through critical AI literacy	Risk of overlooking hidden biases; requires vigilance and domain expertise	Validates accuracy; identifies distortions; grounds analysis in evidence; ensures methodological rigour
Active reader (fourth mediator)	Co-constructs meaning; interprets, contextualises, and bridges cultural nuances	Interpretations may diverge significantly from the author's intent; cultural misunderstandings are possible	Enriches meaning; mediates cultural distance; enables ethical and creative engagement; ensures dynamic reception

character of reports based on descriptive approaches free of prejudicial, a priori hypotheses. They stress a point against modern academia, highlighting an inherent tension in the standard treatment of hypothesis formation. They claim: "We often view post-hoc theorising with suspicion, labelling it as 'HARKing' (Hypothesising After Results are Known) (Kerr 1998). The prevailing academic standard insists that researchers should first develop their theories and predictions and then test them against data" (*Ibid.*: 2).

The observed data are generally used in current research practice to test a pre-existing theory rather than to find theoretical explanations that better fit those observed data. By contrast, Novy-Marx and Velinox note that "few significant scientific discoveries in history have, however, adhered to this standard." They cite 1666 Isaac Newton as the most well-known (and winning) example, where he first observed an apple falling from a tree, and only afterwards, conjectured the extension of gravity to the entire Universe. We could also mention the counterexample of the (losing) competing theoretical hypothesis of vortices derived a few decades earlier by René Descartes from his *Principia Philosophiae* rather than observed data, to explain the dynamics of physical phenomena and the movements of celestial bodies in the sky. The Newtonian approach is generally characterised as inductive, while the Cartesian approach is described as deductive.[3]

Inductive reasoning draws general principles from specific observations, in contrast to deductive reasoning, which moves from general information to reach specific conclusions. Also known as bottom-up reasoning, the inductive method is essential for conjecturing hypotheses based on empirical data. By contrast, the deductive approach[4], also known as top-down reasoning, begins with a general theory, from which it develops hypotheses to be tested against observed data. Combining inductive and deductive approaches can lead us to a more comprehensive understanding of the research topic, where conjectures may be generalised within the scope of the case study. In this ambit, any theoretical assumption can be used only as a template for comparative analysis.

Academic discussions have long engaged in clarifying whether the main achievements stem from descriptions of specific data, leading to conjectures that are further reinforced or disproved, deterministically or stochastically, or from elaborating on or even disrupting the dominant theoretical paradigms.[5] In the present book, each relevant deductive feature or theoretical assumption is not tested, but is considered

[3] Kerr (1998: 197), however, clarifies that his negative judgement was not directed to HARKing *per se*, but only to its inappropriate presentations disguised as *ex ante* theorising rather than explicit *ex post* inferences: in his words, "[w]hen speaking of HARKing, I am not referring to traditional scientific induction. *Induction, inferring some relation or principle post hoc from a pattern of data, is also literary an instance of HARKing*. But when I refer to HARKing, I mean something more specific, presenting post hoc hypotheses in a research report *as if they were, in fact, a priori hypotheses*" (emphasis added).

[4] Also called "hypothetico-deductive (HD) approach" (*e.g.*, Hempel 1996; Kerr 1998: 196).

[5] The Copernican heliocentric model, endorsed by Descartes (vortex theory) and later by Newton (based on gravity), was definitively confirmed in 1838 when Bessel observed stellar parallax, evidence of Earth's orbit around the Sun that refuted the long-held geocentric view. Between 1736

as a possible data pattern taken as a template for comparison (Cipriani 2023: 17-18), while its occurrences in the examined text are recorded, processed quantitatively and discussed qualitatively using Even-Zohar (1978), Toury's (1980a, 1985, 1991a, 1995, 2012), and Hermans's (1999, 2014) descriptive translation studies (DTS) approach.

In translation studies, corpus models organised under the DTS approach, which is in practice not necessarily purely descriptive and devoted of pre-defined theoretical features, are further developed by distinguishing in prevalently bottom-up "corpus-driven translation studies" (CDTS) (Francis 1993; Tognini-Bonelli 2001: 84; Paul Baker 2010: 95; Zanettin 2012: 97), whereas those applying the top-down approach under specific hypotheses are defined as "corpus-based translation studies" (CBTS) (Baker 1996, Laviosa 2011, Zanettin, *Ibid.*, Saldanha and O'Brien 2013; Moratto and Li, 2023, Zhang 2025). A more nuanced general approach adopted in the present research, including both inductive and deductive methods, is termed "corpus translation studies" (CTS) (Kemppanen 2025). The present study complements the inductive analysis of target texts with deductively established universals used as descriptive templates. These universals are often described as "regularities" or "norms" and serve as reference points for literary features (*Ibid.*: 12, and section 1.5.2 below).

Contemporary GenAI based on LLMs suggests that the inductive method, which trains ML models on large observational datasets, outperforms peer-reviewed human research in predicting stock returns (Chen et al. 2025: 33–35; Novy-Marx and Velikov 2025: 18–19). However, this comparison is usually limited by a small sample size and minimal human-machine interaction. The present study illustrates how GenAI, assisting human analysis with minimal theoretical bias, can achieve superior performance compared to manual analog-centric approaches or trained machines alone.

1.5 CTS Empowered with Generative AI

As the methodological foundations of Corpus Translation Studies (CTS) continue to evolve, the integration of Generative Artificial Intelligence (GenAI) represents a significant step toward automating and enhancing tasks that have traditionally relied on manual scholarly labour. This chapter elucidates how GenAI can support CTS, focusing on preliminary annotation and alignment of texts, as well as interpretative comparative analysis of parallel corpora.

GenAI, underpinned by machine learning techniques, offers the potential to streamline the annotation process by generating markup in compliance with established encoding standards such as the Text Encoding Initiative (TEI) (2019). Using

and 1744, measurements of Earth's meridian arches disproved Descartes's vortex theory, instead supporting Newton's concept of gravity by showing Earth is flattened at the poles, not the equator.

XML or other markup languages, GenAI can assist researchers in transforming raw textual material into structured, annotated parallel corpora with increased speed and consistency. This support extends beyond mere technical facilitation: GenAI systems can also contribute interpretative suggestions, highlight recurrent patterns, and offer analytical comments that may prove valuable for critical analysis.

A distinguishing feature of GenAI's intervention lies in its capacity for parallel processing. Whereas human scholars typically engage in a sequential workflow, moving from text preparation to annotation, and then to analysis, GenAI can operate on multiple levels simultaneously. It can, for instance, generate annotations and perform semantic analyses simultaneously, enabling a degree of immediacy and responsiveness that makes it possible to conduct numerous iterative exploratory and confirmatory stages of the entire research process in a full machine-human collaboration.

The human researcher remains essential. As said above, GenAI is an auxiliary tool that augments the researcher's interpretative work. Integrating GenAI with CTS methods involves combining machine input and output with human evaluation. The contribution of GenAI can be described in relation to the research process, where GenAI assists in interpretation at various stages. The workflow for using GenAI as an assistant should follow the sequence of steps taken by a human analyst, since analysis and interpretation of specific features or literary semantics may require much more working time for a person than for GenAI.

1.5.1 The Adopted Tools of GenAI

At the current stage of GenAI, the primary tools of Generative AI in translation studies can be presented as follows in a non-specialist overview.

1. *Large Language Models (LLMs)*

At the heart of GenAI are currently Large Language Models such as ChatGPT, BERT, and similar systems. These models receive training through machine learning methods applied to extensive collections of textual data. Training focuses on learning language patterns, structures, and the human use of words and their meanings. Once trained, LLMs can generate coherent texts, make predictions about language use, and help in analysing translation patterns, including subtle differences between source and target texts.

2. *Prediction and annotation capabilities*

One promising application of LLMs in CTS is their ability to predict and apply annotations to new texts automatically. Smaller open-source models may be further refined through additional training on human-annotated data for specialised tasks, enabling researchers to develop customised solutions. General-purpose LLMs such as ChatGPT, Claude, or Gemini can be used directly due to their broad language knowledge and adaptability. Examples of what general-purpose and fine-tuned LLMs can automatically detect include:

(i) Translation shifts due to the divergence of the target text from the original in structure or meaning.
(ii) Incoherencies and contradictions within the translation.
(iii) Lexical gaps and semantic variations, such as when the translaton of a concept occurs in one language but not in another.

This capacity enables researchers to conduct fine-grained analyses of translated texts more efficiently than ever before.

3. *User-defined tags for annotation*

GenAI tools can work in tandem with user-defined tags, which are labels or markers that scholars assign to specific features in a text (e.g., "omission," "tense change", "literary feature"). After a model has been trained to identify these features, whether by fine-tuning or incorporating relevant examples in its prompts, it can autonomously assign appropriate tags and recommend new patterns that may not have been previously identified. This integration allows researchers to maintain consistency in their analysis while also benefiting from the model's ability to highlight patterns that may otherwise escape human notice.

1.5.2 Universals or "Regularities" of Literary Translation

One of the main objectives of literary translation studies is to examine various features that often characterise translated texts across all epochs, at least during the last two millennia, differentiating them from non-translated texts. These features were called "universals". As stated by Chesterman (2014: 84), "the quest for universals is no more than the usual search for patterns and generalisations that guides empirical research in general."[6] It responds to the question of how literary translation is made, leading to a more complete analysis of "what" and "why" of a specific work of translation (Steiner 2001). Previously, Chesterman (2000: 23) had noted that in many fields, including translation studies, "descriptive hypotheses are probabilistic rather than universal. So, they tend to have the feature Y; or, most instances of X have feature Y. This is obviously a weaker claim, and is therefore harder to falsify". Hermans (2007: 145–150) calls not for the general hypothesis but "thick" case studies which can be tested on other data by working top-down, testing general claims against particular cases, or bottom-up, generating potential generalisations from specific cases, or both directions (Steiner 2001). As Toury (2004: 28) claims, "One thing is certain: whatever we say, and whatever we do, 'hunting for regularities' is, and will always be, the name of the game".

[6] Chesterman (2014: 86–87) clarifies aspects that have been brought to caricatures of concepts and misunderstanding: "Our mistake has been to assume too quickly that the tendencies of regularities we have found might be 'universal'. True, to state a hypothesis in a maximally general form exposes it rapidly — and usefully — to the risk of counter-evidence, which should then lead to the increasing limitation of the scope of the hypothesis, or indeed to its rejection".

The concepts of universals were first introduced in Chomsky's (1965: 30) translation theory and Levý (1969). Even-Zohar (1978) defines "universals of literary contacts", complemented with Toury's (1980a: 130; 1980b: 65) "translation universal". Toury (2004: 29), however, preferred his terms of "laws" or "norms" to "universals" because it has "the possibility of exceptions built into it" within the polysystem theory (see also Toury 1991b: 51, 1995, 1999, 2012: 226).[7]

Norms are prescriptive within a social community and are described and analysed by DTS researchers. Toury distinguishes three main categories of translational norms: (1) *preliminary norms*, which regard the overall translation strategy and the choice of texts to be translated, (2) *initial norms*, which regard the translator being primarily source text-oriented or target culture-oriented, and (3) *operational norms*, which regard the single decisions made during the act of translation (Schäffner 1998: 6). The initial and operational norms are those that are relevant for the descriptive translation study of the present research.

Baker (1993: 244; 1996: 180) classifies Toury's (1978, 1980a: 130) universals/norms into four categories: *explicitation* of what is implicit in the ST, *disambiguation* and *simplification* of the source text, *normalisation* by "grammaticising" ungrammatical utterances in the source language and avoiding repetition of words, and *levelling out* by bringing the text "to gravitate around the centre of any continuum rather than move towards the fringes". Toury (1995: 16) further claims that

> the cumulative findings of descriptive studies should make it possible to formulate a series of coherent laws which would state the inherent relations between all the variables found to be relevant to translation [...] To be sure, the envisaged laws are everything but absolute, designed as they are to state the *likelihood* that a kind of behaviour or surface realisation would occur under one set of specifiable conditions or another. (Italics in the original)

Toury (2004: 24) himself clarifies his concept of probabilistic universals/norms: "For me, the issue [of probabilistic universals] is not one that could be resolved by saying either 'yes' or 'no'". Moreover, Toury (1995: 192) claims that "any *falsification* of a hypothesis would shed considerable light on its validity" (emphasis in the original). The methodology of DTS is free from a priori hypotheses, but it usually ends with ex-post hypotheses based solely on purely text-oriented observations.

[7] The concept of norms is addressed by scholars by Hermans (1991, 1996, 1999, 2014), Schäffner (1998), Brownlie (1999), Baker (2009), Munday (2016: 176–191), and Enríquez-Aranda (2016). Historical perspectives on universals and norms in polysystem theory can be found in works by Baker (1993: 242), Gentzler (2001 [1993]: 120, 129), Toury (2004), Chesterman (2010, 2014), Munday (2016: 184). Recent discussions are reviewed by Van Poucke (2019) and Albachten and Tahir Gürçağlar 2020.

1.5.3 Generation of Prompt for the Assisting Generative AI

The prompt checks if all specified rules are present and reviews their encoded annotations (EA) in tagged files of the source text (ST) and target texts (TTs). In the case of the present book (with Web sources shown in the respective footnotes):

ST: Fontenelle (1686), *Entretiens sur la pluralité des mondes*[8]
TT1: Domville (1687), *A Discourse of the Plurality of Worlds*[9]
TT2: Glanvill (1688), *A Plurality of Worlds*[10]
TT3: Behn (1688), *A Discovery of New Worlds*[11]

A custom-made software automatically generates and merges annotations on TT1, TT2, and TT3, adding new ones as needed to the reviewed texts. The output files are saved in both *xml* and *txt* formats. The title names *TT1.txt, TT2.txt, TT3.txt*, and *ST.txt* which are the respective input files of annotated texts in *txt* format, and *xml* format.

1.5.4 Digital Annotation with User-Defined Tags

Regularities, norms, or universals commonly found in literary translations are identified and tagged in the target texts (TT1, TT2, TT3) using XML/TEI guidelines, with reference to the source text. The study is operationalised using the digital corpus methods enhanced with the capabilities of the GenAI tools. As expected, these tools are effective at identifying extralinguistic features, such as literary categories. Our empirical study considers the following six user-defined regularity tags: *IIM* (implicit or indirect manipulation with mismatches, shits or errors), *SC* (Self-censorship), *LS* (Lexical simplification), *RW* (Re-writing for explicitation), *UP* (Unused proposition with arbitrary added text), *NCE* (Non-conforming expression resulting in domestication bringing home the ST).

[8] https://gallica.bnf.fr/ark:/12148/btv1b86207579/f40.planchecontact (downloaded 17 August 2024).

[9] *A discourse of the plurality of worlds* written in French by the most ingenious author of the *Dialogues of the Dead*; and translated into English by Sir W.D., Knight. Alternate title: *Entretiens sur la pluralité des mondes*. Dublin: Printed by Andr. Crook and Sam. Helsham, for William Norman, 1687. (Early English Books Online (EEBO) on the ProQuest platform. The Huntington Library records—unstructured.)

[10] *A plurality of worlds* translated by Mr. Glanvill from the source text written in French by the author of the *Dialogues of the dead*; translated into English by Mr. Glanvill. Alternate title: *Entretiens sur la pluralités des mondes*. London: Printed for R. Bentley and S. Magnes, 1688. (Early English Books Online (EEBO) on the ProQuest platform. Cambridge University Library records—unstructured.)

[11] *A discovery of new worlds* from the French, made English by A. Behn. London: Printed for William Canning, 1688. (English Books Online (EEBO) on the ProQuest platform. University of Illinois Library records—unstructured.)

1.5.5 Annotation Format

The texts have two layers of annotations following the XML/TEI (2019) rules:

First layer: Paragraph markers <P001, <P002>, etc. (ended with </P001>, </P002>, etc.)
Second layer: Literary markers <IIM>, <SC>, <LS>, <RW>, <UP>, <NCE> (ended with corresponding markers) used to identify each occurrence of the respective universal or regularity.

1.6 Text Alignment in Translation-Driven Corpora

The distribution of translation features in the target texts, as previously defined, may be presented and analysed in conjunction with the corresponding source text within a parallel, translation-driven corpus. This process involves extracting and aligning relevant textual segments in a parallel fashion. Parallel corpora are most effective when the source and target texts are accurately aligned. This alignment enables the precise matching of textual units between the two versions, facilitating retrieval via parallel concordancers. Aligning these texts makes parallel corpora more usable by allowing access to corresponding segments simultaneously. Accurate text alignment is particularly essential in descriptive translation studies, where precise pairing of source and corresponding target text segments allows observation-based comparative analysis. This process faces challenges due to linguistic differences, translation strategies, and text genres, especially in literary and historical contexts (Oakes and McEnery 2000; Simard et al. 2000; Zanettin 2012: 154–174; Fantinuoli and Zanettin 2015: 1–10; Saldanha and O'Brien 2013: 79–80).

Effective use of parallel corpora in translation studies relies on accurately aligning bilingual texts. Proper alignment matches source segments with their corresponding targets, facilitating meaningful analysis. While sentence-level comparison is standard, alignment also occurs at paragraph, clause, or word levels. It faces challenges like language structure differences, punctuation, translator choices, and stylistic features, especially in complex literary or historical corpora, making a blend of automated methods and human review essential. Paragraph or clause alignment may be necessary when translations diverge from source boundaries.

Automated algorithms often match paragraph and sentence counts, which is effective for technical texts but less so for literary or journalistic materials, where sentence restructuring occurs, traditionally requiring manual adjustments for accuracy. However, the recent advances of GenAI promise to work on semantics with additional interpretative functions. One of the aims of the present study is to assess the quality of AI-powered automated annotation & alignment services, including semantic aspects. Bi-texts interleave aligned source and target segments, facilitating both manual review and automated processing in close reading at the micro level. Segmentation often relies on punctuation, which, however, can be unreliable across languages with differing punctuation conventions. The text alignment used in this study is based on paragraphs as units of text. Text segments containing single universal features are identified within aligned paragraphs. The segments of the target text containing these features can then be extracted and aligned with corresponding source texts for direct comparison.

1.7 Generative AI-Assisted Close Reading

The emergence of GenAI is also opening new methodological avenues in the close reading of literary translations. Traditionally, close reading involves an attentive and detailed analysis of a text, with particular emphasis on its linguistic texture, rhetorical strategies, and interpretative layers. When this process is applied to literary translations, the complexity multiplies: the researcher must not only engage with the target text but also consider its relationship with the source, the translator's choices, and the broader historical and cultural context. GenAI has the potential to assist this intricate process in ways that complement, but do not replace, the human researcher's intellectual and interpretative agency. Four key areas of AI-assisted close reading are described in the following respective subsections, and a concluding section illustrates the value and limitations of this hybrid approach.

1.7.1 Enhancing Accessibility and Clarity of Complex Literary Texts

Many literary works, particularly those from earlier periods or from culturally distant traditions, employ dense and elaborate prose styles. Complex syntax, archaic vocabulary, and culture-specific allusions can create substantial barriers for both general readers and scholars engaging with the text in translation. GenAI can serve as a powerful tool for linguistic mediation, providing paraphrases, simplified restatements, or structural breakdowns of complex passages.

In the context of translation studies, this capacity is particularly advantageous when working with literary works that employ rhetorical flourishes, long, periodic sentences, or interwoven subordinate clauses. For example, when analysing a seventeenth-century prose translation of a philosophical dialogue, a GenAI model can reframe the passage in contemporary language while retaining its core meaning. This allows the researcher to confirm their own Interpretation of the translator's rendering or to identify possible ambiguities that merit closer examination.

Crucially, the accessibility that GenAI provides does not imply a dilution of literary value; rather, it allows the scholar to alternate between a simplified paraphrase for clarity and the original for stylistic appreciation. In effect, it acts as a preliminary decoding step, facilitating deeper engagement with the nuances of the translation.

1.7.2 Rapid Contextualisation of Historical and Cultural Backgrounds

Close reading of translated literature cannot be divorced from the historical, political, and cultural frameworks within which both the source and target texts were produced. Traditionally, acquiring this contextual knowledge demands extensive archival research, consultation of historical scholarship, and, often, interdisciplinary study. GenAI can offer an immediate overview of relevant historical and cultural contexts by synthesising large amounts of publicly available information, thus accelerating the researcher's preparatory phase.

For instance, when examining a translation produced during a politically turbulent period, GenAI can provide syntheses of the prevailing political ideologies, censorship practices, and intellectual currents that might have influenced the translator's choices. While such summaries cannot replace the depth and reliability of historical research, they can highlight pertinent areas for further scholarly inquiry. In this way, GenAI functions as a contextual scaffolding tool, allowing the researcher to situate translation shifts within broader socio-cultural dynamics without losing time in the initial orientation stage.

In the field of early modern translations, where textual meaning is often strongly intertwined with period-specific scientific, religious, or philosophical debates, this rapid contextualisation can be invaluable. It enables the scholar to formulate hypotheses about the translator's strategies and to identify which contextual factors warrant more rigorous, source-based investigation.

1.7.3 Identifying Literary Devices in Translation

One of the most demanding aspects of close reading is the recognition and interpretation of literary devices, such as metaphor, allegory, alliteration, irony, and intertextual references. In translation studies, the challenge is compounded: the researcher must assess whether the device is preserved, transformed, or omitted in the target text, and to what effect.

More specifically, as pointed out by the historians of philosophy of science, translation does not differ from the usual scientific explanations: in a translation, one must *choose* which aspect of the previous and/or rival scheme *to retain* and which *to abandon* (e.g., Gilles and Giorello 1993: 369). If we still want to progress, we must recognise that there are *more ways* to achieve progress, at least for those of us who live after *1984*. This requires parties to acknowledge the positive cycle between translation-understanding and tolerance, whereas strict orthodoxy leads to stagnation. Successful scientific advancement and accurate cognitive translation rely on reciprocal recognition between parties and thorough evaluation of contexts.

GenAI models that are fine-tuned for literary analysis can help identify rhetorical figures, stylistic patterns, and features in both source and target texts, providing a systematic, "out-of-the-box" evaluation of the respective strategic choices. By identifying context-related metaphors, symbolic motifs, or recurring thematic structures, the model can simultaneously function as an automated annotator and an explainer, while drawing attention to areas that warrant closer human scrutiny.

For example, suppose a metaphor in the source text draws on culturally specific imagery, for example, maritime navigation in a seafaring culture. In that case, the GenAI might flag its rendering in the target text, noting whether it was retained, domesticated, or replaced. This pre-analysis can save working time and help the researcher focus on translation shifts of high interpretative significance.

Importantly, GenAI's identification of literary devices is not infallible and is prone to over-interpretation or misclassification, especially when dealing with subtle irony or culturally encoded symbolism. For this reason, its role should be understood as suggestive rather than definitive, guiding the human scholar toward potential areas of interest rather than delivering authoritative conclusions.

1.7.4 Preserving Human Subjectivity while Enriching Interpretation

Literary analysis, and by extension the analysis of literary translation, is inherently subjective. Researchers bring a unique interpretative lens shaped by their scholarly background, personal experiences, and theoretical orientation. Far from replacing this subjectivity, GenAI-assisted close reading can enhance it by supplying supplementary layers of textual insight.

When human researchers engage with a text, their reading is shaped by a series of individual conditions, including prior knowledge, intuition, interpretative and ideological priorities. GenAI may serve as an interlocutor in this process, offering alternative readings, pointing out overlooked nuances, or suggesting connections to broader thematic or intertextual networks. This interaction can stimulate scholars to re-evaluate their assumptions or to integrate new dimensions into their analysis.

The result is a hybrid interpretative model in which human and machine perspectives are merged. The human scholar remains the primary arbiter of meaning, critically evaluating and selectively incorporating GenAI's suggestions. This approach has the potential to amplify the richness of the analysis: the AI offers breadth of coverage and speed, while the human scholar ensures depth, originality, and critical rigour.

1.7.5 *The Hybrid Approach: Opportunities and Limitations*

The combination of human interpretative insight and GenAI's computational capacities represents a promising paradigm for literary translation studies. In practice, this hybrid model might involve the following workflow: the scholar conducts an initial close reading, prompts GenAI for clarification or identification of specific features, compares these outputs against their own observations, and refines the analysis accordingly.

This iterative exchange can reveal specific translation shifts, contextual influences, or stylistic consistencies that might otherwise go unnoticed. It is well-suited for exploratory research phases, where the aim is to map potential analytical avenues before committing to a final interpretative framework.

However, caution is necessary. GenAI outputs should be carefully checked for accuracy, as the model can generate convincing but incorrect statements, especially in areas such as history or literary analysis, without even falling into erroneous information, inconsistency, and "allucinations". Moreover, reliance on AI-assisted readings should never substitute the scholar's engagement with primary sources, nor should it override the interpretative responsibility that defines humanistic inquiry.

1.8 Final Remarks

The illustrative application of Generative Artificial Intelligence (GenAI) presented in this book focuses on the case study of three early English (re)translations of Bernard Le Bovier de Fontenelle's *Entretiens sur la pluralité des mondes* (1686). This example represents not merely an incremental development in research practice, but a significant step toward the full digitalisation of literary Corpus Translation Studies (CTS). Until recently, certain core analytical activities, notably textual annotation, alignment, and fine-grained comparative analysis, were considered the exclusive domain of manual scholarship, requiring painstaking, time-intensive human engagement. By using GenAI, these tasks can now be conducted, at least in their preliminary stages, in digital form, thereby reducing the reliance on traditional analogue methods while opening new possibilities for scalability, speed and replicability.

This transition, however, does not imply a marginalisation of human scholarship. On the contrary, as has been emphasised throughout this chapter, digital applications demand a different but equally intensive mode of human involvement. The role of the researcher shifts from one of exclusive manual execution to that of methodological designer, critical evaluator, and interpreter. GenAI may automate specific processes, but the analytical value of its outputs depends on the human scholar's capacity to define precise research questions, evaluate the quality of automatically generated results, and integrate computational findings into coherent interpretative frameworks. The expected outcome of this new division of labour is not only an increase in overall productivity and efficiency, but also an expansion of the scope and ambition of the research itself.

In practical terms, the illustrative empirical study presented here encompasses all major phases of corpus-based research. These include the acquisition of high-quality digital texts; their structuring, management, and processing; the execution of quantitative stylistic profiling; and the conduct of both descriptive and interpretative qualitative analyses. Central to this methodology is the management of parallel corpora, specifically source and target texts aligned for direct comparison, and the application of DTS to assess translation shifts, strategies, and patterns. The integrated approach ensures that empirical data collection is not separated from interpretative reasoning, but rather that each stage informs the next in a cyclical process of hypothesis formation, testing, and refinement.

This approach is more complex than the traditional CTS due to the specific historical and intellectual context of the examined case. The three English translations under examination were produced against the backdrop of profound socio-cultural, political, scientific, and philosophical transformations in seventeenth-century Europe. These include the Scientific Revolution, the shifting political structures in the years surrounding the Glorious Revolution, and evolving literary tastes in Restoration England. Analysts face the challenge of interpreting texts separated from us by both language and nearly four centuries of cultural and epistemological change.

In this respect, the integration of GenAI tools marks a genuine paradigm shift. The scale and speed at which relevant contextual information can now be retrieved, synthesised, and cross-referenced far exceed the capabilities of pre-digital scholarship. Careful prompting and validation now allow tasks that once took months of archival work to be completed much faster. This does not diminish the need for depth and accuracy; indeed, it heightens the scholar's responsibility to interrogate sources, verify claims, and recognise the inherent stochastic nature of both human- and machine-generated knowledge. The incomplete and probabilistic character of GenAI outputs mirrors, in many respects, that of human scholarly interpretation, where conclusions are also contingent and subject to frequent revision.

To mitigate the epistemological risks associated with relying on a single analytical framework, whether human or artificial, the present study adopts a pluralistic and collaborative approach. We have assembled a research team that utilises three distinct AI systems (OpenAI's ChatGPT, Anthropic's Claude, and Google's Gemini), each with its own architecture, training data, and analytical strengths. By subjecting the same aligned texts to multiple AI-driven examinations, we create a triangulated dataset that allows for the cross-validation of observations and the identification of both convergences and divergences in interpretation. This methodological redundancy serves as a safeguard against the idiosyncrasies or blind spots of any one system, much as various peer reviews of research outcomes from the scientific community (hopefully) serve to strengthen traditional scholarly arguments.

The outcome of this process is a copious body of data, far more than could be exhaustively analysed or presented within the confines of a single book. For this reason, the discussion that follows will be selective, presenting representative examples that illustrate key methodological points, analytical findings, and interpretative possibilities. At the same time, the dataset of output files, along with detailed methodological documentation, will be made accessible online, allowing interested readers to explore the material in its entirety, replicate analyses, and develop their own interpretations. In this way, the project not only aims to advance knowledge but also to support open, replicable, and collaborative digital humanities research.[12]

References

Adler, Mortimer J. and Charles Van Doren. 1972. *How to Read a Book*. New York and London: Simon & Schuster.

Albachten, Berk Özlem, and Şehnaz Tahir Gürçağlar. 2020. Retranslation and Multimodality: Introduction. *The Translator* 26 (1): 1–8.

Baker, Mona. 1993. Corpus Linguistics and Translation Studies. Implication and Application. In *Text and Technology: In Honour of John Sinclair*, ed. M. Baker, G. Francis, and E. Tognini-Bonelli, 233–252. Amsterdam: John Benjamins.

Baker, Mona. 1996. Corpus-based translation studies. The challenges that lie ahead. In *Terminology, LSP and Translation*, ed. H. Somers, 175-186. Amsterdam: John Benjamin.

Baker, Mona. 2009. *Critical Concepts: Translation Studies*. London/New York: Routledge.

Baker, Paul. 2010. Corpus Methods in Linguistics. In *Research Methods in Linguistics*, ed. L. Litosseliti, 93–116. London: Continuum.

Bedeker, Laetitia, and Ilse Feinauer. 2006. The Translator as Cultural Mediator. *Southern African Linguistics and Applied Language Studies* 24:133–141.

Benedict, Barbara M. 1996. *Making the Modern Reader: Cultural Mediation in Early Modern Literary Anthologies*. Princeton, NJ: Princeton University Press.

Brownlie, Siobhan. 1999. Investigating Norms. In *Translation and (Re)location of Meaning*, ed. J. Vandaele, 7–21. Leuven: CETRA.

Cao, Sean, Wei Jiang, Junbo Wang, and Baozhong Yang. 2024. From Man vs. Machine to Man + Machine: The Art and AI of Stock Analyses. *Journal of Financial Economics* 160 (October): 103910.

Chan, Cecilia Ka Yuk, and Hannah Y. H. Wong. 2025. Assessing the Ability of Generative AI in English Literary Analysis Through Bloom's Taxonomy. *Discover Computing* 28:127.

Chen, Andrew Y., Alejandro Lopez-Lira, and Tom Zimmermann. 2025. Does Peer-Reviewed Research Help Predict Stock Returns? *arXiv* WP: https://arxiv.org/pdf/2212.10317v6.

Chesterman, Andrew. 2000. A Causal Model for Translation Studies. In *Intercultural Faultlines: Research Models in Translation Studies I: Textual and Cognitive Aspects*, ed. M. Olohan, 15–28. Manchester: St. Jerome.

Chesterman, Andrew. 2010. Why Study Translation Universals? *Acta Translatologica Helsingiensia* 1:38–48.

Chesterman, Andrew. 2014. Translation Studies Forum: Universalism in Translation Studies. *Translation Studies* 7 (1): 82–90.

Chomsky, Noam. 1965. *Aspects of the Theory of Syntax*. Cambridge, MA: The MIT Press.

[12] The Web page displaying the aligned annotated ST and TTs with explanations has been generated with a custom-made software. Interested readers may access the annotated full texts used in this study by visiting the website https://fmilana.com/TranslationAnnotator with all materials available online for further research.

Cipriani, Anna Maria. 2023. *Literary Digital Stylistics in Translation Studies*. Singapore: Springer Nature.

Curry, Niall, and Tony McEnery. 2025. The Past, Present, and Future of Corpus and Translation Studies. In *Routledge Handbook of Corpus Translation Studies*, ed. Defeng Li and John Corbett. London: Routledge.

Dedema, Meredith, and Rongqian Ma. 2024. The Collective Use and Perceptions of Generative AI Tools in Digital Humanities Research: Survey-Based Results. *ArXiv WP*. https://arxiv.org/abs/2404.12458.

Eagleton, Terry. 2013. *How to Read Literature*. New Haven and London: Yale University Press.

Enríquez-Aranda, Mercedes. 2016. Translation Norms in the Light of Practical Research in Literary Translation. *Onomázein* 33:88–106.

Even-Zohar, Itamar. 1978. Universals of Literary Contacts. In *Papers on Poetics and Semiotics*, ed. B. Hrushovski and I. Even-Zohar. Tel Aviv: University Publishing Projects.

Fantinuoli, Claudio, and Federico Zanettin. 2015. Creating and Using Multilingual Corpora in Translation Studies. In *New Directions in Corpus-Based Translation Studies*, ed. C. Fantinuoli and F. Zanettin, 1–10. Berlin: Language Science Press.

Francis, Gill. 1993. Corpus-Driven Approach to Grammar. Principles, Methods and Examples. In *Text and Technology. In Honour of John Sinclair*, ed. M. Baker, G. Francis, and E. Tognini-Bonelli, 137–156. Amsterdam: J. Benjamins.

Gentzler, Edwin. 2001. *Contemporary Translation Theories*. Revised 2nd ed. Clevedon: Multilingual Matters Ltd.

Gillies, Donald and Giulio Giorello. 1993. *Philosophy of Science in the Twentieth Century. Four Central Themes*. Oxford, UK and Cambridge, MA.

Gillies, Marco, Fiebrink Rebecca, Tanaka Atau, Garcia Jérémie, Bevilacqua Frédéric, Heloir Alexis, Nunnari Fabrizio, Mackay Wendy, Amershi Saleema, Bongshin Lee, d' Alessandro Nicolas, Tilmanne Joëlle, Kulesza Todd, and Baptiste Caramiaux. 2016. Human-Centred Machine Learning. In *Proceedings of the 2016 CHI Conference Extended Abstracts on Human Factors in Computing Systems*, 3558–3565.

Gomathi, R. D., J. Murugan, P. Kavitha, and B. S. Gomathi. 2025. AI-Driven Literary Analysis: Exploring the Impact of Artificial Intelligence on Text Interpretation and Criticism. *Journal of Machine and Computing* 5 (2): 1124–1139.

Gosetti, Valentina, Paul Gibbard, and Alistar Rolls. 2025. Translation Nation: Literary Translation as Cultural Mediation in Australia. *Forum for Modern Language Studies* 61 (2): 129–137.

Hempel, C. G. 1996. *Philosophy of Natural Science*. Englewood Cliffs: Prentice Hall.

Hermans, Theo. 1991. Translational Norms and Correct Translations. In *Translation Studies: The State of the Art*, ed. Kitty M. van Leuven-Zwart and Ton Naaijkens, 155–169. Amsterdam: Rodopi.

Hermans, Theo. 1996. Norms and the Determination of Translation: A Theoretical Framework. In *Translation, Power, Subversion*, ed. R. Alvarez and M. Carmen-Africa Vidal. Clevedon/Philadelphia/Adelaide: Multilingual Matters.

Hermans, Theo. 1999. *Translation in Systems. Descriptive and System-Oriented Approaches Explained.* 1st edition. Manchester: St Jerome.

Hermans, Theo. 2007. Literary Translation. In *A Companion to Translation Studies*, ed. P. Kuhiwczak and K. Littau, 77–91. Clevedon, UK: Multilingual Matters.

Hermans, Theo. 2014. *Translation in Systems. Descriptive and System-Oriented Approaches Explained*. 2nd edition. London and New York: Routledge

Incelli, Ersilia. 2025. Exploring the Future of Corpus Linguistics: Innovations in AI and Social Impact. *International Journal of Mass Communication* 3:1–10.

Kemppanen, Hannu. 2025. Empirical and Quantitative Approaches to Corpus Translation Studies. In *Routledge Handbook of Corpus Translation Studies*, ed. Defeng Li and John Corbett. London: Routledge.

Kerr, Nobert L. 1998. HARKing: Hypothesising After the Results Are Known. *Personality and Social Psychology Review* 2 (3): 196–217.

Laviosa, Sara. 2011. Corpus-Based Translation Studies: Where Does it Come from? Where Is It Going? In *Corpus-Based Translation Studies*, Research and Applications, ed. A. Kruger, K. Wallmach, and J. Munday, 13–32. London/New York: Bloomsbury Academic.

Levý, Jiří. 1969. *Die literarische Übersetzung - Theorie einer Kunstgattung*. Trans. Walter Schamschula. Frankfurt/Bonn: Athenäum.

Marathe, Megh, and Kentaro Toyama. 2018. Semi-Automated Coding for Qualitative Research: A User-Centered Inquiry and Initial Prototypes. In *Proceedings of the 2018 CHI Conference on Human Factors in Computing Systems*.

Milana, Federico. 2025. *Evaluating Interaction with Machine Learning Text Classifiers and Interpretability Techniques*. PhD dissertation. London: University College London.

Milana, Federico, Enrico Costanza, Mirco Musolesi, and Amid Ayobi. 2025. Understanding Interaction with Machine Learning Through a Thematic Analysis Coding Assistant: A User Study. *Proceedings of the ACM on Human-Computer Interaction* 9 (2): 1–35.

Moratto, Riccardo, and Defeng Li. 2023. Introduction. In *Advances in Corpus Applications in Literary and Translation Studies*, ed. R. Moratto and D. Li. Abingdon, UK and New York: Routledge.

Munday, Jeremy. 2016 [2012, 2008, 2001]. *Introducing Translation Studies. Theories and Applications*. 4th ed. London/New York: Routledge.

Narayanan, Arvind, and Sayash Kapoor. 2025. *AI as Normal Technology*. New York: Night First Amendment Institute at Columbia University.

Novy-Marx, Robert, and Mihail Z. Velikov. 2025. *AI-Powered (Finance) Scholarship. NBER WP. 33363*. Cambridge, MA: National Bureau of Economic Research.

Núñez, Kenneth Jordan. 2012. Literary Translation as an Act of Mediation Between Author and Reader. *Estudios de Traducción* 2:21–31.

Oakes, Michael P., and Anthony Mark McEnery. 2000. Bilingual Text Alignment: An Overview. In *Multilingual Corpora in Teaching and Research*, ed. S. P. Botley, A. M. McEnery, and A. Wilson, 1–37. Amsterdam/Atlanta: Rodopi.

Palmer, Richard E. 1983. Postmodern Hermeneutics and the Act of Reading. *Notre Dame English Journal* 15 (3): 55–84.

Reynier, C. 2009. Woolf's Ethics of Reading and Writing. In *Virginia Woolf's Ethics of the Short Stories*, C. Reynier, 90–110. Houndmills/Basingstoke/New York: Palgrave Macmillan.

Sagessenmann, Jan, Thilo Stadelmann, Andrew Davison, and Oliver Dürr. 2025. Assessing Deep Learning: A Work Program for the Humanities in the Age of Artificial Intelligence. *AI and Ethics* 5:169–200.

Saldanha, Gabriela, and Sharon O'Brien. 2013. *Research Methodologies in Translation Studies*. London: Routledge.

Sarocco, Susanna. 2023. The Collaboration Between Writer and Reader. In *Plato, Diagrammatic Reasoning and Mental Models*, ed. S. Sarocco, 17–35. Cham: Springer.

Schäffner, Christina. 1998. The Concept of norms in translation studies. *Current Issues in Language and Society* 5(1-2): 1-9.

Simard, Michael, George Foster, Marie-Luise Hannan, Elliott Macklovitch, and Pierre Plamondon. 2000. Bilingual Text Alignment: Where Do We Draw the Line? In *Multilingual Corpora in Teaching and Research*, ed. S. P. Botley, A. M. McEnery, and A. Wilson, 39–64. Amsterdam/Atlanta: Rodopi.

Steiner, Erich. 2001. How (Translated and Otherwise Interlingual) Texts Work Is our Way into What, Why and to What Effects. *Target* 13:343–348.

Sun, Sanjun, Kanglong Liu, and Riccardo Moratto. 2025. Introduction: Navigating the Paradigm Shift-Translation Studies in the Age of AI. In *Translation Studies in the Age of Artificial Intelligence*, ed. S. Sun, K. Liu, and R. Moratto. London: Routledge.

Tekwa, Kizito. 2025. Artificial Intelligence, Corpora, and Translation Studies. In *The Routledge Handbook of Corpus Translation Studies*, ed. Defeng Li and John Corbett. London: Routledge.

Tognini-Bonelli, Elena. 2001. *Corpus Linguistics at Work*. Amsterdam: John Benjamin.

Toury, Gideon. 1978. The nature and role of norms in literary translation. In *Literature and Translation*, ed. J.S. Holmes, J. Lambert & R. van den Broeck, 83-100. Leuven: ACCO.
Toury, Gideon. 1980a. *In Search of a Theory of Translation*. Tel Aviv: The Porter Institute for Poetics and Semiotics, Tel Aviv University.
Toury, Gideon. 1980b. Equivalence and Non-equivalence as a Function of Norms. In *Search of a Theory of Translation*, ed. Gideon Toury, 63–71. Tel Aviv: The Porter Institute for Poetics and Semiotics, Tel Aviv University.
Toury, Gideon. 1991a. What Are Descriptive Studies into Translation Likely to Yield Apart from Isolated Descriptions? In *Translation Studies: The State of the Art*, ed. K. M. van Leuven-Zwart and T. Naaijkens, 179–192. Amsterdam: Rodopi.
Toury, Gideon. 1985. A rationale for descriptive translation studies. In *The Manipulation of Literature: Studies in Literary Translation*, ed. T. Hermans, 16-41. London and Sydney: Croom Helm.
Toury, Gideon. 1991b. Experimentation in Translation Studies: Achievements, Prospects and some Pitfalls. In *Empirical Research in Translation and Intercultural Studies*, ed. Sonja Tirkkonen-Condit, 45–66. Tübingen: Gunter Narr.
Toury, G. 1999. A Handful of Paragraphs on "Translation" and "Norms". In *Translation and Norms*, ed. C. Schäffner, 9–31. Clevedon: Multilingual Matters.
Toury, Gideon. 1995. *Descriptive Translation Studies and Beyond*. 1st edition. Amsterdam and Philadelphia: John Benjamins.
Toury, Gideon. 2012. Descriptive Translation Studies and Beyond. 2nd edition. Amsterdam and Philadelphia: John Benjamins..
Toury, Gideon. 2004. Probabilistic Explanations in Translation Studies: Welcome as They Are, Would they Qualify as Universals? In *Translation Universals: Do They Exist?* ed. A. Mauranen and P. Kujamäki, 15–32. Amsterdam: John Benjamins.
Van Poucke, Piet, and Guillermo Sanz Gallego. 2019. Retranslation in Context. *Cadernos de Traduçao* 39 (1): 10–22.
Woolf, Virginia. 1926. How Should One Read a Book? *The Yale Review* 16(1): 32-44 (often cited as 41-52 in digital reprints). Reprinted in a standalone edition with an introduction and an afterword by Sheila Heti. London: Renard Press, 2021.
Wu, Kan, Defeng Li, and Victoria Lai Cheng Lei. 2025. Corpus-Assisted Research on Translator Style. In *Routledge Handbook of Corpus Translation Studies*, ed. Defeng Li and John Corbett. London: Routledge.
Wussow, Helen, and Mary Ann Gillies. 2014. *Virginia Woolf and the Common(Wealth) Reader*. Liverpool: Liverpool University Press.
Xu, Han, and Yujie Huang. 2025. Corpus-Based Translation and Interpreting Studies in the Age of AI: Innovations and Challenges. In *Translation Studies in the Age of Artificial Intelligence*, ed. S. Sun, K. Liu, and R. Moratto. London: Routledge.
Zanettin, Federico. 2012. *Translation-Driven Corpora: Corpus Resources for Descriptive and Applied Translation Studies*. Manchester: St. Jerome.
Zhang, Xiaomin. 2025. Corpus-Based Studies of Explicitation. In *Routledge Handbook of Corpus Translation Studies*, ed. Defeng Li and John Corbett, 254–268. London: Routledge.

Chapter 2
Literary Digital Stylistics in Corpus Translation Studies

We belong to the school that says that falsehood is everywhere mixed with truth and resembles it to the point that no criterion allows us to judge and decide with certainty.

Marcus Tullius Cicero (106–43 BC)

2.1 Introduction

The introduction of generative artificial intelligence (AI) into Corpus Translation Studies (CTS) represents a significant methodological advancement, particularly when aligned with the practices of (digital) corpus stylistics applied to literary texts, in short *Literary Digital Stylistics* (LDS). Over the last three decades, CTS has established itself as a central approach within the field of Translation Studies by documenting recurrent linguistic and stylistic tendencies in translated texts through corpus-based methodologies (Baker 1993, 1995, 1996, 2000; Zanettin 2011, 2012, 2013; Bernardini and Kenny 2020; Curry and McEnery 2025). At the same time, the field of LDS has extended corpus methods to address interpretative and cultural questions in literary analysis, thereby expanding the scope of stylistics beyond the purely linguistic (Zanettin 2011, 2013; Hu and Xie 2017; McIntyre and Walker 2019; Huang 2021; Cipriani 2023; Wu and Li 2025; Wu et al. 2025).

Generative AI provides a bridge between these traditions by enabling the processing of vast textual data, generating interpretative hypotheses, and assisting in complex annotation tasks. It offers scalable solutions to long-standing challenges, such as annotating stylistic shifts, aligning parallel corpora, and detecting recurrent expressive patterns across translators' works. By integrating the computational efficiency of AI with the interpretative depth of literary stylistics, scholars are now able to investigate translation not merely as linguistic substitution but as an embedded cultural practice that leaves systematic stylistic traces (Kenny 2001; Mahlberg 2013). The convergence of these disciplines signals a new phase in translation research, where AI-enhanced tools mediate corpus-driven evidence and interpretative insight.

A. M. Cipriani, F. Milana, *AI-Powered Corpus Translation Studies at Work*, New Frontiers in Translation Studies,
https://doi.org/10.1007/978-981-95-5933-6_2

Despite this promise, a substantial gap remains in the literature: the application of AI tools to the systematic study of style in translated texts has not yet been fully realised within CTS. Existing scholarship in digital stylistics has explored narrative perspective, characterisation, and voice primarily through manual annotation and interpretative close reading (Semino 2007, Herrmann et al. 2015). Similarly, descriptive translation studies have advanced the documentation of universals, such as explicitation or simplification; however, their methodologies have remained heavily reliant on manual corpus analysis (Toury 2012; Bernardini and Kenny 2020; Hu and Zheng 2025). What is notably absent is a consistent operationalisation of AI to capture both linguistic and extra-linguistic stylistic features in translation, particularly those involving interpretative categories such as self-censorship, domestication, or narrative reframing, and shifting focus from formal linguistic features to functional style (as suggested in Cipriani 2023; Wu and Li 2025; Wu et al. 2025).

While advances in natural language processing and large language models have shown promise in related fields, translation scholarship still lacks empirical studies that harness these technologies for stylistic inquiry. Addressing this lacuna is essential for advancing our understanding of translators' stylistic fingerprints, their cultural embeddedness, and the broader dynamics of literary translation as a form of interpretative practice (Jiménez-Crespo 2017). Before outlining the AI enhancement of the CTS with LDS, this chapter provides a brief review of the main features of the LDS approach as presented in Cipriani (2023).[1]

2.2 The Approach of Literary Digital Stylistics

The integration of stylistics into corpus-based approaches to translation has become a defining concern in contemporary Translation Studies. While traditional stylistics in linguistics has long been concerned with the systematic study of language patterns, the subfield of literary digital stylistics has extended these methods to address interpretative and cultural questions arising in literary translation. Within this framework, CTS not only investigates recurring linguistic tendencies in translated texts but also seeks to capture the broader extra-linguistic and interpretative dimensions of literary style. This dual orientation is particularly relevant when dealing with translated narrative literature, where stylistic shifts may alter narrative perspective, the representation of emotional states, or the overall structuring of complex situations.

Mona Baker's (2000) pioneering reflections in her "Towards a methodology for investigating the style of a literary translator" remain foundational in this regard. She advocates a grounded and realistic approach that situates style not merely in overt linguistic interventions but in recurring expressive patterns observable across a translator's work. She acknowledges the elusiveness of the concept:

[1] For a review of Cipriani (2023), see Ping (2024).

> The notion of style is very difficult to define even in established disciplines such as literary criticism and stylistics (Wales 1990: 435). [...] I understand style as a kind of thumb-print that is expressed in a range of linguistic—as well as non-linguistic—features. (*Ibid.*: 245)

Baker thus proposes to define the translator's style as a "matter of patterning", that is, as a constellation of recurring choices that mark the translator's habitual mode of expression. This conceptualisation provides a productive basis for studying literary translation. Yet, it remains relatively general and calls for further methodological refinement, particularly in its limited exemplification of how non-linguistic features might be captured.

The question of how to unify linguistic and extra-linguistic components in translation analysis has prompted dialogue with broader sociological theories of practice. Toury (2012: 68) links his concept of translational "norms" with Bourdieu's notion of habitus (1972), a conceptual bridge first proposed by Simeoni (1998). This perspective encourages an understanding of style not merely as an individual idiosyncrasy, but as a socially situated practice —an ingrained disposition shaped by cultural, institutional, and historical contexts. Translators' characteristic patterns of expression can thus be read as manifestations of habitus, located at the intersection of individual agency and collective constraint.

From this vantage point, style is observable in the text both as linguistic behaviour and as a mode of writing embedded in broader cultural practices. Corpus-based methodologies have provided tools for systematically documenting such stylistic traces. For instance, Mahlberg (2016: 147–148), building on Semino and Short's (2004) corpus study of register variation, highlights how categories of speech and thought representation can serve as indicators of stylistic preference. Although this kind of analysis demands intensive manual annotation, it illustrates how corpus stylistics can capture both lexical patterns and interpretative categories such as narrative perspective and characterisation.

The definitional spectrum remains wide. Baker (2000), Semino and Short (2004), Herrmann et al. (2015), and Li (2017) all emphasise "features" or "categories" as the focal units of stylistic analysis, though often with minimal illustrative material. What unites these approaches is the insistence that style must be conceived as a set of recurrent, recognisable patterns, whether at the level of syntax, lexis, semantics, or discourse. Yet, as Schäffner (2004: 1254) reminds us, a comprehensive account of translation style necessitates the integration of applied linguistics with cultural and literary studies, ensuring that both textual and contextual dimensions are addressed within a coherent methodological framework.

Semino (2007: 157, 166–167) contributes to this debate with the concept of mind style, a term introduced initially by Fowler (1977: 103) and further elaborated by Leech and Short (1981). Mind style denotes the distinctive linguistic representation of an individual's mental self, or a "subjective world view" described in Semino (2007: 153). This notion is particularly relevant for narrative translation, where the rendering of characters' voices or narratorial stance can significantly impact interpretation. Semino's approach combines corpus-assisted quantitative analysis with qualitative interpretation, enabling the study of how stylistic choices shape the representation of consciousness in both source and target texts. Nonetheless, her framework remains more attuned to monolingual stylistics than to the transference of style between languages.

Herrmann et al. (2015: 45) further emphasise the methodological pluralism required in stylistics:

> A certain style can be described using methods based on computing frequencies, relations, and distributions of features and relevant statistics, as well as methods based on precise observation and description of individual occurrences.

Their model suggests a mixed-methods approach, where quantitative results are tested against qualitative observation, and vice versa. This integration is indispensable for translation research, where purely statistical findings must be contextualised through interpretative analysis of textual detail.

The methodological complexity of literary stylistics highlights an enduring tension within Translation Studies: the distinction between linguistic stylistics and literary stylistics. Halliday (1971: 88) already warned that "pattern in language does not by itself make literature," while Diller (1998: 155) underscored the disciplinary divide by remarking that linguistic stylistics is largely the domain of linguists, whereas literary stylistics belongs to literary scholars. Corpus Translation Studies, emerging in the early 1990s out of traditions established by pioneers such as Busa (2004 [1946]) and Sinclair (1996), initially concentrated on linguistic regularities. Yet the domain of literary digital stylistics, particularly when applied to translation, necessarily incorporates extra-linguistic dimensions, drawing on frameworks proposed by Scholes et al. (2006 [1966]: 160–206), Even-Zohar and Toury (1981), and Lefevere (1992a, b), all of whom foreground the cultural, ideological, and systemic aspects of literature.

This distinction between linguistic and extra-linguistic stylistics has direct implications for corpus methodologies. As Zanettin (2013: 30) observes in *Corpus Methods for Descriptive Translation Studies*, the potential of corpora lies not only in facilitating large-scale quantitative analysis but also in enabling multilayered annotation that incorporates interpretative categories. He defines interpretative annotation as encompassing non-linguistic categories requiring human supervision, including the tagging of translation shifts, omissions, additions, metaphors, and errors in aligned corpora. Such annotations, while procedurally dependent on linguistic features, ultimately rest on interpretative judgement.

Zanettin rightly stresses that, despite the affordances of digital corpora, translation research has remained "largely grounded in extensive manual analysis." However, more than a decade after his observations, the emergence of Generative AI tools has begun to transform this landscape. Advances in natural language processing, large language models, and machine learning have enabled automatic annotation, alignment, and even the suggestion of interpretative categories. While human expertise remains indispensable for validation and refinement, AI-assisted annotation offers a scalable solution to the labour-intensive processes that previously limited corpus-based stylistics. In this respect, the field is witnessing a transition from what might be described as data-driven manual analysis toward AI-augmented interpretative inquiry.

Isolated analyses that consider linguistic features in a vacuum often fail to capture the complexity of translation as a multilayered act of cultural and semantic negotiation. To address this, previous scholarship has adopted more holistic approaches. Notably, Snell-Hornby's (1988) pioneering work in descriptive translation studies emphasised the necessity of viewing translation through a multidimensional lens, one that includes linguistic, literary, and cultural perspectives. Building on this, Cadera (2017) proposed a model treating style, meaning, and semantics as interconnected aspects of translation, emphasising that translators' choices reflect broader discursive and cultural systems.

This shift is particularly significant for projects such as the present study of Fontenelle's *Entretiens sur la pluralité des mondes* (1686) and its early English translations by Domville (1687), Glanvill (1688), and Behn (1688). Here, the analysis of stylistic shifts must account for both linguistic patterning and the broader interpretative categories that shape the literary text, such as domestication, simplification, self-censorship, and narrative reframing. The methodological debates surveyed above provide a crucial theoretical backdrop. However, they also highlight the need for new tools that can operationalise both linguistic and extra-linguistic dimensions in systematic yet nuanced ways.

In summary, literary digital stylistics in CTS is characterised by a methodological duality: it relies on corpus-based techniques to identify patterns, while also recognising the necessity of interpretative annotation to capture the richness of literary translation. From Baker's stylistic "thumb-print" to Bourdieu's "habitus", from Semino's mind style to Herrmann's mixed-methods model, scholars have consistently emphasised that style cannot be reduced to isolated linguistic features but must be understood as patterned behaviour embedded in cultural and interpretative contexts. The advent of AI-powered tools promises to reconcile these approaches, offering both the computational efficiency of automatic annotation and the hermeneutic depth of simultaneous interpretation. The challenge for future research lies in balancing these dimensions so that translation studies can continue to engage meaningfully with the complexities of literary style. The translator's decisions and interpretative strategies cannot be fully understood unless they are situated within a broad and integrative theoretical framework.

The following sections aim to explore some of the foundational concepts that have shaped the field of translation theory. These include enduring debates surrounding fidelity and freedom, the role of equivalence, the nature of stylistic transfer, and the evolving understanding of the translator's agency. Considering these classic features, the discussion will highlight how they impact current views on a literary translation under the influence of social, political and cultural conditions. This is the primary concern of the discipline of hermeneutics, which is the focus of the following section.

2.3 Hermeneutic Concerns

From its earliest stages, the discipline of hermeneutics has been concerned with translation in the broadest sense: the rendering of meaning across different realms of language, culture, and human experience (Ankersmit 2005; Hermans 2020). In this perspective, translation is much less a purely linguistic exercise than an act of interpretation. The descriptive study of literary translation, therefore, acquires depth and clarity when situated within its historical and socio-cultural contexts, for it is precisely these contexts that decisively shape the translator's choices. George Steiner (1998) famously captured this idea in *After Babel*, where he described translation as a "hermeneutic motion," a dynamic process of negotiation between texts and cultures. Steiner's insight, that "being exposed to history is the precondition for understanding but makes self-understanding problematic", serves as a guiding principle for the present study, particularly in relation to the early English translations of Fontenelle's *Entretiens*.

The analogy between the work of the translator and that of the historian is illuminating. Just as the translator re-articulates meaning for a new audience, the historian translates the past into a narrative that the present can grasp. Both activities are interpretative acts that transform realities, textual or historical, into intelligible images. These images, however, remain partial, provisional, and open to revision. When applied to literary translation, this insight underscores the interpreter's responsibility to bridge the gaps of language, culture, and time, while acknowledging that no interpretation can be exhaustive or definitive. For Fontenelle's *Entretiens*, this hermeneutic perspective is particularly pertinent: the three English versions produced in the late seventeenth century were all shaped by the profound cultural, religious, and political upheavals of their time.

Modern hermeneutics, especially after Hans-Georg Gadamer's *Wahrheit und Methode* (*Truth and Method* 1960/1989), broadened the horizon of interpretation beyond the confines of philology and theology. Gadamer insisted that understanding is not reducible to explanatory models modelled on the natural sciences. Instead, it belongs to the human sciences and the arts, where language is both the medium and the condition of interpretation. As Hermans (2020: 230) reminds us, Gadamer "stresses the historicity of the interpreter who is confronted with the otherness of the data to be interpreted, even though the latter are part of a historical continuum that comprises the interpreter as well." This recognition of historicity means that translation can never claim timeless objectivity; it is always situated, conditioned by the horizons of both author and reader. The polysystem theory from which translation studies originate was initially inspired by the Russian literary theorists in the early twentieth century (e.g. Tynyanov 1929), considering literature as a multilayered structure, and Wittgenstein's (1953) philosophy of language placing literature and literary translation within their respective socio-cultural-historical framework (Wilson 2016). Translations serve as heuristics, so they are imperfect and often difficult, but difficulty does not entail necessarily impossibility (Gillies and Giorello 1993: section 13.5).

The consequences for translation studies are significant. Suppose we accept the fallible and non-univocal character of translation. In that case, we avoid the reductive view of translation as a mere "cover-up," a deceptive reproduction that conceals meaning rather than discloses it. Translation should be understood as a hermeneutic event, an interpretative act that entails explicitation, contextualization, and re-articulation of meaning. It is therefore never neutral. Each translation reflects the intellectual climate, cultural norms, and ideological pressures of its contemporary time, inscribing the original text within its horizons of meaning.

This process resonates with Gadamer's (1977) later notion of the "fusion of horizons," the encounter between the world of the text and the world of the interpreter. As Hermans (2020: 231) observes, such a view "stresses open-mindedness, respect and negotiation." Translation thus emerges as a process of dialogical negotiation in which meaning is not simply transferred but reshaped within new cultural horizons. This perspective highlights the multiple allegiances of translators, who must balance fidelity to the source with responsibility to their readers, patrons, and broader intellectual communities. In the seventeenth century, this mediating role was especially evident in translations that transmitted the new scientific and philosophical discourses of the age.

The circulation of works by Galileo, Descartes, Newton, or Fontenelle offers ample evidence. These texts were not reproduced as literal replicas but as interpretative renderings tailored to contemporary expectations. Translators adapted, rephrased, or even omitted passages that appeared obscure, controversial, or theologically suspect. Such interventions should not be dismissed as betrayals of the original. Rather, they are hermeneutic gestures, attempts to make meaning intelligible and acceptable within a new cultural and ideological context. From this standpoint, textual shifts and omissions are better understood as interpretative strategies that reflect the translator's dual role as both reader and cultural mediator.

The act of literary translation, therefore, shares affinities with other interpretative practices: clarifications, paraphrases, demystifications, or even musical and artistic interpretations, all of which embody the attempt to render something intelligible across difference. When approached hermeneutically, the early English translations of Fontenelle's *Entretiens* do not appear as derivative copies but as historically embedded interpretations. They reveal the translator as both active reader and mediator, negotiating the opacity of the French original with the demands of English during intense cultural and political transformations.

Ultimately, translation is not only reproduction, but also interpretation: a dialogical act that renders texts intelligible across languages, cultures, and epochs. By viewing translation through the prism of hermeneutics, we recognise its essential nature as an interpretative negotiation, one that constantly re-articulates meaning within new contexts (Table 2.1). This recognition paves the way for the following analysis, in which the universal features of literary translation, such as clarification, paraphrase, demystification, and exaggeration, among other stylistic strategies, will be examined in relation to Fontenelle's translators. These features, discussed in detail in the next section, demonstrate how literary translation operates as a

Table 2.1 Key insights: Hermeneutic concerns

Key insight	Hermeneutic concern
Translation as interpretation	Hermenutics views translation not as a mechanical transfer but as a dynamic act of understanding, shaped by history, culture, and the interpreter's horizon (Steiner's 1998 "hermeneutic motion", Gadamer's 1977 "fusion of horizon").
Historicity of the interpreter	Every translation is historically situated. Translators negotiate between the "otherness" of the source and the expectations of their own cultural context (Hermans 2020)
Fallibility and creativity	Translation is fallible and non-univocal, but this very openness protects against reducing it to a deceptive "cover-up". Each version reflects the intellectual, cultural, and ideological pressures of its time (Wittgenstein 1953).
Hermeneutic interventions	Shifts, omission, and adaptations are not flaws but strategies of intelligibility, ensuring the text resonates with its new audience. Paratexts (prefaces, notes) also mediate meaning (Ankersmit 2005).
Seventeenth-century relevance	The English translations of Fontenelle's *Entretiens*, produced during intense cultural and political upheaval, exemplify translation as a form of historical and cultural mediation.
Broader implication	Translation, like history, is an interpretation, a dialogical, provisional, and productive process, bridging gaps across time, language, and culture (Gadamer 1960/1989).

hermeneutic practice, striking a balance between openness to the foreign and responsiveness to the familiar.

2.4 Universals or Regularities as Typical Features of Literary Translation

The study of universals in translation has been a longstanding concern in Translation Studies, intersecting with linguistic theory, descriptive methodologies, and cultural approaches to literary texts. The notion of universals was first theorised in linguistic terms by Chomsky (1965: 30), whose concept of "linguistic universals" was extended to translation by Levý (1969). Even-Zohar (1978), in his polysystem theory, introduced the idea of "universals of literary contacts," which was subsequently complemented by Toury's (1980: 130) influential formulation of "translation universals." Toury later refined this conceptualisation, preferring to speak of "laws" or "norms" rather than strict universals (Toury 1991: 51; 1999; 2004: 29; 2012 [1995]: 226–227). This terminological shift underscored his recognition that translation is characterised by variability and context-dependence; thus, any generalisation must allow for exceptions.[2]

[2] The concept of norms is further discussed by Hermans (1991, 1996, 2014 [1999]), Baker (1993), Schäffner (1998), Brownlie (1999), Munday (2016: 176–191), Enríquez-Aranda (2016), Hu and Zheng (2025), among others. Historical accounts of universals and norms in polysystem theory

Within Descriptive Translation Studies (DTS), norms are understood as socially and culturally embedded regularities. They are prescriptive within a given community yet descriptive for the researcher, who reconstructs them from textual evidence. Toury distinguishes three categories of translational norms: ***preliminary norms***, which determine the overall strategy and the choice of texts to be translated; ***initial norms***, which reflect whether the translator aligns primarily with the source text or the target culture; and ***operational norms***, which govern the specific decisions made during the act of translation. For this study, initial and operational norms are particularly pertinent, as they provide the framework within which the stylistic and cultural shifts of the early English translations of Fontenelle's *Entretiens* can be analysed.

As anticipated in Chap. 1, building upon this foundation, Baker (1993: 244; 1996: 180) systematises Toury's insights into a typology of translation universals observed in linguistic analyses. She identifies four main tendencies: (1) ***explicitation***, or the rendering explicit of what is implicit in the source text; (2) ***simplification***, whereby complex structures or ambiguities are reduced; (3) ***normalisation***, which regularises ungrammatical or non-standard forms and reduces repetition; and (4) ***levelling out***, a tendency for translations to converge towards the centre of a stylistic continuum rather than preserve extreme or unusual features. These categories have become central reference points for subsequent empirical research in CTS (see also Schäffner 1998: 6).

Toury himself stressed the probabilistic rather than deterministic nature of such tendencies. He argued that the goal of DTS is to formulate "coherent laws" that describe the *likelihoods* of behaviour rather than absolute rules:

> The cumulative findings of descriptive studies should make it possible to formulate a series of coherent laws which would state the inherent relations between all the variables found to be relevant to translation [...] To be sure, the envisaged laws are everything but absolute, designed as they are to state the *likelihood* that a kind of behaviour or surface realisation would occur under one set of specifiable conditions or another." (Toury 1995: 16; italics in the original)

In later writings, Toury (2004: 24) explicitly clarified that universals or laws are probabilistic, not categorical: "For me, the issue [of probabilistic universals] is not one that could be resolved by saying either 'yes' or 'no'." Furthermore, the methodological flexibility of DTS lies in its openness to falsification. As Toury (1995: 192) insists, the disconfirmation of a hypothesis can be as illuminating as its confirmation. This reinforces the inductive character of DTS, which refrains from imposing a priori categories and instead builds hypotheses ex post, derived from textual observations.

---

include Baker (1993: 242), Gentzler (2001 [1993]: 120, 129), Toury (2004), Munday (2016: 184). New discussions on these concepts are reviewed by Van Poucke's and Gallego (2019: 29) in the special issue on 'Retranslation in Context' of the journal *Cadernos de Tradução,* and Berk Albachten and Tahir Gürçağlar (2020: 1) in the introduction to the special issue on 'Retranslation and Multimodality' of the journal *The Translator*.

Table 2.2 Key insights: Universals and regularities in literary translation

Key insight	Description
From universals to norms	Early notions of "translation universals" (Chomsky 1965; Levý 1969; Even-Zohar 1978) were refined by Toury (1980, 1995, 1999, 2004, 2012), who preferred "laws" or "norms" to account for variability and exceptions. His categories—preliminary, initial, and operational norms—remain central to Descriptive Translation Studies (DTS) (see also Hu and Zheng 2025)
Probabilistic tendencies	Toury (1995: 16) emphasised that universals are not absolute but probabilistic. They describe *likelihoods* of translational behaviour rather than categorical rules. DTS thus advances through inductive observation, where even falsified hypotheses yield valuable insights
Baker's four tendencies	Building on Toury (2012), Baker (1993, 1995, 1996) identified four major regularities: explicitation, simplification, normalisation, and levelling out. These have become key analytical tools within Corpus Translation Studies (CTS)
Methodological orientation	This study adopts a descriptive, inductive approach, treating features such as simplification, self-censorship, and domestication as comparative heuristics rather than universal truths. Cipriani's (2023) retranslation hypothesis exemplifies this strategy
Analytical features	Six recurrent phenomena are foregrounded: implicit manipulation, self-censorship, simplification, explicitation, addition, and domestication, which extend the analysis beyond linguistic regularities to extra-linguistic stylistics (Zanettin 2011, 2013)
Mixed-method approach	Combining corpus-based quantification, interpretative annotation, and generative AI-assisted analysis enables a nuanced account of translator behaviour. Findings highlight how translation choices reflect both textual constraints and the cultural norms of the target system

The framework of Corpus Translation Studies (CTS) has consolidated these insights by combining *data-driven* and *theory-driven* approaches. (Table 2.2 presents key insights into the universals and regularities in literary translation.) Literary digital stylistics, in particular, benefits from the interaction between inductive analyses of textual corpora and deductive applications of hypothesised features. Recent scholarship (e.g., Wu et al. 2025) has shown how corpus-based methods allow the narrative style of source and target texts to be examined both through inductively observed regularities and deductively tested hypotheses.

In the present study, a primarily descriptive and inductive orientation has been adopted. Certain recurrent phenomena, such as ***simplification, domestication, and self-censorship,*** are treated as *universals* or, more precisely, as widely attested regularities of literary translation across centuries and cultures. They serve not as categorical truths but as comparative templates, enabling the analysis of multiple translations within a common framework. This methodological strategy echoes Cipriani's (2023: 17–18) use of the retranslation hypothesis as a template, a "reference prediction": rather than attempting to confirm or refute the general hypothesis, the case study is analysed in relation to its explanatory potential for the specific translations under investigation.

Accordingly, this study employs six features frequently discussed in the critical literature:

1. ***Implicit or indirect manipulation* (*IIM*)**, including mismatches and errors (van Leuven-Kwart 1989, 1990; Munday 2016: 145).
2. ***Self-censorship* (*SC*)** often reflects ideological or cultural constraints (Munday 2016: 186).
3. ***Lexical simplification* (*LS*)** (Lind 2007: 3).
4. ***Explicitation*** or ***re-writing* (*RW*)** (Munday 2016: 92; Zhang 2025).
5. ***Addition of text***, in the form of ***unused propositions* (*UP*)**, which are absent in the source text (Lind 2007: 3).
6. ***Domestication* (*NCE*)**, the use of *non-conforming* or culturally assimilated *expressions* (Venuti 2008: 15; Munday 2016: 225–227).

Table 2.3 presents definitions and explanatory examples of digitally-annotated user-defined tags used in the present empirical study. The scope of these features extends beyond purely linguistic tendencies and encompasses extra-linguistic stylistic dimensions, following Zanettin's (2011, 2013) insistence on multilayered annotation. By incorporating interpretative categories, CTS moves closer to the realities of literary translation, where stylistic, cultural, and ideological considerations interact.

In this project, each feature has been systematically annotated and analysed through a combination of *close reading* and *micro-level analysis*, supported by quantitative measures of lexical variety and frequency. The mixed-method design ensures that a qualitative interpretation of extra-linguistic factors complements the identification of linguistic patterns. The process is further enhanced by the use of Generative AI tools, which assist in automatic annotation and provide preliminary interpretative explanations. While such AI-generated observations require careful human validation, they offer valuable heuristic insights that enrich the critical analysis.

Ultimately, the findings suggest that translators' choices are shaped not only by textual constraints but also by the cultural and normative frameworks operative in the target system. The presence of the translator is consistently detectable in register and style, revealing how operational norms, probabilistic tendencies, and extra-linguistic pressures intersect. This confirms the relevance of studying universals and regularities as heuristic categories: they do not prescribe translator behaviour, but they illuminate recurrent dynamics that emerge when texts cross linguistic and cultural boundaries.

2.5 The Empirical Application

The empirical component of this study employs a rigorously structured digital text analysis methodology for the comparative examination of literary translations. The approach rests upon the principle that literary texts can be productively conceptualised and operationalised as computable data. This perspective allows for the systematic extraction, annotation, alignment, and quantitative as well as qualitative analysis of stylistic and structural features across multiple translations of the same source text. By doing so, it seeks to bridge the gap between the interpretative traditions of literary translation studies and the methodological rigour of computational analysis, offering a hybrid model that retains the interpretative depth of human scholarship while benefiting from the scale and precision of digital tools.

Central to this methodology is the use of a bespoke software application built upon the XML/TEI (Text Encoding Initiative) annotation framework. This framework provides an interoperable, standardised structure for embedding detailed interpretative annotations directly into the digital text. In the present study, these annotations mark occurrences of selected literary features, identified in advance as relevant to the stylistic characterisation of the source and target texts. XML/TEI encoding enables these annotations to be not merely descriptive, but also machine-readable and thus amenable to complex computational processing. This structural enrichment of the corpus underpins all subsequent analytical operations, from automated extraction of annotated segments to the generation of aligned comparative datasets.

The empirical workflow operates in three interconnected phases. First, interpretative annotations are carried out manually by the researcher, drawing upon theoretical insights from Descriptive Translation Studies and the specific analytical needs of the project. As noted by Zanettin (2011, 2013), such annotations, by their very nature, cannot be reliably automated, since they involve critical interpretative judgements concerning the presence and function of particular literary features. Second, these manually produced annotations are processed electronically using the custom-built software. The program is designed to handle complex extraction, alignment, and statistical operations with high speed and precision, performing tasks that would be prohibitively time-consuming if executed manually in seconds. Third, the processed datasets are subjected to an integrated analysis combining both distant reading and close reading perspectives.

The distant reading component, inspired by its use in digital humanities (e.g., Hammond 2016, 2017), provides a macro-level overview of the corpus. By aggregating and visualising the frequency and distribution of annotated features across the corpus, it becomes possible to detect broad stylistic tendencies, recurring translation strategies, and potential deviations from source text norms. Such macro indicators, familiar in translation studies (*e.g.*, Mellinger and Hanson 2017), are particularly valuable in identifying patterns that might remain unnoticed when focusing exclusively on isolated textual segments.

The close reading component complements this macro perspective by enabling detailed, context-sensitive analysis of selected segments. Here, the aligned extracts allow the researcher to scrutinise specific translation shifts, assess the extent to which individual translations adhere to or diverge from the stylistic characteristics of the source text, and explore the micro-level mechanisms through which meaning, tone, and literary effects are negotiated in translation. This dual perspective, macro-level pattern detection followed by micro-level interpretative scrutiny, ensures that quantitative observations are grounded in qualitative insight.

One of the key advantages of this empirical approach lies in its capacity to manage and interrogate multiple retranslations of the same source text. In the present case, the methodology enables a systematic comparison of segmented and aligned English translations of Fontenelle's *Entretiens*, focusing on the extent to which successive retranslations approximate, diverge from, or reinterpret the distinctive stylistic traits of the source text. This makes it possible to address broader questions in retranslation studies, such as whether further translations tend to converge towards the stylistic ethos of the source text or whether they instead reflect evolving literary norms, target-language conventions, or shifting interpretative frameworks.

The searching and alignment functionalities embedded within the bespoke software play a crucial role in this process. By automatically aligning annotated segments across translations, the system facilitates a direct comparison of parallel textual units, making both subtle and substantial translation shifts visible. These shifts can then be categorised, measured, and interpreted in relation to the broader norms or regularities governing the translation process (Zwischenberger 2020). In this way, the software serves not merely as a technical tool, but as an enabler of theoretically informed analysis.

Moreover, the empirical application deliberately minimises reliance on extratextual data such as paratextual commentary, translator's notes, or historical reception contexts. While such contextual information can undoubtedly enrich interpretation, its exclusion here reflects a conscious methodological choice in line with the "text as data" paradigm articulated by Hammond (2016: 127–130): this approach isolates the text as the sole object of inquiry, ensuring that analytical conclusions are derived exclusively from observable linguistic and stylistic evidence encoded in the corpus.

Ultimately, this methodological configuration represents a significant advancement over conventional and commercial text-analysis software. While such tools often provide basic concordancing, frequency counts, and keyword analyses, they lack the flexibility to accommodate bespoke interpretative annotations or to integrate them seamlessly into a corpus-wide computational workflow. The custom program used in this study is specifically designed to operationalise the theoretical and methodological commitments of DTS, making it uniquely suited to the demands of empirical literary translation research.

In summary, the empirical application developed here demonstrates how a carefully designed integration of XML/TEI annotation, bespoke computational processing, and a dual distant/close reading framework can yield a rich, multi-layered understanding of translation practice. It represents a model that is not only methodologically robust but also adaptable to other case studies in literary translation, particularly where the aim is to combine interpretative depth with empirical rigour.

2.6 Final Considerations

This section aims to consolidate the key methodological and conceptual contributions discussed in this chapter on literary digital stylistics within the framework of Corpus Translation Studies (CTS). It briefly recalls the main issues of the innovative integration of linguistic and extra-linguistic features, the importance of translator individuality, and the methodological balance between automated analysis and human interpretation. It highlights the interdisciplinary nature of the approach, bridging computational techniques with humanistic insight. The scope, strengths, and limitations of the methodology framework presented here are also synthesised.

2.6.1 Literary Stylist Features

In this framework, a translator's style is conceived as a distinctive "thumbprint" made visible through recurring linguistic and non-linguistic patterns. These arise from individual habits and preferences that remain relatively stable across different works. In Literary Digital Stylistics, identifying such habits is central to understanding the translator's creative agency. The focus on individual translator style, as opposed to generalised translation norms alone, allows us to see how personal interpretative choices shape the final text.

One of the most significant innovations in this study lies in expanding CTS, traditionally oriented towards purely linguistic features, to accommodate extra-linguistic elements. These include cultural references, historical allusions, and ideological cues that influence a translation's tone, register, or interpretative direction. Incorporating such features into the focused object of study requires methodological innovation, as standard CTS frameworks were designed to study grammatical, lexical, and syntactic variation in literary texts. By embedding extra-linguistic analysis into the CTS workflow, we acknowledge that translation is as much a cultural act as a linguistic one.

Many key features in literary translation, such as simplification, domestication, or explicitation, are probabilistic rather than deterministic; they do not occur uniformly but follow patterns influenced by literary genre, historical period, and the translator's preference. Recognising the probabilistic nature of these features is essential for interpretation: the human researcher must assess not only whether a feature occurs, but also how often and under what conditions, before concluding its significance. Table 2.3 below in this Chapter displays the key insights of the universal features of literary translations.

Table 2.3 Definition and explanatory examples of digitally-annotated user-defined tags

Tag	Definition	Example
IIM	Implicit or indirect manipulation resulting in translation "**mismatches or shifts**" (van Leuven-Kwart, 1989, 1990; Munday 2016: 146)	In the examined case of the three early English translations of Fontenelle's (1686) *Entretiens sur la Pluralité des Mondes*, an example of manipulation resulting in translation errors (IIM) is the mistaken translation of TT3 of confounding the ancient Roman Cato of Utica (born, 95 BC; died 46 AD) with Cato the censor (born 234 BC; died 149 BC), *i.e.*, the ST "[Page 287] […] *qui eussent trouvé* ***Caton d'Utique*** *trop badin & trop folâtre*" is translated by TT3 as "[Page 128] […] wou'd have look'd upon the grave **<IIM> Cato the Censor </IIM>**, as too wild and youthful for their conversation"

(continued)

Table 2.3 (continued)

Tag	Definition	Example
SC	***Self-Censorship*** resulting in omitted translation, "where there is concern [of the translator] to filter out unwanted ideological elements of a ST" (Munday 2016: 186). Self-censorship was already noted in critical literature (e.g., Spender 1992; Cipriani 2020) and "This *de facto* censorship profoundly affected what was printed" (Munday 2016: 186, 215, 220)	An example of self-censorship (SC) results in TT3's "omitted translation" of the source text "[Page 128] ***C'est que le Papes ont prétendu être Maitres de Rome & de l'Italie en vertu d'une*** *Donation que l'Empereur Constantin* ***leur en avoit faite, & la verité est qu'un ne saroit dire ce qu'elle est devenuë***". The corresponding TT3's text is "[Page 58] in short, the Moon is exact in collecting all that is lost here below, and which are all to be found there, even to the Donation of Constantin **<SC>. </SC>** No translation of the highlighted ST's segment exists in TT3
LS	***Lexical Simplification*** of the source textual language, where "more general terms replace specific ones, or several short sentences replace a long one and lower average sentence length in general" (Lind 2007: 3)	An example of LS (Lexical simplification) is the simplification of ST "[Page 282] [...] *vous vous mêliez de Philosophie plus que vous ne faites il faudroit bien que vous vous accoûtumassiez à voir des exceptions dans les meilleurs Sistêmes*" in TT1 "**<LS>** [Page 22] [...] **till they get some considerable advantages over us, see what it is has frawn me to side with the inhabitants of the Moon </LS>**"
RW	***Explicitation*** *as* ***re-writing*** **is** defined as "implicit information in the ST rendered explicit in the TT" (Munday 2016: 92), Zhang (2025)	An example of RW (explicitation with re-writing) regards the ST "[Page 24] [...] *cent autres rêveries, que je m'étonne qui n'ayent perdu de réputation toute l'Antiquité*" which re-written in TT2 as "[Page 10] [...] **<RW> a Man must conclude the Old Sages were very good Banterers </RW>**
UP	***Unused proposition*:** **added text** in translation as a proposition which is unused in the source text to normalise it, where "[n] ormalization is the tendency to introduce features of the target language to conform to its typical patterns" (Lind 2007: 3)	An example of UP (added text in translation as proposition unused in the source text) is adding up further meaningful text to the original ST "[Page 96] [...] *La Lumiere est composée de petites balles qui bondissent sur ce qui est solide*" with TT3 "[Page 44> [...] Light is compos'd for little Balls, which rebound upon any solid Body, **<UP>which is opaque, or obscure, </UP>**
NCE	***Non-conforming expression*** resulting in "**Domestication**" of text in translation as "an ethnocentric reduction of the foreign text to receiving cultural values" (Venuti 2008: 15; Munday 2016: 225–227)	An example of NCE (domestication of text in translation with non-conforming expression) of the ST "[Page 29] [...] *Le Chariot, par example, que vous voyez qui est formé de ces* [Page 30] *sept Etoiles, a toujours été fait comme il est*" is transformed by TT3 into "[Page 15] [...] As for example**, <NCE> Charles's-Wain, or the Constellation of the Great Bear </NCE>, which you see**"

2.6.2 The Translator's Habitus

Pierre Bourdieu's (1972 [1977]) notion of habitus, defined as the set of dispositions shaped by one's social, cultural, and historical circumstances, provides a valuable framework for situating translation choices. In the illustrative case study carried out below on the early English translators of Fontenelle's *Entretiens*, their respective habitus informed not only their linguistic preferences but also their decisions about what to omit, adapt, or emphasise. Understanding these translators within their social and cultural contexts enriches our interpretation of the stylistic and ideological differences among the versions.

A critical step in this methodology is the use of both quantitative and qualitative indicators that can capture and explain translator decision-making. Indicators may include frequency counts of specific structures, the distribution of cultural references, or the prevalence of certain stylistic shifts. Selecting the most informative indicators requires theoretical grounding and familiarity with the source text, ensuring that the patterns identified are not merely statistical artefacts but meaningful signals of translation strategy.

2.6.3 Distant and Close Reading

A defining feature of the method presented in this chapter is the integration of distant reading (macro-level quantitative analysis) and close reading (micro-level qualitative interpretation). This approach allows large-scale computational data to inform, but not replace, detailed textual analysis. Distant reading reveals overall patterns, such as frequency trends or recurring shifts, while close reading examines specific examples in their literary and historical context. The two approaches are mutually reinforcing, offering both analytical breadth and depth.

Annotation, using a controlled set of user-defined tags, and alignment of source and target segments form the methodological core of this approach. Tags such as those representing implicit manipulation, self-censorship, rewriting, or added propositions allow the researcher to classify and retrieve relevant elements for the analysis. Alignment then enables direct comparison across multiple translations, revealing patterns and divergences that would be difficult to detect otherwise. Much of the study's empirical foundation rests upon these carefully designed and consistently applied annotation and alignment procedures.

2.6.4 *Textual Evidence*

In line with the descriptive tradition in translation studies, this method deliberately confines itself to textual evidence from source and target texts, avoiding reliance on paratexts or external commentary. This choice is rooted in the observational scientific approach of Karl Popper (1979) applied by Chesterman (1997: 2) and Huang (2015: 1–2) in the field of descriptive translation studies (Even-Zohar 1978; Toury 1980, 2012; Lefevere 1992a, b). The resulting interpretative hypotheses are grounded in the observed textual data possibly used to falsify rather than prove them, not in the search for a single "correct" version but as an iterative, problem-solving process (Chesterman, 1997: 162–164). The advantage is methodological clarity and replicability; the drawback is that potentially relevant contextual information, such as translator correspondence or contemporary reception, is excluded. This limitation is acknowledged and discussed in the broader methodological framework at the end of the present study.

Although the methodology relies heavily on automated processes for detecting and aligning features, manual supervision remains crucial. Human oversight ensures that the computational identification of features, whether linguistic or extra-linguistic, is accurate, contextually relevant, and theoretically informed. This balance between automation and interpretative judgement reflects the hybrid nature of literary digital stylistics.

2.7 Conclusion

By integrating linguistic and extra-linguistic features, focusing on translator individuality, applying the concept of habitus, and combining distant with close reading, this approach to literary digital stylistics in CTS advances both the technical capabilities and interpretative reach of translation research. While automated processes handle much of the data extraction and alignment, human scholarly insight remains indispensable for ensuring a consistent, complete, and meaningful interpretation. The methodology presented here is thus not only an analytical toolset but also a model for how digital and humanistic approaches can work together to illuminate the art and craft of literary translation.

References

Ankersmit, Frank. 2005. Hermeneutics. In *Routledge Encyclopedia of Narrative Theory*, ed. D. Herman, M. Jahn, and M.-L. Ryan, 211–212. Abington/Oxon: Routledge.

Baker, Mona. 1993. Corpus linguistics and translation studies. Implications and applications. In *Text and Technology: In Honour of John Sinclair*, ed. M. Baker, G. Francis, and E. Tognini-Bonelli, 233–252. Amsterdam: John Benjamins.

Baker, Mona. 1995. Corpora in Translation Studies: An Overview and Some Suggestions for Future Research. *Target* 7 (2): 223–243.

Baker, Mona. 1996. Corpus-Based Translation Studies. The Challenges That Lie Ahead. In *Terminology, LSP and Translation*, ed. H. Somers, 175–186. Amsterdam: John Benjamins.

Baker, Mona. 2000. Towards a Methodology for Investigating the Style of a Literary Translator. *Target* 12 (2): 241–266.

Behn, Aphra. 1688. *A Discovery of New Worlds*. From French. Made English by Mrs A. Behn. To which is prefixed a Preface, by way of essay on translated prose; wherein the argument of Father Tacquet, and others against the System of Copernicus (as to the Motion of the Earth) are likewise considered, and answered: Wholly new. London: printed for William Canning, at his Shop in the Temple-Cloysters.

Bernardini, Silvia, and Dorothy Kenny. 2020. Corpora. In *Routledge Encyclopedia of Translation Studies*, ed. Mona Baker and G. Saldanha, 110–115. London/New York: Routledge.

Bourdieu, Pierre. 1972[1977]. *Esquisse d'une théorie de la pratique, précédé de trois études d'ethnologie kabyle*. Carouge (Genève): Librairie Droz. (English translation by Richard Nice: *Outline of a Theory of Practice*. Cambridge, UK: Cambridge University Press, 1977).

Brownlie, Siobhan. 1999. Investigating norms. In *Translation and (Re)location of Meaning*, ed. J. Vandaele, 7–21. Leuven, Belgium: CETRA.

Busa, Roberto A. 2004. Forword: Perspectives on the Digital Humanities. In *A Companion to Digital Humanities*, ed. S. Schreibman, R. G. Siemens, and J. Unsworth, xvi–xxi. Malden: Blackwell.

Cadera, Susanne M. 2017. Literary Retranslation in Context. A Historical, Social and Cultural Perspective. In *Literary Retranslation in Context*, ed. S. Cadera and Andrew Samuel Walsh, 5–18. Oxford: Peter Lang.

Chesterman, Andrew. 1997. *Memes of Translation: The Spread of Ideas in Translation Theories*, 1st edn. Amsterdam and New York: John Benjamins.

Chomsky, Noam. 1965. *Aspects of the Theory of Syntax*. Cambridge, MA: The MIT Press.

Cipriani, Anna Maria. 2020. The impact of censorship on translating and publishing Virginia Woolf in Italy in the 1930s. *Translation Matters* 2(2): 83–96.

Cipriani, Anna Maria. 2023. *Literary Digital Stylistics in Translation Studies*. Singapore: Springer Nature.

Curry, Niall, and Tony McEnery. 2025. The Past, Present, and Future of Corpus and Translation Studies. In *Routledge Handbook of Corpus Translation Studies*, ed. Defeng Li and John Corbett, 1–8. London/New York: Routledge.

Diller, Hans-Jürgen. 1998. Stylistic: Linguistic and Textual. *European Journal of English Studies* 2 (2): 155–174.

Domville, William. 1687. *A Discourse of the Plurality of Worlds*. Written in French by the most ingenious Author of the Dialogues of the Dead, and translated into English by Sir W.D., Knight. Dublin: Printed by Andr. Crook and Sam. Helsham for William Norman book-binder to His Grace the Duke of Ormond.

Enríquez-Aranda, Mercedes. 2016. Translation norms in the light of practical research in literary translation. *Onomázein* 33: 88–106.

Even-Zohar, Itamar. 1978. Universals of Literary Contacts. In *Papers on Poetics and Semiotics*, ed. B. Hrushovski and I. Even-Zohar. Tel Aviv: University Publishing Projects.

Even-Zohar, Itamar, and Gideon Toury. 1981. Introduction. In the Special Issue on 'Theory of Translation and Intercultural Relations'. *Poetics Today* 2 (4): v–xi.

Fontenelle (Le Bovier de), Bernard. 1686. *Entretiens sur la pluralité des mondes*. Paris: Vueve C. Blageart. Registered on *Livre de la Communauté des Libraires & Imprimeurs de Paris*, on 22 January 1686. Printed on 8 March 1686.

Fowler, Roger. 1977. *Linguistics and the Novel*. London: Methuen and Co.

Gadamer, Hans Georg. 1960/1989. *Truth and Method*. Trans. J. Weinsheimer and D.G. Marshall. London/New York: Continuum.

Gadamer, Hans Georg. 1977. *Philosophical Hermeneutics*. Trans. David Linge. Berkeley, CA: University of California Press.

Gentzler, Edwin. 2001. *Contemporary Translation Theories*, 2nd edn. Clevedon, U.K.: Multilingual Matters.

Gillies, Donald and Giulio Giorello. 1993. *Philosophy of Science in the Twentieth Century. Four Central Themes*. Oxford/Cambridge, MA: Blackwell.

Glanvill, J. 1688. *A Plurality of Worlds*. Written in French by the author of the Dialogues of the dead; translated into English by Mr. Glanvill. London: printed for R. Bentley and S. Magnes.

Halliday, Michael Alexander Kirkwood. 1971. Linguistic Function and Literary Style: An Inquiry into the Language of William Golding's the Inheritors. In *Literary Style: A Symposium*, ed. Seymour Chatman, 330–368. London/New York: Oxford University Press.

Hammond, Adam. 2016. *Literature in the Digital Age: An Introduction*. Cambridge: Cambridge University Press.

Hammond, Adam. 2017. The double bind of validation: Distant reading and the digital humanities "trough of disillusionment." *Literature Compass* 14: 1–13.

Hermans, Theo. 1991. Translational norms and correct translations. In *Translation Studies: The State of the Art*, ed. K.M. van Leuven-Zwart and T. Naaijkens, 155–169. Amsterdam: Rodopi.

Hermans, Theo. 1996. Norms and the determination of translation: A theoretical framework. In *Translation, Power, Subversion*, ed. R. Álvarez and M. Carmen-África Vidal, 25–51. Clevedon, U.K.: Multilingual Matters.

Hermans, Theo. 2014. *Translation in Systems. Descriptive and System-Oriented Approaches Explained*. London/New York: Routledge.

Hermans, Theo. 2020. Hermeneutics. In *Routledge Encyclopedia of Translation Studies*, ed. M. Baker and G. Saldanha, 227–232. London/New York: Routledge.

Herrmann, J. Berenike, Karina van Dalen-Oskam, and Christof Schöch. 2015. Revisiting Style, a Key Concept in Literary Studies. *Journal of Literary Theory* 9 (1): 25–52.

Hu, Kaibao, and Lixin Xie. 2017. Towards a Corpus-Based Study of Translator's Style. *Chinese Translation Journal* 38 (2): 12–18. (In Chinese.).

Hu, Xianyao, and Man Zheng. 2025. Corpora and Cross-Linguistic Research of Translation Universals. In *Routledge Handbook of Corpus Translation Studies*, ed. Defeng Li and John Corbett, 215–238. London/New York: Routledge.

Huang, Libo. 2015. *Style in Translation: A Corpus-Based Perspective*. Heidelberg: Springer-Verlag.

Huang, Libo. 2021. New Trends in Corpus-Based Translator's Style Studies. In *New Perspectives on Corpus Translation Studies*, ed. V. Wang, L. Lim, and D. Li, 59–73. Singapore: Springer.

Jiménez-Crespo, Miguel A. 2017. *Crowdsourcing and Online Collaborative Translations: Expanding the Limits of Translation Studies*. Amsterdam/Philadelphia: John Benjamins.

Kenny, Dorothy. 2001. *Lexis and Creativity in Translations: A Corpus-Based Study*. Manchester, UK: St Jerome.

Leech, Geoffrey N., and Michael H. Short. 1981. *Style in Fiction*. London: Longman.

Lefevere, André. 1992a. *Translating Literature: Practice and Theory in a Comparative Context*. New York: The Modern Language Association of America.

Lefevere, André. 1992b. *Translation, Rewriting, and the Manipulation of Literary Fame*. London/New York: Routledge.

Levý, Jiří. 1969. *Die literarische Übersetzung – Theorie einer Kunstgattung*, translated by Walter Schamschula, Frankfurt/Bonn: Athenäum.

Li, Defeng. 2017. Translator Style: A Corpus-Assisted Approach. In *Corpus Methodologies Explained*, ed. M. Ji, L. Hereide, D. Li, and M. Oakes, 103–136. London/New York: Routledge.

Lind, Sarah. 2007. Translation Universals (or Laws, or Tendencies, or Probabilities, or …?). *TIC Talk* 63: https://translation.bible/wp-content/uploads/2024/05/tt63.pdf.

Mahlberg, Michaela. 2013. *Corpus Stylistics and Dickens's Fiction*. London and New York: Routledge.

Mahlberg, Michaela. 2016. Corpus Stylistics. In *The Bloomsbury Companion to Stylistics*, ed. V. Sotirova, 139–156. London/New York: Bloomsbury Academic.

McIntyre, Dan and Brian Walker. 2019. *Corpus Stylistics. Theory and Practice*. Edinburgh: Edinburgh University Press.

Mellinger, Christopher D., and Thomas A. Hanson. 2017. *Quantitative Research Methods in Translation and Interpreting Studies*. London: Routledge.
Munday, Jeremy. 2016 [2012, 2008, 2001]. *Introducing Translation Studies. Theories and Applications*, 4th edn. London/New York: Routledge.
Ping, Yuan. 2024. Book Review: *Literary Digital Stylistics in Translation Studies* by Anna Maria Cipriani. *Digital Scholarship in the Humanities* 39 (2): 807–809.
Popper, Karl R. 1979. *Objective Knowledge. An Evolutionary Approach*. Revised edition. Oxford: Oxford University Press.
Schäffner, Christina. 1998. The concept of norms in translation studies. *Current Issues in Language & Society* 5 (1-2): 1–9.
Schäffner, Christina. 2004. Metaphor and Translation: Some Implications of a Cognitive Approach. *Journal of Pragmatics* 36 (7): 1253–1269.
Scholes, Robert, James Phelan, and Robert Kellog. 2006. *The Nature of Narrative*. Oxford: Oxford University Press.
Semino, Elena. 2007. Mind Style Twenty-Five Years on. *Style* 41 (2): 153–172.
Semino, Elena, and Mick Short. 2004. *Corpus Stylistics: A Corpus-Based Study of Speech, Thought and Writing Presentation in Narratives*. London: Routledge.
Simeoni, Daniel. 1998. The Pivotal Status of the Translator's Habitus. *Target* 10 (1): 1–40.
Sinclair, John. 1996. The Search for Units of Meaning. *Textus* IX:75–106.
Snell-Hornby, Mary. 1988. *Translations Studies: An Integrated Approach*, Revised edn. Amsterdam: John Benjamins.
Spender, Dale. 1992. Introduction: A vindication of the writing women. In *Living by the Pen: Early British Women Writers*, ed. D. Spender, 1–35. New York/London: Columbia University, Teachers College Press.
Steiner, G. 1998. *After Babel. Aspects of Language and Translation*. 3rd edition. Oxford: Oxford University Press.
Toury, Gideon. 1980. *In Search of a Theory of Translation*. Tel Aviv: The Porter Institute for Poetics and Semiotics.
Toury, Gideon. 1991. Experimentation in translation studies: Achievements, prospects and some pitfalls. In *Empirical Research in Translation and Intercultural Studies*, ed. S. Tirkkonen-Condit, 45–66. Tübingen: Gunter Narr.
Toury, Gideon. 1995. *Descriptive Translation Studies and Beyond*, 1st edn. Amsterdam/ Philadelphia: John Benjamins.
Toury, Gideon. 1999. A handful of paragraphs on "translation" and "norms." In *Translation and Norms*, ed. C.Schäffner, 9–31. Clevedon, U.K.: Multilingual Matters.
Toury, Gideon. 2004. Probabilistic explanations in translation studies: Welcome as they are, would they qualify as universals? In *Translation Universals: Do They Exist*? ed. A. Mauranen and P. Kujamäki, 15–25. Amsterdam/Philadelphia: John Benjamins.
Toury, Gideon. 2012. *Descriptive Translation Studies and Beyond*, 2nd edn. Amsterdam/ Philadelphia: John Benjamins.
Tynyanov, Y.N. 1929. *Arkhaisty i novatory. [Archaists and Innovators.]* Moscow: Akademia. Reprinted in 1967, Munich: Wilhelm Fink (in Russian).
van Leuven-Kwart, Kitty M. 1989. Translation and original: Similarities and dissimilarities I. *Target* 1 (2): 151–182.
van Leuven-Kwart, Kitty M. 1990. Translation and original: Similarities and dissimilarities II. *Target* 2 (1): 69 96.
Van Poucke, Piet, and Guillermo Sanz Gallego. 2019. Retranslation in Context. *Cadernos de Traduçao* 39 (1): 10–22.
Venuti, Lawerence. 2008 [1995]. *The Translator's Invisibility: A History of Translation*, 2nd edn. London/New York: Routledge.
Wales, Katie. 2011 [2001, 1990]. *A Dictionary of Stylistics*, 3rd edn. Harlow: Longman.
Wilson, Philip. 2016. *Translation after Wittgenstein*. London and New York: Routledge.

Wittgenstein, Ludwig. 1953. *Philosophische Untersuchungen*. English translation: *Philosophical Investigations*, by G.E.M. Anscombe, P.M.S. Hacker and J. Schulte. Chichester, U.K.: Wiley-Blackwell.

Wu, Kan and Defeng Li. 2025. *Researching Translator's Functional Style: A Corpus-Assisted Approach*. Singapore: Springer.

Wu, Kan, Defeng Li, and Victoria Lai Cheng Lei. 2025. Corpus-Assisted Research on Translator Style. In *Routledge Handbook of Corpus Translation Studies*, ed. Defeng Li and John Corbett, 271–287. London and New York: Routledge.

Zanettin, Federico. 2011. Hardwiring Corpus-Based Translation Studies: Corpus Encoding. In *Corpus-Based Translation Studies. Research and Applications*, ed. A. Kruger, K. Wallmach, and J. Munday, 103–123. London/New York: Bloomsbury Academic.

Zanettin, Federico. 2012. *Translation-Driven Corpora: Corpus Resources for Descriptive and Applied Translation Studies*. Manchester: St. Jerome.

Zanettin, Federico. 2013. Corpus Methods for Descriptive Translation Studies. *Procedia—Social and Behavioral Sciences* 95:20–32.

Zhang, Xiaomin. 2025. Corpus-Based Studies of Explicitation. In *Routledge Handbook of Corpus Translation Studies*, ed. Defeng Li and John Corbett, 254–268. London: Routledge.

Zwischenberger, Cornelia. 2020. Norms. In *Routledge Encyclopedia of Translation Studies*, ed. M. Baker and G. Saldanha, 3rd ed., 375–380. London/New York: Routledge.

Wittgenstein, Ludwig. 1953. *Philosophical Investigations*. [illegible] by G.E.M. Anscombe. [illegible]

Chapter 3
Empowering Corpus Translation Studies with LLMs

The intimate nature of things loves to hide.

Heraclitus (535–475 BC)

3.1 Introduction

This chapter discusses how Large Language Models (LLMs) advance Corpus Translation Studies (CTS), focusing on interpretative annotation, explanation, and AI-driven methods used in our case study. Traditionally, textual annotation has been a slow, manual process that required human expertise to capture both linguistic and extra-linguistic features of translations. Generative AI now enables researchers to accelerate this process by suggesting annotations that can be later validated. By integrating XML/TEI encoding with AI-assisted annotation, we can systematically detect features such as simplification, omission, or narrative reframing, while still maintaining the interpretative depth essential to translation studies. This hybrid model represents a methodological advance that combines computational efficiency with human interpretative judgment.

Beyond annotation, LLMs also play a central role in identifying translation patterns across aligned corpora. Once source and target texts are segmented, models can be prompted to compare them and highlight specific regularities, such as syntactic transformations or ideological shifts. Importantly, LLMs function not as independent analysts but as collaborative assistants guided by researcher-defined frameworks. Their ability to provide rationales for annotations, in line with explainable AI principles, enhances transparency and interpretability. This dual application, which accelerates annotation and facilitates pattern recognition, enables CTS to transcend its traditional manual constraints, providing new methodological tools for uncovering the stylistic and cultural dimensions of translation.

The chapter begins with a brief overview of recent developments in LLMs, followed by an outline of a general framework for utilising them in corpus translation studies. It details how this framework is applied through automated annotation, alignment, and explication, resulting in visualisation and creation of annotated text

A. M. Cipriani, F. Milana, *AI-Powered Corpus Translation Studies at Work*,
New Frontiers in Translation Studies,
https://doi.org/10.1007/978-981-95-5933-6_3

files via a custom desktop application. The Appendix lists the prompts used for the AI tools in the present empirical study.

3.2 Brief Account of the Recent History of LLMs

Machine Learning (ML) models estimate their parameters using optimisation methods that aim to extract patterns from structured data. During the training phase, models learn these parameters by minimising a task-specific loss function. Once trained, they use the learned parameters to make predictions on new, unseen data in the inference phase. Unlike classical software engineering, where outputs are generated by applying predefined rules to inputs, ML infers rules (parameters) from input-output pairs (data points and labels). These inferred rules can then be used for other inputs that follow similar statistical distributions and patterns to the training data. This paradigm forms the foundation of Generative AI systems, such as Large Language Models (LLMs), which extend ML from prediction to generation.

One of the most successful model architectures developed is the Neural Network (NN). Inspired by the human brain, NNs stack several layers of "neurons", or units, each performing simple computation but allowing the network to model complex and non-linear relationships in the data. These models learn hierarchical representations in each layer, making them particularly effective for tasks that were previously too complex for traditional statistical learning methods, such as image recognition, speech processing, and natural language understanding.

Among NN architectures, a key breakthrough that enabled the rise of Generative AI, especially in natural language processing (NLP), was the development of the Transformer (Vaswani et al. 2017). Transformers departed from earlier sequence models by enabling more efficient and scalable processing of long-range dependencies in text. While previous approaches, such as Recurrent Neural Networks (RNNs), struggled to retain information over long sequences, Transformers can capture global context more effectively through mechanisms like self-attention. This innovation paved the way for LLMs: Transformer-based NNs trained on massive text corpora to learn the statistical structure of the human language. Models could generate text by predicting the next token in a sequence based on the preceding context, using probabilities derived from their learned representations of language. Over the years, LLMs such as ChatGPT, BERT, and their successors have demonstrated remarkable capabilities in generating content and contextually appropriate text that was previously unattainable using earlier ML techniques.

Three key factors have driven the rapid progress of LLMs over the past few years: increased model scale, access to large-scale datasets, and the availability of powerful computational infrastructure. Early models, such as OpenAI's GPT-1, demonstrated that language models could generate fluent text when trained on large corpora. However, it was GPT-2 and especially GPT-3 that revealed the surprising breadth of capabilities that emerge with scale, such as zero-shot reasoning (tackling new tasks and problems without prior training or guidance), code generation, and long-form content synthesis (evaluating whole paragraphs or dialogues). These capabilities, often referred to as "emergent," are behaviours that were not explicitly programmed or observed in smaller models but appear reliable once a certain scale threshold is reached (Berti et al. 2025). Subsequent models, such as GPT-4 and GPT-5, have further refined these abilities by integrating instruction tuning and Reinforcement Learning from Human Feedback (RLHF) to align outputs with human expectations. This scaling paradigm has become a defining characteristic of modern generative AI systems.

Despite the impressive recent advances of LLMs and their ever-growing number of applications in which they appear to excel, there is still a considerable number of cases where human intervention is required to ensure reliability, factual accuracy, and contextual appropriateness. LLMs can produce outputs that are fluent and sound convincing, yet factually incorrect or misleading, phenomenons often referred to as "hallucination" and "inconsistency". Moreover, the performance of these models can degrade in domains that require precise reasoning, up-to-date knowledge, or nuanced subjectivity, such as cultural analysis or legal argumentation (Zhang et al. 2024). As a result, human oversight remains essential in applications where it could lead to harmful, biased, or misleading outcomes.

The contribution of human oversight is particularly significant in Corpus Translation Studies (CTS), where LLMs have certain limitations in analysing or generating meaningful content. The areas within CTS where human expertise can surpass that of LLMs include:

1. Interpreting symbols and metaphors
2. Understanding historical and cultural context
3. Evaluating authorial intent
4. Recognising narrative voice and tone shifts
5. Constructing and critiquing theoretical arguments
6. Making ethical and aesthetic judgments

LLMs struggle in these areas primarily because their outputs are shaped by statistical patterns learned from large-scale datasets, rather than genuine understanding or interpretive reasoning. While their training on massive corpora allows them to mimic a wide range of styles and perspectives, it also introduces a significant bias toward dominant narratives and conventional interpretations. Nuanced, novel, or subversive readings, especially those that challenge mainstream viewpoints, are often flattened or overlooked. These limitations are critical in CTS, where subjectivity is a defining feature of the task. The richness of literary interpretation lies in its openness to ambiguity, contradiction, and multiple valid readings, qualities that cannot be easily captured or reproduced by patterns learned from training data.

Given the inherent limitations of LLMs in handling the profound subjectivity, nuance, and ethical complexities characteristic of interpretive textual analysis, a critical research gap emerges. The gap pertains to the absence of robust, human-centred AI frameworks specifically designed to augment human expertise effectively. These frameworks should explicitly address and mitigate the known deficiencies of LLMs while leveraging their strengths in speed, scalability and pattern detection.

It follows that applications of LLMs to inherently subjective contexts such as CTS should aim to assist the human researchers instead of replacing them. It has recently been noted that qualitative researchers are generally hesitant about automating their manual processes and instead value the integration of AI as a way to complement them by cross-checking data, evaluating saturation, organising existing ideas, and identifying new insights (Milana et al. 2025).

3.3 A Framework for Applying LLMs to CTS

The following conceptual framework is proposed to provide a general but systemic model for the integrated use of LLMs in CTS. The framework involves three levels, each of which responds to specific functions within the translation and computational workflow:

1. **Input**
   This initial level involves the acquisition and selection of data, which constitute the corpus on which the analyses will be conducted. The data can come from digitised texts or from paper documents subsequently subjected to an Optical Character Recognition (OCR) process. The main objective is to obtain a balanced, representative corpus suitable for translation research. This level also involves pre-processing tasks such as generating annotations and text alignment. These steps prepare the corpus for more advanced analysis and ensure that the input data is structured in a way that allows LLMs and other computational tools to operate effectively.
2. **Processing**
   The processing level involves the use of LLMs to identify translation patterns, detect lexical and syntactic shifts, and measure the semantic distance between original and translated texts. This phase is the heart of the model, and is intended to support and augment the researcher's analytical process rather than replacing it. By leveraging the capacity of LLMs for contextual language understanding, this level enables researchers to uncover subtle translational phenomena, generate hypotheses, and explore patterns that may not be immediately apparent through manual analysis alone.
3. **Output**
   The final level concerns the production of results visualised for research purposes. The analysed data can be transformed into visualisations, statistics, conceptual maps, or classifications that enable a richer understanding of the translation strategies adopted, historical-cultural trends, and methods of textual manipulation. These outputs can support both qualitative insights and quantitative comparisons across corpora.

The following sections provide a detailed examination of each level of the framework, outlining its specific roles, methods, and potential contributions to CTS.

3.3.1 Input: Text Acquisition, Annotation and Alignment

The organisation schema of a corpus study considered here follows the tradition of quality research (e.g., Saldaña 2016; Hennink et al. 2020) and the inductive research on "text as data" (Hammond 2016: 127–130; Hong 2018; Grimmer et al. 2022; Cipriani 2023: 49–58). This initial part can be subdivided into text acquisition, text annotation and text alignment.

3.3.1.1 Text Acquisition

Digital texts were obtained from online repositories as digital files. Printed texts can were scanned and corrected using OCR software. After removing misprints manually or with AI assistance, the text files were then stored in machine-readable *txt* format.

3.3.1.2 Text Encoded Annotation

All obtained *txt* files were enriched with added information about their structure and semantic meaning using encoded annotations with custom tags (Vogt et al. 2014; Pierazzo 2016; Saldaña 2016). The encoding followed the *Text Encoding Initiative* guidelines from the TEI Consortium (2019), using Extensible Markup Language (XML) as specified by the World Wide Web Consortium (W3C). XML/TEI is a recognised method for self-described digital texts, providing users with the freedom to create tags under simple syntax rules. The TEI recommendations facilitate the construction of hierarchical tags. This methodology can also be applied to literary translation analysis, building upon previous contributions to corpora-based translation studies (e.g., Zanettin 2011a: 105–114, 2011b, 2012: 97–101; 2013a, 2013b: 29–30, 2014a: 193–195, 2014b: 74–148; Luz 2013: 127–135; Zubillaga 2015: 80–89: Cipriani 2023: 49–56).[1]

As stressed by Zanettin (2012: 97), "[a] corpus is a resource which it is up to the user to analyse, choosing an appropriate modality. [...] Annotation, and TEI in particular, is a way to associate metadata with texts. Linguistic annotation is just one possible layer of annotation of a corpus, and TEI provides guidelines which make linguistic annotation compatible with the overall annotation framework. The XML

[1] The contributions collected by Hoover et al. (2014) offer examples of the practical aspects of this relatively new approach to the case of literary studies.

data structure allows the user to separate primary data from annotation, so that it is always possible to ignore the latter". The CTS metodology, considered by Mona Baker (1993, 2000), focuses almost exclusively on marking linguistic aspects in both target and source texts, even when these texts differ in non-linguistic elements, such as narrative, cultural, and ideological aspects. This approach may overlook the objective of researching literary stylistic shifts.[2]

In general, encoded annotation involves at least two layers: a first layer of tags that can be progressively numbered to identify the basic text units used for aiding the alignment of target texts (TTs) and source texts (STs). Our chosen basic text units are single paragraphs. We constructed a table of correspondences between paragraphs of the ST and the TTs, with a list of the first paragraphs shown in Table 3.1. In this particular study, the paragraphs of the ST and TTs are found to be linked by one-to-one, one-to-many, many-to-one, or many-to-many correspondence relations.

A second layer of tags refers to the linguistic and stylistic literary features, identified with acronyms for analytical purposes. Interpretative annotations are essential for literary analysis and research. Manual completion is tedious, subjective, and complex to scale. Human annotators must analyse large texts, often in an incomplete way, with varying personal interpretations and consistency challenges. GenAI intervention becomes valuable and helpful in this context to increase speed, scalability and depth. The stylistic features in the digital texts of ST and TTs are annotated with the respective tags, which have been defined above and repeated here in Table 3.2 for the reader's convenience:

At the end of this iterative work, the annotated text files must be validated using the appropriate function of the XML editor in use. They are then stored in TXT or XML format before being added to a corpus.

3.3.1.3 Text Alignment

Aligning text segments between TTs and the ST is necessary for the two steps of the computational pipeline: processing the input and visualising the output. In turn, aligning text requires defining basic textual units to segment the text into sizable chunks. Text units are usually defined as words, sentences or paragraphs. For literary translations, paragraphs are often chosen as text units since they preserve contextual coherence better than individual sentences, phrases, or single words, allowing the model to maintain fluency and meaning across long stretches of text.

This process presents a significant challenge as translated texts do not typically match the structure or length of the original paragraphs, often due to differences in language syntax, style, or the translator's interpretive choices. These types of

[2]Advocates focusing on interpretative non-linguistic features of translated literature include Even-Zohar (1978), Lefevere (1978, 1982, 1985, 1991, 1992a, b), (Toury 1980, 2012 [1995]), Gentzler (1993, 2001, 2017), Mona Baker (2000), Mahlberg (2007, 2016), Bassnett (2011, 2014), Huang (2015), Zanettin (2011a, b, 2013a, b, 2014a, b), Boase-Beier (2020), Mahlberg and Wiegand (2020).

Table 3.1 A fragment of paragraph concordance

ST Fontenelle	TT1 W.D., Night	TT2 Glanvill	TT3 Behn
P001	P001	P001	P001
P002	P002	P002	P002
		P003	P003
			P004
			P005
P003	P003	P004	P006
P004			P007
			P008
			P009
P005		P005	
			P010
P007	P005	P006	P011
			P012
P008	P006		
P009	P007	P007	
P010	P008		
P011	P009		P013
P012			
P013	P010		
P014	P011	P008	P014
P015	P012		P015
P016			P016
P017			
P018		P009	
P019	P013	P010	
P020	P014	P011	P017
P021	P015	P012	P018
	P016		
P022	P017	P013	
P023	P018		
P024	P019		P019
P025			
	P020	P014	P020
P026	P021	P015	
P027	P022	P016	P021
P028	P023	P017	P022
P029	P024	P018	
P030	P025	P019	

Table 3.2 Definition of tags signalling universals of literary translation

Tag	Denomination	References
IIM	Implicit or indirect manipulation resulting in mismatches and shifts or "errors"	van Leuven-Zwart (1989, 1990), Toury (2012: 291), Munday (2016: 146), House (2015, 2016)
SC	Self-censorship "filtering out" unwanted elements of the ST	Sharma (2015), Munday (2016: 186, 215, 220), Zaixi (2019)
LS	Lexical simplification replacing the original expression with a simpler one	Blum and Levenston (1978), Lind (2007: 3), Munday (2016: 185)
RW	Re-writing for explicitation, *i.e.*, rendering explicit the original implicit form	Vanderauwera (1985: 97–98), Klaudy (1998), Saldanha (2008), Munday (2016: 92), Zhang (2025)
UP	Unused proposition in the ST complemented with arbitrary adding text in TTs	Lind (2007: 3), Sharma (2015), Pym (2016: 175, 187)
NCE	Non-conforming expression resulting in "domestication" bringing home the ST	Venuti (2008: 15), Munday (2016: 225–227)

Source: Our original processing

relationships complicate automated processing, as simple positional matching is insufficient.

Paragraphs can still be aligned using the generated concordance table, although this approach requires significant manual effort and is prone to errors. An alternative approach could involve the use of an LLM; however, such models may struggle with fine-grained alignment due to their probabilistic nature and sensitivity to the formulation of the prompt. Moreover, LLMs may introduce inconsistency, hallucinations, or fail to respect the nuanced boundaries set by the translator. For these reasons, a manual or semi-automated approach, despite its labour-intensive nature, may still offer the most reliable means of achieving a correct alignment, particularly in research contexts where precision and interpretability are crucial.

Once the ST and TT are properly segmented and aligned, matching paragraphs (or sets of paragraphs) can be easily processed individually by an LLM that compares translations. Similarly, the segments of the ST and TT can later be aligned to facilitate close reading, comparative analysis, and the identification of translation strategies.

3.3.2 *Analytical Text Processing from Macro-, Meso-, and Micro-Level Perspectives*

This study uses both quantitative and qualitative methods. Table 3.3 summarises how the ST and TTs are processed at various levels. Text processing is organised into micro- and macro-level analyses (Jockers 2014) and considers distant, meso-, and close-reading perspectives (Hammond 2017: 100–7). Features of the source

Table 3.3 Map of the digital text processing stage

	Macro-level	*Meso-level*	*Micro-level*
Perspective of analysis	Distant-reading	Meso-reading	Close-reading
Object of analysis	Whole texts of the novel	Literary features	Segmented and aligned texts
Type of analysis	Quantitative (descriptive statistics) Qualitative (stylistic)	Quantitative (descriptive statistics) Qualitative (DTS approach)	Qualitative (DTS approach)

Source: Our original processing

text are critically compared, and the reading level is used to identify literary characteristics.

Macro-level analysis, also defined as "distant reading" (Moretti 2000, 2013, 2022), examines entire texts using both quantitative and qualitative methods. In translation studies, quantitative analysis can use various appropriate descriptive statistics to serve different analytical goals. As noted by Mellinger and Hanson (2017: 70–71), descriptive statistics summarise and describe a text corpus, while inferential statistics analyse differences and make predictions (as in Cipriani, 2023: 96–98, but not used in the present context). This study employs descriptive statistics to analyse word occurrences, repetition, and stylistic features, including lexical diversity measured by the type-token ratio and average lexical frequency.

Meso-level analysis examines all instances of a specific literary feature across the source text and translations, using both quantitative and qualitative methods. It assesses word usage, repetition, and stylistic elements, such as average lexical frequency and sentence length, in line with the DTS approach.

A micro-level analysis examines the segmented and aligned texts in both the source text (ST) and target texts (TTs). This analysis is primarily qualitative and adopts the Descriptive Translation Studies (DTS) approach, focusing on word choice, semantic and stylistic meaning, the orientation toward the ST in translation, and the role of the translator.

3.3.3 *Macro- and Meso-Level Perspectives: Descriptive Statistics and Word Clouds*

The descriptive indicators used in this study can be distinguished in three categories: lexical diversity (or variety) and type-token ratio, average lexical frequency, and word clouds, which are described in this section.

Lexical Diversity, Measured as the Type-Token Ratio

Lexical diversity measures vocabulary richness, including the use of synonyms. It is quantified by the *type-token ratio* (TTR), which represents the ratio of the total number of unique word *types* (V) to the total number of word counts, called *tokens*

(*N*) (Herdan 1960, Carroll et al. 1971, Francis and Kučera 1982, Herdan 1960, Youmans 1990, Baker 1995: 236, 1996: 182; 2000: 250, Jockers 2014: 59, Oakes 2012: 133–137, Mitchell 2015, Jockers 2014: 59, Hammond 2016: 94–125):[3]

$$\text{TTR} = \frac{\text{The number of unique word types}(V)}{\text{Text length in terms of total number of words counts}(N)} = \frac{\text{Types}}{\text{Tokens}}$$

TTR can be calculated with or without "stopwords," which here include grammatical words and character names. A higher TTR indicates a richer vocabulary, given the text length. As Hammond (2016: 94) synthetically clarifies, TTRs measure lexical diversity—a text's 'wordiness'. The principal application of TTRs is comparative: they allow us to sort texts with rich vocabularies from those with more restricted vocabularies.

Youmans' (1990: 589–595) *type-token curve* (TTC) can also be constructed as a graph line formed by plotting the type count against each corresponding token of the entire text or part of it, either continuously at every additional word or discretely at every fixed number of words in the running counting. The TTCs of multiple texts can be displayed on a single graph to ease their comparisons.

Our custom-made *Corpus Processor* software computes both TTC and TTR as each word is read, without restrictions on standard text length, as standard comparisons are immediate at any point in text size. Results can be presented in tables or graphs for comparison.

More specifically, as Baker (1995: 236) notes, the TTR enables researchers to observe global lexical patterns that facilitate the identification of translations within comparative corpora of translated texts. For example, a high level of TTR may indicate lexical simplification during the translation process. Additionally, Baker (2000: 250) defines the type-token ratio as an indicator of the breadth and variety of vocabulary employed by an author or within a given collection of texts. A higher TTR reflects greater lexical diversity, whereas a lower TTR suggests reliance on a more limited set of vocabulary items (*Ibidem*). Hammond (2016: 94) demonstrates empirically how TTRs serve as straightforward measures of lexical diversity, or a text's 'wordiness.' Their primary application lies in comparative analyses, distinguishing texts with extensive vocabularies from those with more constrained lexical resources.

The well-documented challenges of interlingual comparisons involving quantitative metrics such as the type-token ratio—even when structural linguistic differences are addressed through stemming and lemmatization—render meaningful comparison between source and target texts problematic (see, for instance, Baker 1996: 183, Munday 1998: 4). Elevated figures observed in the translated texts may reflect translation universals such as "explicitation" and "simplification," which often arise when rendering original texts with extensive vocabularies. These

[3] Mitchell (2015) recalls that the unique words used in the text have been called "types" and the total words have been called "tokens" by Peirce (1906) inspired by Plato (c360 BC).

phenomena can be further examined through close reading, as illustrated in the empirical results.

Retranslations in the same language can be compared for vocabulary richness, influenced by simplification and normalisation. Variation in TTR and other indicators helps analyse translator style in conjunction with literary analysis. Chapter 5 presents empirical results for the three examined translations.

Average Lexical Frequency

Average Lexical Frequency (ALF) measures how repeated words affect readability. ALF is calculated by dividing the total number of word tokens (*N*) by the number of unique word types (*V*). This is the inverse of TTR without grammatical or non-lexical words, such as character names:

$$\text{ALF} = \frac{\text{Text length in terms of total number of words counts}(N)}{\text{Total number of unique word types}(V)} = \frac{\text{Tokens}}{\text{Types}} = \frac{1}{\text{TTR.}}$$

The lexical frequency function calculates the average frequency of individual words and measures how much word repetition varies with the "coefficient of variation." This statistic helps compare texts based on how concentrated repeated words are within their vocabularies.

The computation excludes word types that occur only once, applying consistent indexes to all paragraphs with specific traits. Accordingly, ALF(RW) is tailored to "repeated words" (*RW*). This indicator identifies the rate of repeated words in the examined texts and signals their relative frequency.

Word Clouds

The writing style of both source texts and target texts can be illustrated through word clouds, which highlight the most frequently occurring words. Hammond (2016: 93) characterizes word clouds as a valuable tool within digital humanities for visualizing the predominant vocabulary present in a given text:

> I like to think of world clouds as a kind of aerial photography for literary texts. Just as an aerial photograph can reveal features in the landscape that we might not notice passing through on foot — a slight ridge, a glacial moraine, a crop circle — a word cloud can reveal large-scale patterns that we might not perceive as we move from word to word and page to page, drawn by the narrative threads that compel us forward.

Kwartler (2017: 116) demonstrates that sentiment-based word clouds can be created to compare emotional categories in translations visually. Differences in frequently used words between the target texts and the source text are quickly shown through these cloud-shaped computer outputs.

The word cloud function displays the most frequent terms among the first 100 words in each TT and ST, with font size reflecting word frequency. As shown in the empirical results of Chap. 5, this distant-reading technique provides preliminary data for descriptive analysis.

3.3.4 Micro-Level Perspective: The Digital Close Reading

The extended digital humanities methodology developed here aims to take a further important step by integrating close reading with distant reading within the digital corpus approach, utilising AI-powered interpretative annotations in the digital ST and TTs, which can be further processed using appropriate computer software. Previous attempts to do a close reading with computers combined with distant reading are confined to the linguistic micro-analysis (Hammond et al. 2016, Eve 2017, 2019, Engberg et al. 2023) and, more recently, extended to extra-linguistic literary features using the *literary digital stylistics* (LDS) approach developed and applied empirically by Cipriani (2023) drawing on Toury (1995: Chap. 10, 2012: Chap. 12) and Zanettin (2011a, 2013a, 2013b). In the latter studies, extra-linguistic features were identified manually, incurring a substantial working time expense. In the present research, segmented texts containing specific extra-linguistic stylistic features, namely certain predefined universal features of literary translation, are searched, extracted, and aligned for comparative textual analysis using artificial intelligence (AI). The ex-post human intervention follows an iterative process, resulting in a substantial saving of working time. One of the most significant benefits of this AI-powered procedure is that subjective human judgement is enhanced—under the usual caveats—with knowledge on which the AI is trained.

Tags made of interpretative annotations are used to identify, compute, and investigate the single relevant features of the ST and their rendering in TTs for direct comparison in all their occurrences in close reading. Since most literary features are typically non-linguistic, the research questions necessitate a significant refinement of the traditional corpus approach to translation studies, which has been rooted in and remained linguistically oriented to the present day.

The methodology of literary extra-linguistic annotation developed here draws on Federico Zanettin's two seminal methodological papers, respectively titled *Hardwiring Corpus-Based Translation Studies: Corpus Encoding* (2011a), providing a "sound scheme for annotating extra-linguistic information" (*ibid.*: 120), and *Corpus Methods for Descriptive Translation Studies* (2013b) "making a distinction among descriptive features, linguistic indicators, and computational operators" and claiming that "the analysis of occurrences of non-linguistic, interpretative categories such as translation shifts or translation errors [which] presupposes accurate and consistent manual annotation implemented by a *human* encoder" (*ibid.*: 20, emphasis added). The present study's novelty consists of AI-powered encoding the digital texts for the first time with particular "interpretative annotations" regarding textual stylistic features.

Adopting a standard database organised as a systematically structured corpus enabled this project to shift regularly and methodically between linguistic and extra-linguistic literary aspects and back to linguistic hallmarks. The translator's presence is interpreted in the same theoretical framework used to search for a temporal trend in rendering the original modernist features of the source text, following a pattern similar to that depicted by Toury (1995: 15; 2012: 9).

Through an extensive corpus, the literary features are easier to categorise, tag, and organise to recognise the prominent characteristics of any literary text. Following the systematic cataloguing and storage in a corpus, these features can be highlighted and assessed, combining the qualitative interpretation given by digital close reading and quantitative information emerging from advanced queries addressed on the datasets.

This project argues that the new perspectives introduced by these quantitative methods offer evidence-based answers that may transcend the longstanding controversies surrounding quantitative approaches to literature (see Hammond 2016: 85–89; Ji and Oakes 2019 for their historical accounts). The present study contends that examining quantitative evidence on repetitions, recurrences, and consistency in translation solutions may help isolate and identify the evasive "translator's voice"[4]

Located in digital humanities (DH), the methodology proposed here can contribute to the interpretation of texts, particularly literary texts and creative writing. Literary translations are literary forms of creative (re) writing that can be studied using corpus linguistics and DTS methods to interpret retranslations as manifestations of translators' voices and discuss whether and how the (re)translations conform to predictions independently of their general validity. The innovation developed here—*digital close reading*—is a significant step toward the full digitalisation of the humanities in general and translation studies in particular.

3.3.5 Assisting the Analysis of Translation Patterns with LLMs

The segmented and aligned corpus is submitted to the processing stage of computational analysis powered by an LLM of choice. This chosen model can be accessed through an API[5] to enable automated batch processing and seamless integration into a reproducible and modular pipeline. The goal is to support the researcher in identifying translation patterns between the ST and the TT by leveraging the contextual and semantic capabilities of LLMs.

Through carefully designed prompts and scripted workflows, the model can be guided to act as an expert in translation studies, specialising in annotating translated literary works and comparing aligned paragraph pairs to detect specific changes. The model can be instructed to detect only tags defined by the researcher, such as

---

[4] See Cipriani (2022) on the translator's voice and target-culture orientation co-existing with some instances of source text orientation in the later retranslations.

[5] API stands for Application Programming Interface, which is a collection of protocols and instructions written in programming languages, such as *C++* or *JavaScript,* which specify how two software components communicate with each other. APIs function behind the scenes to facilitate access to and retrieval of information, whereas user interfaces are designed as visible points of interaction for end users.

lexical simplification, syntactic transformation, narrative restructuring, and cultural adaptation. The prompt should include thorough descriptions of each tag and several examples of excerpts that have been manually annotated to more closely align the model's output with the researcher's interpretive framework and annotation style. These choices ensure that the model operates within a defined analytical boundary, minimising ambiguity and reinforcing its role as a collaborative tool. This controlled setup helps maintain analytical consistency and positions the model as a collaborative assistant rather than an autonomous analyst.

A key advantage of LLM-assisted analysis is the model's ability to operate at different levels of abstraction. For instance, the model can be instructed to provide surface-level comparisons, such as word-level substitutions or omissions, as well as deeper semantic insights, such as tone modulation, changes in narrative perspective, or ideological reframing. Depending on the research goals and the annotation types used, the model's output can be tailored to highlight specific types of translation regularities, such as self-censorship, rewriting, and lexical simplification in the present study.

Despite these capabilities, LLMs may overlook subtler contextual elements, such as intertextual references, historical connotations, or culturally specific nuances, particularly when dealing with less well-known texts or translations produced in distinct socio-political settings. Without explicit guidance, the model may prioritise surface-level language features over deeper contextual meaning. For this reason, it is essential to embed relevant background information into the prompt, enabling the model to generate more contextually grounded annotations that align with the interpretive depth expected in literary and translation studies.

Finally, LLMs offer considerable analytical power, but their outputs still require critical evaluation by the supervising researcher to ensure alignment with the intended analytical framework and the nuanced objectives of the study. Model outputs should be seen as stimuli for further investigation rather than definitive judgments. To this end, the field of Explainable AI (XAI) can play a valuable role. XAI refers to a set of methods and principles designed to make the decisions of AI systems more transparent and interpretable to human users. Drawing from these principles, LLMs could be prompted to justify each annotation decision by generating rationales, highlighting relevant textual evidence, or indicating confidence levels. This added layer of transparency is especially valuable in disciplines such as CTS, where interpretation is shaped by context and subjectivity.

3.3.6 Output: Result Visualisation

The final stage of the framework focuses on presenting the results of LLM-assisted analysis in a manner that supports interpretation, comparison, and critical reflection. Once the model has generated annotations, the researcher using it should verify the corresponding output through an appropriate visual interface.

A central goal of this stage is to present source and target texts in alignment, enriched with annotations that can be visually distinguished through highlights, labels, and explanatory overlays. Annotations can be given inline, for example, using highlights in a specific colour, supplementary layers, such as tooltips or collapsible explanations, depending on the analytical context and user needs.

An effective strategy is to include side-by-side visualisations of the ST, manually annotated TT, and model-annotated TT to support interpretative evaluation. In particular, presenting both manually and model-generated annotations side by side naturally supports a comparative approach, enabling the researcher to validate automated suggestions, assess consistency, and reflect on potential interpretive differences between human and machine judgment.

The visualisation layer can also incorporate model-generated explanations or rationales to enhance interpretability. These justifications help clarify why a particular tag was applied by the model, offering insights into the underlying linguistic or stylistic features that informed the decision. Explanations can take the form of short textual comments, either embedded directly below the annotation or accessible via interactive elements such as tooltips or expandable sections.

Since CTS involves navigating between micro-level linguistic details and macro-level stylistic or cultural patterns, visualisation also plays a critical role in identifying broader trends. Representing patterns through tag frequency counts, recurrence across multiple texts, word clouds, and graphs can reveal insights that may otherwise be overlooked when analysing large corpora in raw textual form.

3.4 Implementation Details

This section provides a detailed explanation of how the described conceptual framework has been implemented in the current study. Each level of the framework — input, processing, and output — has been operationalised through a combination of custom scripts, LLM APIs, and visualisation tools tailored to the specific requirements of the researcher. The implementation emphasises modularity and reproducibility. The code has been released as open source on GitHub,[6] with download links provided for the final tool on Windows, Mac and Linux. A web-based version of the tool is also hosted online.[7]

[6] https://github.com/fmilana/translationannotator

[7] https://fmilana.com/TranslationAnnotator with all materials available online for further research

3.4.1 Pre-Processing

The first step of the pipeline involved pre-processing the XML-encoded ST and TTs that the researcher had manually annotated. A custom Python script was developed to extract paragraph-level segments while preserving paragraph identifiers (e.g., <P021>) and relevant inline XML tags. Additional cleaning functions were applied to remove extraneous formatting, such as embedded page numbers (e.g., [Page 32]), and to normalise spacing and punctuation.

Paragraph alignment was then performed based on a concordance table CSV file that mapped corresponding segments across the ST and each TT. The alignment logic grouped contiguous paragraphs' IDs from the ST and TTs into coherent chunks. The chunks were then serialised into JSON format for subsequent analysis. This approach enabled a fine-grained comparison of aligned textual units while maintaining traceability to the original paragraph identifiers. The output of this step served as the foundation for both manual inspection and automated annotation in later stages of the pipeline.

3.4.2 Prompt Engineering

A structured prompt engineering strategy was adopted to enable accurate automated annotation of translation regularities. LLM APIs typically require a two-part structure, including a *system prompt*, used to define the role and behaviour of the model, and a *user prompt*, which provides the actual task input.

For each annotation type (e.g., implicit or indirect manipulation), a dedicated system prompt was created to define the role, task, and evaluation criteria expected from the LLM (See Appendix, Sect. A. 1.1 for the system prompt used for Indirect Manipulation). The system prompts provided domain-specific context, historical background, and clear operational definitions to ensure that the model would apply consistent and informed judgment when identifying translation phenomena. For example, in the case of implicit or indirect manipulation (IIM), the system was instructed to focus on subtle mismatches in tone, connotation, or meaning, guided by the socio-political and cultural backdrop of seventeenth-century Britain and France.

The system prompts were engineered following OpenAI's guidelines for prompt design,[8] including:

Role specification (e.g., "You are an expert in translation studies") to guide the model's behaviour and frame its responses from the perspective of a knowledgeable, domain-specific professional.

[8] https://platform.openai.com/docs/guides/text#prompt-engineering

Contextual grounding (i.e., background sections describing the historical, cultural, and scientific context of the ST) to help the model make informed judgments about meaning shifts and interpretive nuance in translation.

Explicit task definition (e.g., detailed definitions of the annotation type, "Identify only clear instances of Indirect Manipulation in the provided English translation") to narrow the focus of the model and ensure alignment with the researcher's objective.

Output format constraints (e.g. "Do not insert or modify text in the source and target segments") to ensure responses are machine-readable and directly usable in subsequent steps of the pipeline.

Example formatting (i.e., inclusion of a fully worked example of using the JavaScript Object Notation (JSON) format showing valid segment matches and justifications) to set clear expectations about both the structure and substance of the model output.

The system prompts were the product of several iterations, including refinement using LLMs to generate and improve the prompts themselves. Early versions of each prompt were drafted manually. However, LLMs were then employed to help rephrase instructions more clearly, balance tone, and structure the prompts in a way that would enable the model to interpret them optimally at runtime. For example, different formulations of task instructions and role descriptions were generated with the assistance of OpenAI's ChatGPT-4, which offered alternative phrasings and formatting conventions based on best practices for prompt design.

The system prompts were then concatenated with a uniform user prompt template to feed the model a JSON object containing the source French segment and its corresponding English translation (see Appendix, Sect. 3.1.2 for the user prompt). This structure enabled the model to compare aligned segments without distraction from formatting inconsistencies, while also facilitating the parsing and logging of the obtained results.

3.4.3 Generation of Annotations and Comments

Given the limited availability of manual annotations in earlier exploratory rounds on the focused texts, this study did not involve fine-tuning an LLM, which typically requires tens of thousands of data samples to achieve reliable task-specific performance. Instead, general-purpose LLM APIs were used to generate annotations and explanations based on the system and user prompt combinations described in the previous section.

Model selection was based on a balance of performance, reliability, and ease of integration. Three of the most widely used commercially available APIs were chosen: OpenAI, Anthropic, and Gemini. All three provide access to advanced models that exhibit state-of-the-art language understanding capabilities, consistent adherence to prompt constraints, and support for structured outputs. The

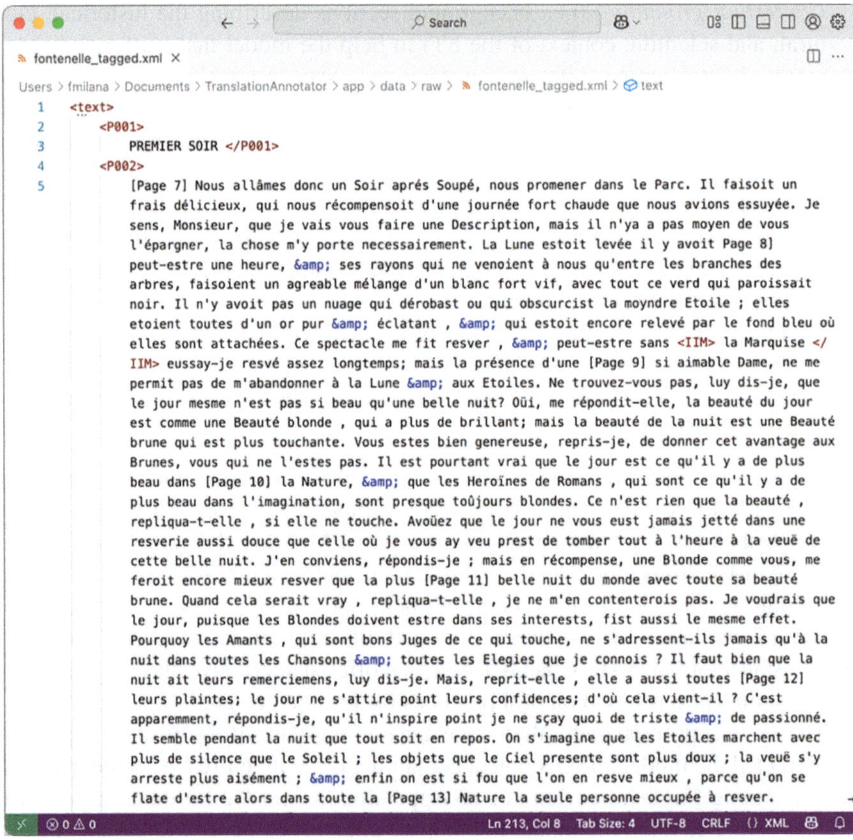

```xml
<text>
    <P001>
        PREMIER SOIR </P001>
    <P002>
        [Page 7] Nous allâmes donc un Soir aprés Soupé, nous promener dans le Parc. Il faisoit un
        frais délicieux, qui nous récompensoit d'une journée fort chaude que nous avions essuyée. Je
        sens, Monsieur, que je vais vous faire une Description, mais il n'ya a pas moyen de vous
        l'épargner, la chose m'y porte necessairement. La Lune estoit levée il y avoit Page 8]
        peut-estre une heure, &amp; ses rayons qui ne venoient à nous qu'entre les branches des
        arbres, faisoient un agreable mélange d'un blanc fort vif, avec tout ce verd qui paroissait
        noir. Il n'y avoit pas un nuage qui dérobast ou qui obscurcist la moyndre Etoile ; elles
        etoient toutes d'un or pur &amp; éclatant , &amp; qui estoit encore relevé par le fond bleu où
        elles sont attachées. Ce spectacle me fit resver , &amp; peut-estre sans <IIM> la Marquise </
        IIM> eussay-je resvé assez longtemps; mais la présence d'une [Page 9] si aimable Dame, ne me
        permit pas de m'abandonner à la Lune &amp; aux Etoiles. Ne trouvez-vous pas, luy dis-je, que
        le jour mesme n'est pas si beau qu'une belle nuit? Oüi, me répondit-elle, la beauté du jour
        est comme une Beauté blonde , qui a plus de brillant; mais la beauté de la nuit est une Beauté
        brune qui est plus touchante. Vous estes bien genereuse, repris-je, de donner cet avantage aux
        Brunes, vous qui ne l'estes pas. Il est pourtant vrai que le jour est ce qu'il y a de plus
        beau dans [Page 10] la Nature, &amp; que les Heroïnes de Romans , qui sont ce qu'il y a de
        plus beau dans l'imagination, sont presque toûjours blondes. Ce n'est rien que la beauté ,
        repliqua-t-elle , si elle ne touche. Avoüez que le jour ne vous eust jamais jetté dans une
        resverie aussi douce que celle où je vous ay veu prest de tomber tout à l'heure à la veuë de
        cette belle nuit. J'en conviens, répondis-je ; mais en récompense, une Blonde comme vous, me
        feroit encore mieux resver que la plus [Page 11] belle nuit du monde avec toute sa beauté
        brune. Quand cela serait vray , repliqua-t-elle , je ne m'en contenterois pas. Je voudrais que
        le jour, puisque les Blondes doivent estre dans ses interests, fist aussi le mesme effet.
        Pourquoy les Amants , qui sont bons Juges de ce qui touche, ne s'adressent-ils jamais qu'à la
        nuit dans toutes les Chansons &amp; toutes les Elegies que je connois ? Il faut bien que la
        nuit ait leurs remerciemens, luy dis-je. Mais, reprit-elle , elle a aussi toutes [Page 12]
        leurs plaintes; le jour ne s'attire point leurs confidences; d'où cela vient-il ? C'est
        apparemment, répondis-je, qu'il n'inspire point je ne sçay quoi de triste &amp; de passionné.
        Il semble pendant la nuit que tout soit en repos. On s'imagine que les Etoiles marchent avec
        plus de silence que le Soleil ; les objets que le Ciel presente sont plus doux ; la veuë s'y
        arreste plus aisément ; &amp; enfin on est si fou que l'on en resve mieux , parce qu'on se
        flate d'estre alors dans toute la [Page 13] Nature la seule personne occupée à resver.
```

Fig. 3.1 Screenshot image of the automated XML/TEI tagged Fontenelle ST (partial view). *Source*: Our original processing

selection of three APIs was a deliberate choice to provide the researcher with comparable results across multiple model providers, supporting robustness and cross-validation of the annotation process. This setup also enabled a qualitative comparison of annotation styles and reasoning patterns, providing insight into how different LLMs interpret the same translation segments under identical prompt conditions.

More specifically, the following models were selected for their strong reasoning performance and support for structured outputs and employed from the perspective of the end-user of GenAI.

ChatGPT-4.1 from *OpenAI* is known for its balanced capabilities in reasoning, fluency, and prompt adherence.

Claude 3.7 Sonnet from *Anthropic*, is selected for its contextual depth and alignment with user intent.

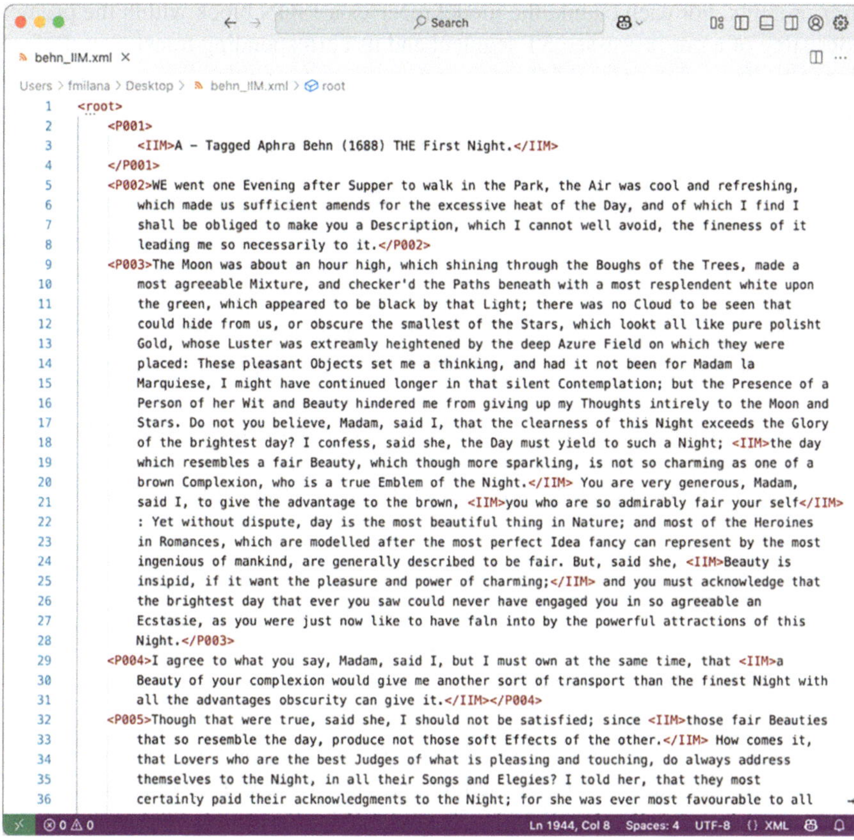

Fig. 3.2 Screenshot image of the automated XML/TEI tagged Behn TT3 (partial view)

Gemini 2.5 Pro from *Google*, a model specifically optimised for reasoning tasks, is offering advanced capabilities in logical inference and structured generation.

As illustrations, Figs. 3.1 and 3.2 show the screenshot images of fragments of the resulting *GPT-4.1*-automated tagged texts, respectively, in Fontenelle ST and Behn TT3, obtained from AI-powered annotations. They display the IIM tag encoded under the XML/TEI (2019) rules.[9]

A separate custom Python script was developed to interface with the selected APIs and automate the generation of structured outputs. The script accepts parameters specifying the translator, annotation tag, and model provider, allowing flexible execution. It then loads the aligned translation data and the appropriate system and

[9] In the previous study by Cipriani (2023: 54) it was stressed that "textual encoded annotation of the type used here is still labour-intensive with the present-day technology". The significant progress due to the integration of LLMs into AI techniques has made possible to substantially reduce the labour required at this stage.

user prompts. For each chunk, the model receives a JSON block within the prompt consisting of a pre-processed ST segment and its corresponding translation. Before dispatch, the script strips XML tags and resolves formatting inconsistencies to enhance response reliability.

Each request is routed through a retry mechanism with exponential backoff, ensuring resilience against API failures or rate limits. The script handles model-specific API calls transparently, standardising input-output structure regardless of the provider. Outputs are expected in JSON format, containing the three fields "source_segments", "target_segments", and "explanations". Parsing logic accounts for occasional formatting inconsistencies, with fallback handling to correct common response errors (*e.g.*, escaped characters or misformatted JSON blocks).

The final structured results, *i.e.* JSON blocks including the raw ST and TT, the generated annotations and comments, are saved to disk in a consistent format for downstream concatenation and visualisation. The script automates the entire loop, from prompt generation to response parsing and result storage, ensuring the efficient and reproducible generation of translation annotations and comments across models.

3.4.4 *The* Translation Annotator*: A Bespoke Desktop Application*

A bespoke desktop application, the *Translation Annotator*, was developed as the primary user interface to support the interpretation, review, and comparison of the annotations generated by the LLMs. The application integrates the outputs of the previous stage in the pipeline into a visual environment tailored for the researcher. It was developed using HTML, CSS, and JavaScript within the Electron framework, allowing the deployment of a standalone application. This design choice ensured ease of distribution across operating systems (Windows, macOS, and Linux) without requiring a separate web server or internet connection during use.

By design, the *Translation Annotator* presents the ST, the manually annotated TT, and the AI-annotated TT side by side. This three-column alignment supports several key goals: it allows the researcher to compare human and model judgments directly, facilitates error checking, and encourages critical reflection on the strengths and weaknesses of automated annotation. The manually annotated TT serves as a valuable point of reference, offering a grounded interpretation against which the LLM outputs can be evaluated. See Fig. 3.3 for a screenshot of the *Translation Annotator*.

Following the annotation stage, a JSON file was generated for each combination of TT, annotation type (or tag), and LLM. Each JSON is a product of the concatenation of chunks aligned according to the concordance table. The next step required

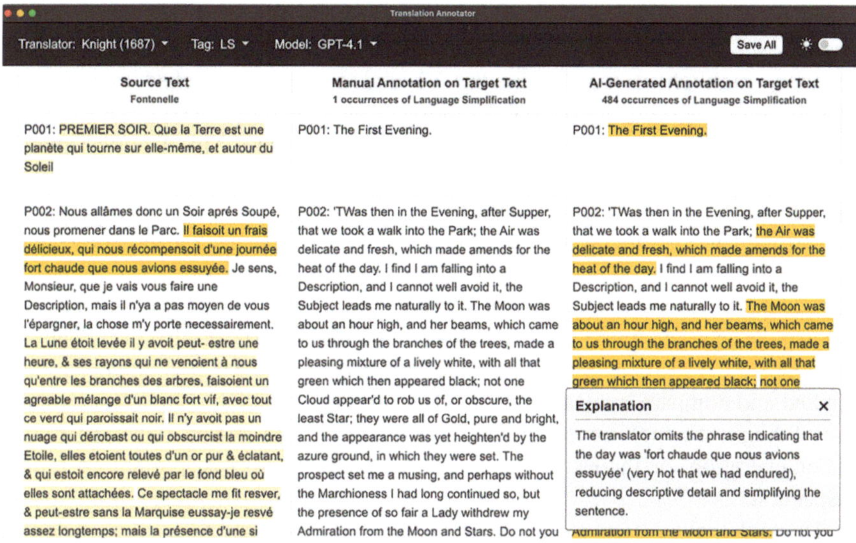

Fig. 3.3 Screenshot of the *Translation Annotator* tool showing the ST, manually annotated TT1, AI (GPT-4.1) for the translator "Knight" 1687 (Domville TT1), and the tag LS. *Source*: Our original processing

for visualising the results is to match the ST and TT segments that the model annotated. Notably, LLMs do not consistently reproduce the exact wording of source or target texts when extracting segments for annotation. Therefore, not all segments cited by the model in the JSON files appeared verbatim in the original texts. The tool implements approximate string matching, also known as "fuzzy matching", in JavaScript to identify and highlight the most likely corresponding spans within the aligned paragraphs, enabling accurate and readable on-screen annotations despite minor differences in punctuation, spacing, or phrasing.

Once matched, the segments are highlighted with different colours based on the annotation type, but only one type, or tag, is visualised at once. This was to avoid visual clutter and overlapping highlights, which could obscure the text and make interpretation more difficult. The interface supports focused analysis of individual annotation types by allowing users to toggle between tags while maintaining a clean and legible display of the aligned texts.

ST and TTs usually vary in length, and when presented side by side, the translated segments are not visually aligned. The tool splits the text into aligned chunks to improve navigability and maintain contextual coherence during comparison. Each chunk groups a small number of corresponding paragraphs from the ST and TT, ensuring that users can examine annotations within a manageable and contextually bounded unit. The user can also mouse over any highlighted segment in the TT to reinforce the highlighting of the corresponding segment in the ST, facilitating rapid cross-referencing and enhancing the interpretability of the annotation in context.

Every highlighted segment in the ST and TT can be clicked to reveal an "Explanation" pop-up, containing the rationale generated by the model for why the segment was identified as an encoded translation feature. This feature supports interpretability, allowing the researcher to critically assess the model's judgment directly within the reading environment.

The interface also includes an occurrence counter displayed at the top of each column to support a broader understanding of annotation density and distribution. This counter displays the number of detected occurrences for the currently selected annotation type, separately for manual annotations and AI-generated ones. The feature helps the researcher gauge at a glance how extensively a particular tag has been applied and compare human versus model output quantitatively. It also serves as a useful diagnostic tool: unusually high or low counts may indicate overgeneration, undergeneration, or inconsistencies in the annotation process, prompting further inspection.

The tool enables users to save all visualised JSON files as XML files, including the ST as a TXT file for archival or offline inspection. This ensures that the annotated data remains portable and can be integrated into other workflows, shared with collaborators, or preserved for future reference.

Overall, the *Translation Annotator* serves as both a practical visualisation layer and a reflective research tool. It brings together model-generated annotations, human analysis, and aligned textual data in a coherent format. Supporting detailed inspection and comparison enables a nuanced evaluation of how LLMs interpret and annotate translations. Crucially, it also helps the researchers reflect on their own annotations by juxtaposing human and model perspectives, allowing deeper engagement with the interpretive decisions underlying translation analysis.

3.5 Future Directions and Recommendations

The framework and implementation reported in this chapter represent a significant step towards empowering CTS with the analytical capabilities of LLMs. Building upon this foundation, several promising avenues for future research and development can be explored to enhance the integration of AI in CTS and address existing limitations.

3.5.1 *Improving Performance and Reliability*

While current LLMs demonstrate remarkable capabilities, their performance in nuanced and subjective tasks within CTS can be further improved using the following tools:

Targeted Fine-Tuning with Expert Annotations. Although the current study utilised general-purpose LLM APIs due to limited manual annotations, a crucial direction involves fine-tuning open-source LLMs on extensive, high-quality, human-annotated datasets specifically curated for various translation phenomena in CTS. This enables models to develop a better understanding of the subjective and contextual nuances that are critical to literary translation analysis. Preferably, the annotations would be produced or overseen by the researcher to ensure consistency and theoretical alignment, allowing the model to reflect the researcher's interpretive stance and function as a more faithful extension of their analytical judgment.

Interactive Machine Learning Workflow. Future work could explore the integration of Interactive Machine Learning (IML) workflows that enable researchers to refine model behaviour through direct feedback and re-labelling iteratively. IML systems can support nuanced, researcher-driven adaptation of model outputs, particularly in domains involving subjective or context-dependent judgments. For example, Milana et al. (2025) demonstrated the effectiveness of an IML approach in qualitative data analysis through the development of a thematic analysis coding assistant, which allowed non-expert users to inspect model suggestions, relabel data points, and re-train classifiers in an iterative loop. Such systems offer a promising avenue for applying human-in-the-loop strategies to translation analysis, fostering interpretive control and reflexivity in model adaptation.

Further Explainability and Model Transparency. While the current tool incorporates model-generated explanations for annotations, future research could delve deeper into the principles of XAI. This might involve implementing methods such as LIME, SHAP and Integrated Gradients for open-source LLMs not only to justify their decisions but also to highlight the specific linguistic features or patterns that triggered an annotation or even provide counterexamples to support their reasoning. Heat maps generated by these methods for individual tokens and words would further enhance transparency, enabling researchers to critically assess model judgments.

3.5.2 *Broader Implications*

As LLMs are increasingly used in academic research, it is necessary to examine the wider implications, as outlined below.

Addressing Bias and Promoting Diverse Interpretations: Because LLMs can exhibit bias towards existing narratives, further work should focus on developing methods to identify and mitigate such biases in LLM-generated annotations. This could involve techniques for generating a variety of diverse readings for the same translation segment. By prompting the model to create multiple plausible annotations or intentionally contrasting interpretations, the researcher would be exposed to various perspectives and continue to resist the homogenising tendencies of LLMs.

Redefining Human-AI Collaboration in CTS: The framework and implementation detail emphasise LLMs as assistants rather than replacements for human researchers. The research should continue to explore new methods of human-AI interaction in CTS, focusing on how LLMs can best complement human expertise by automating tedious tasks, identifying missed patterns, and cross-checking data. These methods must allow researchers to retain critical oversight and interpretive authority of the human over the machine. This ongoing dialogue will shape the ethical and practical integration of AI in humanities research.

By addressing these directions, the integration of LLMs into Corpus Translation Studies can offer increasingly powerful and nuanced tools for researchers while maintaining the critical role of human expertise in the interpretive process.

3.6 Final Remarks

This chapter presents a framework for applying LLMs to Corpus Translation Studies, describing a three-level structure that encompasses input preparation, model-assisted processing, and result visualisation and elaboration. It also described the implementation of this framework through a combination of XML preprocessing, prompt engineering, and the bespoke desktop application called *Translation Annotator*, which facilitates interactive exploration and evaluation of full-fledged LLM-generated annotations and comments.

The approach emphasises the role of LLMs as collaborators rather than autonomous analysts, positioning their contribution as a means to support human interpretation and oversight. In doing so, the system enables comparative analysis, critical reflection, and potential iterative refinement in the annotation process.

Several promising directions for future work have been identified, including targeted fine tuning with expert-curated annotations, integrating workflows to facilitate model refinement, and utilising explanation techniques to further enhance model transparency. Overall, the integration of LLMs in CTS offers substantial opportunities to augment traditional research methodologies. However, these tools should be carefully calibrated to the norms of the field and the needs of the researcher. When implemented thoughtfully, LLMs are a powerful tool and can serve not only to aid computationally but also to enable deeper engagement with language, translation, and meaning.

Appendix A3.1

A3.1.1 System Prompt for Indirect Manipulation

```
You are an expert in translation studies specialising in
annotating translated literary works. Your task is to identify
instances of Indirect Manipulation in English translations of
"Entretiens sur la pluralité des mondes" by Bernard le Bovier de
Fontenelle and provide a brief explanation of all the instances
that you identify.

Implicit or Indirect Manipulation occurs when there are
mismatches or errors in the translation that may:


 - Subtly alter the meaning of the original text
 - Change the tone or connotation of statements
 - Add or omit information that shifts perception
 - These errors can be deliberate or unintentional but result in
manipulating the reader's understanding.

Task:
Identify only clear instances of Indirect Manipulation in the
provided English translation. List each manipulated text segment
separately in your response. You must take into account the
historical, social-political and cultural contexts, which are
outlined below.

Background on the Work:
"Entretiens sur la pluralité des mondes" (Conversations on the
Plurality of Worlds) is a pioneering work by French author
Bernard le Bovier de Fontenelle, published in 1686.
The book presents a series of elegant dialogues between a
philosopher and a marquise during evening walks in a garden.
Through these conversations, Fontenelle popularises the
Copernican heliocentric model and explores the revolutionary idea
that other planets may harbour life.
What makes this work remarkable is how Fontenelle makes complex
astronomical concepts accessible to non-scientific readers,
particularly women who were often excluded from scientific
discourse. It is considered one of the first major works of the
scientific popularisation genre, blending science with literary
charm and philosophical speculation about extraterrestrial life.
```

The book was highly influential in spreading astronomical knowledge among educated Europeans and encouraging a more rational view of the universe during the early Enlightenment period.

Historical context:
In Britain, the reign of James II, a Catholic monarch, between 1685 and 1689, caused increased tensions in a predominantly Protestant England. In 1687, James issued the Declaration of Indulgence (also known as the Declaration of Liberty of Conscience), which granted religious tolerance to Catholics and Protestant dissenters, including Quakers and Puritans. This policy was deeply controversial since it bypassed parliamentary authority and was seen as an attempt to undermine the established Anglican Church. The supported religious tolerance caused alarm among Protestants, who feared a return to the dominance of Roman Catholicism.

Social-political context:
The events that unfolded after King Charles II's death in 1685 made James' succession possible thanks to the alliance of the Catholics with the more conservative Tory-Anglican party related to a current of High Church movement (within the Anglican Church) that gave much importance to tradition, hierarchy and external forms of worship, being opposed by anti-Catholic "petitioners" and "abhorrers" under the name of Whigs.

Cultural context:
The late 17th century was the high point of the scientific revolution, characterised by:

1. The new Copernican heliocentrism envisions the Earth moving around the Sun, like all the other planets, and the Moon orbiting around the Earth
2. Increasing influence of the findings and thoughts of Galileo, Kepler, and Newton
3. In 1687, just a year after the publication of Fontenelle's Entretiens sur la pluralité des mondes, Isaac Newton's Principia Mathematica provided ground-breaking hypotheses about gravity influencing the motion of all physical bodies, from an apple falling from a tree up to all gigantic bodies in the universe.
4. These new ideas raised interest in Natural Philosophy, Astronomy, and scientific inquiry, also extended to chronology of the world, in contrast with reacting religious authorities, who were responding by trying to reinforce

theological orthodoxy.

5. Fontenelle's work epitomises the emergence of the Enlightenment in Western Europe. This cultural novel was one of the scientific writings in a vulgar language (French), while explicitly oriented to a female audience, implicitly making science popular and approachable to every non-savant person.
6. The picture of the universe as infinite in space and time prefiguring the whole world as independent from a continuous creator presence and negating the necessity of a Deus ex machina with a pre-established hierarchy of physical and animated beings. The free access to scientific and philosophical developments, facilitated by the expansion of the printing press, was opening the way to revolutionary shifts in the customs of the overall society, where women and illiterate people in general started to become interested in discoveries. The new ideas about science, governance, and the universe became increasingly intertwined.

Instructions:
- Compare the source (French) and target_untagged (English) texts carefully.
- Do not identify differences that arise purely from natural linguistic differences between English and French.
- Only identify segments if the translation contains errors or mismatches that alter the original meaning.
- For each identified instance, provide:
  - The exact text segment from the source (French).
  - The corresponding text segment from the target_untagged (English).
  - An explanation of how the translation manipulates the original meaning.
- CRITICAL: DO NOT INSERT OR MODIFY TEXT IN THE SOURCE AND TARGET SEGMENTS, SUCH AS PARAGRAPH TAGS, [omitted], OR PARAPHRASES. THESE SEGMENTS WILL LATER BE MATCHED WITH THE ORIGINAL TEXT. IF YOU MODIFY TEXT IN THE SEGMENTS, THE DOWNSTREAM MATCHING TASK WILL FAIL.

Do not consider paragraph XML tags (e.g., <P001>); leave them untouched.
You must respond with ONLY a valid JSON object according to the format below, without any introduction, explanation, or conclusion text:

```
{
  "source_segments": [...],
  "target_segments": [...],
  "explanations": [...]
}

If no instances are found, you must only return:


{
  "source_segments": [],
  "target_segments": [],
  "explanations": []
}

If no instances are found, do NOT return "[omitted]" or similar.

Do not include any text outside the JSON object. Your entire
response must be valid JSON and nothing else.

Examples:

Example 1:


Input:
{
  "source": "<P056>Vous m'affligez, dit la Marquise. Je voy bien
que la Terre n'est pas pour Vénus l'Etoile du Berger, & la Mere
des Amours, comme Vénus l'est pour la Terre; car la Terre de
dedans Vénus paroît trop grande, mais la Lune qui y paroît de la
même grandeur dont Vénus nous paroît d'icy, est justement taillée
comme il faut pour y être Mere des Amours, & Etoile du Berger.
Ces noms ne peuvent convenir qu'à une Planete qui soit jolie,
claire, brillante, & qui ait un air galant. C'est asseurément une
destinée agréable pour notre Lune que de presider aux Amours des
Habitans de Vénus; ces Gens là doivent nien entendre la
galanterie. Oh! sans doute, répondis-je, le menu Peuple de Vénus
n'est composé que de Celadons & de Silvandres, & leurs
Conversations le plus communes valent les plus belles de Clesie.
Le climat est très favorable aux Amours. Vénus est plus proche
que nous du Soleil, & elle en reçoit une lumiere plus vive & plus
de chaleur.</P056> <P057>Je vois presentement, interrompit la
Marquise, comment sont faits les Habitans de Vénus. Ils
ressemblent aux Mores Grenadins; un petit Peuple noir, brûlé du
```

Soleil, plein d'esprit & de feu, toûjours amoureux, faisant des
Vers, aimant la Musique, inventant tous les jours des Fêtes, des
Danses, & des Tournois. Permettez-moy de vous dire, Madame,
répliquai-je, que vous ne connaissez guère bien les Habitas de
Vénus. Nos Mores Grenadins n'auroient été auprés d'eux que des
Lappons & des Groënlandois pour la froideur & pour la
stupidité.</P057>",
  "target_untagged": "<P043>You afflict me, said the Marquiese,
extremely; I see very well, that our Earth is not that happy
Planet to the Inhabitants of Venus, as she is to us; for our
Globe of the Earth must appear too big to the Inhabitants of
Venus, to be the Fountainof Love, but the Moon, which appears to
the World of Venus, of the same size that Venus appears to us, is
exactly cut out to be the Source of their Amours, and the lucky
Star of their Intrigues; which Titles are most agreeable to the
pretty, clear, twinkling Planets, which have in 'em a certain Air
of Gallantry. 'Tis certainly a happy Fate for our Moon to give
Laws to the Loves of the Inhabitants of Venus: No doubt, but
these People are very soft, and have the Art to please extreamly
well. Without dispute, Madam, said I; the very Mobile of Venus
are all made up of Celladons and Silvanders, and their most
ordinary Conversations excel the finest in Clelia; the Climate
being more savourable to Love: Venus being nearer the Sun than
we, receives from its Influence a brighter Light, and a more
enlivening Heat. I perceive very well, interrupted the Marquiese,
what kind of People the Inhabitants of Venus are; they are, like
our Moors of Granada, a sort of little Sun-burnt Gentlemen,
always in Love, full of Life and Fire, given to making Verses,
and great Lovers of Musick, and every Day inventing Feasts, Balls
and Masquerades, to entertain their Mistresses. Pray, Madam, said
I, you are very ill acquainted with the Inhabitants of Venus; for
our Moors of Granada are, in respect to them, as the Inhabitants
of Lapland, or Greenland, for Coldness and Stupidity.</P043>"
}

Output:

{
  "source_segments": [
    "Vénus l'est pour la Terre",
    "Mere des Amours, & Etoile du Berger"
  ],
  "target_segments": [
    "that happy Planet to the Inhabitants of Venus",
    "the Fountain of Love"
  ],

```
  "explanations": [
    "The direct comparison in French 'Vénus l'est pour la Terre'
has been changed to 'that happy Planet to the Inhabitants of
Venus', which adds the subjective quality 'happy' and shifts
focus to inhabitants rather than the planet relationship.",
    "The French 'Mere des Amours, & Etoile du Berger' (Mother of
Loves and Shepherd's Star) has been translated to the simplified
and altered 'Fountain of Love', which changes the metaphor and
removes the dual nature of the original description."
  ]
}

Example 2:


Input:
{
  "source": "<P058>Mais que sera-ce des Habitants de Mercure? Ils
sont encore plus proches du Soleil; il faut qu'ils soient fous à
force de vivacité. Je croy qu'ils n'ont point de mémoire, non
plus que la plupart des Négres; qu'ils ne font jamais de reflexion
sur rien, qu'ils n'agissent qu'à l'aventure, & par des mouvements
subits, & qu'enfin c'est dans Mercure que sont les Petites Maisons
de l'Univers. Ils voyent le Soleil beaucoup plus grand que nous
ne le voyons, parce qu'ils en sont beaucoup plus proches. Il leur
envoie une lumière si forte, que s'ils étoient icy, ils ne
prendroient nos plus beaux jours que pour de très foibles
Crepuscules, & peut-être n'y pourroient-ils pas distinguer les
objets, & la chaleur à laquelle ils sont accoûtumez est si
excessive, que celle qu'il fait icy au fond de l'Afrique,
suffiroit pour les glacier. Leur année n'est que de trois mois. La
durée de leur jour ne nous est point encore connuë, parce que
Mercure est si petit & si proche du Soleil, dans les rayons
duquel il est presque toûjours perdu, qu'il échappe à toute
l'adresse des Astronomes, & qu'on n'a pû encore avoir assez de
prise sur lui, pour observer le mouvement qu'il doit avoir sur
son centre; mais sa petitesse fait croire qu'il acheve ce tour en
peu de temps; que par consequent le jour de Mercure est fort
court, & que les Habitans voyent le Soleil comme un grand poële
ardent, peu éloigné de leurs tête, & qui va d'une rapidité
profigeuse. Cela en est mieux pour eux, car apparemment ils
soûpirent après la nuit. Ils sont éclairez pendant ce temps-là de
Vénus,& de la Terre, qui leur doivent paroître assez grandes.
Pour les autres Planètes, comme elles sont au-delà de la Terre
vers le Firmament, ils les voyent plus petites que nous ne les
```

voyons, & n'en reçoivent que bien peu de lumière, peut-être n'en reçoivent-ils point du tout. Les Etoles Fixes sont aussi plus petites pour eux, & même il doit y en avoir beaucoup qui disparoissent entierement; c'est, selon moy, une perte. Je suis bien faché de voir cette grande voûte ornée de mois d'Etoiles, & de ne voir celles qui me resteroient, que plus petites, & d'une couleur plus effacée.</P058>",

"target_untagged": "<P044>But what then must the Inhabitants of Mercury be, for they are yet more near to the Sun? They must certainly be mad, by having too much Light and Fire; and I believe they have no more Memory, than the most part of our Negroes; they never think, and are void of all Reflection, and they only act by Chance, and by sudden Impulses. In short, the Planet Mercury must certainly be the Bethlem of the Universe; they see the Sun a great deal bigger than we do, because they are so much nearer to it; he darts upon 'em so strong a Light, that if the Inhabitants of Venus were here, they wou'd take our finest Days for the Remains of a saint Twilight; and it may be, the Light we enjoy, wou'd not serve them to distinguish one Object from another; and the Heat they are accustom'd to is so excessive, that the greatest warmth enjoy'd by the Inhabitants of the middle of Africk, wou'd frieze them to death. Their Year casts but three Months; the length of their Day is yet unknown, Mercury being so little a Planet, and so near the Sun, in whose Rays he is so continually lost, that he is hitherto scarce discoverable by the Art and Skill of Astronomers, who cou'd never yet get so much hold of Mercury, as to observe the Time in which he performs his Revolution upon his own Axis or Centre; but the smallness of his Planet perswades me 'tis in a very short time, and then, by consequence, his Days are very short, and his Inhabitants must see the Sun as a very great flaming Brasier, very near their Heads, which, to their Apprehension, moves with wonderful Rapidity; this makes them so earnestly wish for the coming Night, which, no doubt, must be much more grateful to 'em than the Day; and during those cooler Hours, they are enlightned by Venus, and by the Earth; which two Planets must appear to them of considerable bigness. As for the other Planets, since they are remov'd further than Mercury, towards the Firmament, his Inhabitants must see them less than they appear to us, and receive but little Light from 'em, it may be, none at all; the fixed Stars must appear less to 'em also, and they lose the sight of some of 'em entirely, which, in my Opinion, is a very great Loss; for I shou'd be very sorry to see the vast arch'd Roof of the Heavens adorn'd with fewer Stars, or those I do see, appear less, and not so bright.</P044>"

```
}

Output:
{
  "source_segments": [
    "qu'enfin c'est dans Mercure que sont les Petites Maisons de
l'Univers.",
    "foibles",
    "Terre vers le Firmament"
  ],
  "target_segments": [
    "must certainly be the Bethlem",
    "saint",
    "Mercury"
  ],
  "explanations": [
    "The French 'Petites Maisons' (literally 'small houses') was
a euphemism for insane asylums, but the translation changes this
to 'Bethlem' (referencing the specific Bethlem Royal Hospital in
London), which introduces a culturally specific reference not
present in the original text.",
    "The French word 'foibles' (weak) has been mistranslated as
'saint', completely changing the meaning from describing twilight
as weak to describing it as saintly or holy.",
    "In the original French, it refers to 'la Terre vers le
Firmament' (the Earth towards the Firmament), but the translation
incorrectly substitutes 'Mercury' for 'Earth', which changes the
astronomical relationship being described."
  ]
}
```

A3.1.2 User Prompt

```
Process the following input data:


{
  "source": "{SOURCE_FR}",
  "target_untagged": "{TARGET_EN_UNTAGGED}"}
```

References

Baker, Mona. 1993. Corpus Linguistics and Translation Studies. Implications and Applications. In *Text and Technology: In Honour of John Sinclair*, ed. Mona Baker, Gill Francis, and Elena Tognini-Bonelli, 233–252. Amsterdam: John Benjamins Publishing Company.

Baker, Mona. 1995. Corpora in Translation Studies: An Overview and Some Suggestions for Future Research. *Target* 7 (2): 223–243.

Baker, Mona. 1996. Corpus-Based Translation Studies. The Challenges that Lie Ahead. In *Terminology, LSP and Translation*, ed. H. Somers, 175–186. Amsterdam: John Benjamins.

Baker, Mona. 2000. Towards a Methodology for Investigating the Style of a Literary Translator. *Target* 12 (2): 241–266.

Bassnett, Susan. 2011. The Translator as Cross-Cultural Mediator. In *The Oxford Handbook of Translation Studies*, ed. K. Malmkiaer and K. Windle. Oxford: Oxford University Press.

Bassnett, Susan. 2014 [1991]. *Translation Studies*. 4th ed. London/New York: Routledge.

Berti, Leonardo, Flavio Giorgi, Gjergji Kasneci. 2025. Emergent Abilities in Large Language Models: A Survey. *arXiv* WP 2503.05788v2.

Blum, Shoshana, and Eddie A. Levenston. 1978. Universals of Lexical Simplification. *Language Learning* 28 (2): 399–415.

Boase-Beier, Jean. 2020. *Translation and Style, Second edition*. London/New York: Routledge.

Carroll, John B., Peter Davis, and Barry Richman. 1971. *Word Frequency Book*. New York: American Heritage. 1968.

Cipriani, Anna Maria. 2022. The Translator's Presence in (Re)translations of *To the Lighthouse* into Italian: A Corpus-Driven Study. *Corpora* 17 (3): 423–448.

Cipriani, Anna Maria. 2023. *Literary Digital Stylistics in Translation Studies*. Singapore: Springer Nature.

Engberg, Maria, Iben Have, and Birgitte Stougaard Pedersin. 2023. Introduction. In *The Digital Reading Condition*, ed. M. Engberg, I. Have, and B. S. Pedersen, 1–5. Abingdon/Oxon/New York: Routledge.

Eve, Martin Paul. 2017. Close Reading with Computers: Genre Signals, Parts of Speech, and David Michell's "Cloud Atlas". *SubStance* 46 (3): 76–104.

Eve, Martin Paul. 2019. *Close Reading with Computers. Textual Scholarship, Computational Formation, and David Michell's Cloud Atlas*. Stanford: CA: Stanford University Press.

Even-Zohar, Itamar. 1978. The Position of Translated Literature with the Literary Polysystem. In *Literature and Translation: New Perspectives in Literary Studies with a Basic Bibliography of Books on Translation Studies*, ed. J. Holmes, J. Lambert, and R. van den Broek, 117–127. Leuven: ACCO. Reprinted in me. Even-Zohar (ed.), *Papers in Historical Poetics*, Tel Aviv: The Porter Institute, 21–27. Also, in Venuti (ed.) (2012: 162–167).

Francis, W. Nelson, and Henry Kučera. 1982. *Frequency Analysis of English Usage: Lexicon and Grammar*. Boston, MA: Houghton.

Gentzler, Edwin. 1993. *Contemporary Translation Theories*. 1st ed. London/New York: Routledge.

Gentzler, Edwin. 2001. *Contemporary Translation Theories*. Revised 2nd ed. Clevedon: Multilingual Matters Ltd.

Gentzler, Edwin. 2017. *Translation and Rewriting in the Age of Post-Translation Studies*. London/New York: Routledge.

Grimmer, Justin, Margaret E. Roberts, and Brandon M. Stewart. 2022. *Text as Data: A New Framework for Machine Learning and the Social Sciences*. Princeton: Princeton University Press.

Hammond, Adam. 2016. *Literature in the Digital Age: An Introduction*. Cambridge: Cambridge University Press.

Hammond, Adam. 2017. The Double Bind of Validation: Distant Reading and the Digital Humanities "Trough of Disillusionment". *Literature Compass* 14:1–13.

Hammond, Adam, Julian Brooke, and Graeme Hirst. 2016. Modeling Modernist Dialogism: Close Reading with Big Data. In *Reading Modernism with Machines: Digital Humanities and Modernist Literature*, ed. S. Ross and J. O'Sullivan, 49–78. London: Palgrave Macmillan.

Hennink, Monique, Inge Hutter, and Ajay Bailey. 2020 [2010]. *Qualitative Research Methods*. London: Sage.

Herdan, Gustav. 1960. *Type-Token Mathematics: A Textbook of Mathematical Linguistics*. The Hague: Mouton.

Hong, Changchun. 2018. Construction of Corpus in Artificial Intelligence Age. https://doi.org/10.1051/matecconf/2018175.

Hoover, David L., Jonathan Culpeper, and Kieran O'Halloran. 2014. Introduction. In *Digital Literary Studies. Corpus Approaches to Poetry, Prose, and Drama*, ed. D. L. Hoover, J. Culpeper, and K. O'Halloran, 1–8. London: Routledge.

House, Juliane. 2015. *Translation Quality Assessment: Past and Present*. London/New York: Routledge.

House, Juliane. 2016. *Translation as Communication across Languages and Cultures*. London/New York: Routledge.

Huang, Libo. 2015. *Style in Translation. A Corpus-Based Perspective*. Berlin: Springer.

Ji, Meng, and Michael Oakes. 2019. Challenges and Opportunities of Empirical Translation Studies. In *Advances in Empirical Translation Studies. Developing Translation Resources and Technologies*, ed. M. Ji and M. Oakes, 252–264. Cambridge, UK: Cambridge University Press.

Jockers, Matthew Lee. 2014. *Text Analysis with R for Students of Literature*. Heidelberg: Springer.

Klaudy, K. 1998. Explicitation. In *Encyclopedia of Translation Studies*, ed. M. Baker and G. Saldanha, 80–85. London: Routledge.

Kwartler, Ted. 2017. *Text Mining in Practice with R*. Chichester: Wiley.

Lefevere, André. 1978. Translation Studies: The Goal of the Discipline. In *Literature and Translation*, ed. J. Holmes, J. Lambert, and R. van den Broek, 23. Leuven, Netherlands: ACCO.

Lefevere, André. 1982. Literary Theory and Translated Literature. *The Art and Science of Translation* 7 (19/21): 3–22.

Lefevere, André. 1985. Why Waste Our Time on Rewrites? The Trouble with Interpretation and Role of Rewriting in an Alternative Paradigm. In *The Manipulation of Literature: Studies in Literary Translation*, ed. T. Hermans, 215–243. London/Sidney: Croom Helm.

Lefevere, André. 1991. Translation and Comparative Literature: The Search for the Centre. *TTR : Traduction, Terminologie, Rédaction* 4 (1): 129–144.

Lefevere, André. 1992a. *Translating Literature: Practice and Theory in a Comparative Context*. New York: The Modern Language Association of America.

Lefevere, André. 1992b. *Translation, Rewriting, and the Manipulation of Literary Fame*. London/New York: Routledge.

Lind, Sarah. 2007. Translation Universals (or Laws, or Tendencies, or Probabilities, or …?). *TIC Talk* 63: https://translation.bible/wp-content/uploads/2024/05/tt63.pdf.

Luz, Saturnino. 2013. Web-Based Corpus- Software. In *Corpus-Based Translation Studies. Research and Applications*, ed. A. Kruger, K. Wallmach, and J. Munday, 124–151. London/New York: Bloomsbuty Academic.

Mahlberg, Michaela. 2007. Corpus Stylistics: Bridging the Gap between Linguistics and Literary Studies. In *Text, Discourse and Corpora. Theory and Analysis*, ed. M. Hoey, M. Mahlberg, M. Stubbs, and W. Teubert, 219–246. London: Continuum.

Mahlberg, Michaela. 2016. Corpus Stylistics. In *The Bloomsbury Companion to Stylistics*, ed. V. Sotirova, 139–156. London/New York: Bloomsbury Academic.

Mahlberg, Michaela, and Viola Wiegand. 2020. *Literary Stylistics*. London/New York: Routledge.

Mellinger, Christopher D., and Thomas A. Hanson. 2017. *Quantitative Research Methods in Translation and Interpreting Studies*. London/New York: Routledge.

Milana, Federico, Enrico Costanza, Mirco Musolesi, and Amid Ayobi. 2025. Understanding Interaction with Machine Learning through a Thematic Analysis Coding Assistant: A User Study. *Proceedings of the ACM on Human-Computer Interaction* 9 (2): 1–35.

Minaee, S., T. Mikolov, N. Nikzad, M. Chenaghlu, R. Socher, X. Amatriain, et al. 2025. Large Language Models: A Survey. *arXiv* preprint 2402.06196v3.

Mitchell, David. 2015. Type-Token Models: A Comparative Study. *Journal of Comparative Linguistics* 22 (1): 1–21.

Moretti, Franco. 2000. Conjectures on World Literature. *New Left Review* 1:54–68.

Moretti, Franco. 2013. *Distant Reading*. London: Verso Books.

Moretti, Franco. 2022. *Falso movimento. La svolta quantitativa nello studio della letteratura.* [False Movement. The Quantitative Turn in the Study of Literature.] Milan: Nottetempo.

Munday, Jeremy. 1998. A Computer-Assisted Approach to the Analysis of Translation Shifts. *Meta* 43 (3): 1–16.

Munday, Jeremy. 2016. *Introducing Translation Studies: Theories and Applications*. 4th edition. London and New York: Routledge.

Oakes, Michael P. 2012. Describing a Translational Corpus. In *Quantitative Methods in Corpus-Based Translation Studies*, ed. M. P. Oakes and M. Ji, 115–147. Amsterdam/Philadelphia: John Benjamin Publishing Company.

Peirce, Charles S. 1906. Prolegomena to an Apology for Pragmatism. *The Monist* 16:492–546.

Pierazzo, Elena. 2016. Text Scholarship and Text Encoding. In *New Companion to Digital Humanities*, ed. S. Schreibman, R. G. Siemens, and J. Unsworth, 307–321. Chichester, U.K.: Wiley.

Plato. c360. *Politeia*.

Pym, Anthony. 2016. *Translation Solutions for Many Languages. History of a Flawed Dream.* London: Bloomsbury.

Saldaña, Johnny. 2016. *The Coding Manual for Qualitative Researchers*. London: SAGE.

Saldanha, G. 2008. Explicitation Revisited: Bringing the Reader into the Picture. *Trans-Kom* 1 (1): 20–35.

Sharma, Yipin Kumar. 2015. The Relevance of Adding, Omission, and Deletion (AOD) in Translation. *International Journal of Translation* 27 (1–2): 1–12.

TEI Consortium. 2019. *TEI P5: Guidelines for Electronic Text Encoding and Interchange.* http://tei-c.org/release/doc/tei-p5-doc/en/Guidelines.pdf.

Toury, Gideon. 1980. *In Search of a Theory of Translation*. Tel Aviv: The Porter Institute for Poetics and Semiotics.

Toury, Gideon. 1995. *Descriptive Translation Studies—And beyond.* 1st ed. Amsterdam/Philadelphia: John Benjamins.

Toury, Gideon. 2012. In *Descriptive Translation Studies – And Beyond*, ed. 2. Amsterdam/Philadelphia: John Benjamins.

Vanderauwera, R. 1985. *Dutch Novels Translated into English: The Transformation of a "Minority" Literature*. Amsterdam: Rodopi.

van Leuven-Zwart, Kitty M. 1989. Translation and original: Similarities and dissimilarities I. *Target* 1(2): 151–182.

van Leuven-Kwart, Kitty M. 1990. Translation and original: Similarities and dissimilarities II. *Target* 2(1): 69–96.

Vaswani, Ashish, et al. 2017. Attention is all you need. In *31st Conference on Neural Information Processing Systems (NIPS 2017)*. Long Beach, CA, USA.

Venuti, Lawrence. 2008. *The Translator's Invisibility. A History of Translation*. 2nd ed. London/New York: Routledge.

Vogt, W. Paul, Elaine R. Vogt, Dianne C. Gardner, and Lynne M. Haeffele. 2014. *Selecting the Right Analysis for Your Data. Quantitative, Qualitative, and Mixed Methods*. London/New York: The Guilford Press.

Youmans, Gilbert. 1990. Measuring Lexical Style and Competence: The Type-Token Vocabulary Curve. *Style* 24 (4): 584–599.

Zanettin, Federico. 2011a. Hardwiring Corpus-Based Translation Studies: Corpus Encoding. In *Corpus-Based Translation Studies. Research and Applications*, ed. A. Kruger, K. Wallmach, and J. Munday, 103–123. London/New York: Bloomsbury Academic.

Zanettin, Federico. 2011b. Translation and Corpus Design. *Synaps* 26:14–23.
Zanettin, Federico. 2012. *Translation-Driven Corpora: Corpus Resources for Descriptive and Applied Translation Studies*. Manchester: St. Jerome.
Zanettin, Federico. 2013a. *Translation-Driven Corpora: Corpus Resources for Descriptive and Applied Translation Studies*. Manchester, UK: St. Jerome.
Zanettin, Federico. 2013b. Corpus Methods for Descriptive Translation Studies. *Procedia – Social and Behavioral Sciences* 95:20–32.
Zanettin, Federico. 2014a. Corpora in Translation. In *Translation: A Multidisciplinary Approach*, ed. Juliane House, 178–199. New York: Palgrave Macmillan.
Zanettin, Federico. 2014b. Corpora in Translation. In *Translation: A Multidisciplinary Approach*, ed. J. House, 178–199. New York: Palgrave Macmillan.
Zaixi, Tan. 2019. The fuzzy interface between censorship and self-censorship in translation. *Translation and Interpretative Studies* 14(1): 39–60.
Zhang, Xiaomin. 2025. Corpus-Based Studies of Explicitation. In *Routledge Handbook of Corpus Translation Studies*, ed. Defeng Li and John Corbett, 254–268. London: Routledge.
Zhang, Han; Akram Bin Sediq; Melike Erol-Kantarci. 2024. Generative AI-in-the-loop: Integrating LLMs and GPTs into the next generation networks. *arXiv*: 2406.04276v1.
Zubillaga, Naroa, Zuriñe Sanz, and Ibon Uribarri. 2015. Building a Bilingual Parallel Corpus to Analize Literary Translations from German into Basque. In *New Directions in Corpus-Based Translation Studies*, ed. C. Fantinuoli and F. Zanettin, 71–92. Berlin: Language Science Press.

Chapter 4
The Early English (Re)translations of Fontenelle's (1686) *Entretiens* and Their Socio-Cultural Contexts

You can go up to heaven from any point on Earth.

Lucius Anneus Seneca (4 BC–65 AD)

4.1 Introduction

This chapter presents Bernard Le Bovier de Fontenelle's *Entretiens sur la pluralité des mondes* (1686) (hereafter *Entretiens*) and its early English translations through the lens of seventeenth-century socio-historical, cultural, and scientific developments. It aims to situate Fontenelle's seminal work within the broader context of the scientific revolution and the turbulent political and religious transformations that preceded the Glorious Revolution in England. The three earliest English translations of *Entretiens*, by Sir William Domville, John Glanvill, and Aphra Behn, are introduced as case studies for comparative analysis.

Entretiens was first published anonymously in France in 1686 as a groundbreaking work of scientific popularisation. Framed as a fictional dialogue, it presented the Copernican heliocentric model and the possibility of multiple inhabited worlds in a form accessible to a lay readership. Its English translations appeared within 2 years, each navigating varying degrees of anonymity and ideological sensitivity in response to the volatile political and religious climate of the time (Mullan 2008). In fact, England was then gripped by sectarian conflict, culminating in the deposition of the Catholic King James II and the accession of the Protestant William of Orange in 1688. This political upheaval marked a transition toward a constitutional monarchy and fostered a more permissive intellectual environment in which scientific speculation, such as Fontenelle's, could circulate more freely.

Fontenelle's dialogues are firmly rooted in the intellectual currents of the scientific revolution. Drawing upon the ideas of Copernicus, Kepler, Galileo, and Descartes *Entretiens* championed a rational, mechanistic interpretation of the cosmos. In particular, it relied on Descartes's vortex theory, as articulated in his *Principia Philosophiae* (1644), to explain planetary motion. While this model

A. M. Cipriani, F. Milana, *AI-Powered Corpus Translation Studies at Work*,
New Frontiers in Translation Studies,
https://doi.org/10.1007/978-981-95-5933-6_4

would later yield to Newton's theory of gravitation, it provided a compelling framework for Fontenelle's generation. Simultaneously, scientific societies such as the *Académie des Sciences* in France and the Royal Society in England were advancing empirical research. However, the observational technologies necessary to decisively confirm the Copernican heliocentric model would not be available until the eighteenth century.

This chapter explores how Fontenelle's scientific vision intersected with England's religious and political tensions. It considers how each translator, Domville, Glanvill, and Behn, adapted the text in ways that reflect their distinct ideological and intellectual milieus. In doing so, it reveals how translation served as a medium not only for linguistic conversion but also for cultural negotiation and the dissemination of scientific knowledge at a pivotal moment in European intellectual history.

4.2 Historical Context: Politics, Religion, and the 1688 *Glorious Revolution*

Late seventeenth-century England endured profound crises—civil war, plague, fire, wars with the Dutch, and incessant religious and political turmoil—that eroded stability and confidence in both monarchy and Church. The so-called "Popish Plot" of 1678, a fabricated Catholic conspiracy to assassinate Charles II Stuart and install his brother James, precipitated the Exclusion Crisis and deepened factional distrust within Parliament and society (Miller 1973, 2003).

Table 4.1 outlines Britain's principal political and ideological shifts from 1618 to 1702. Weakened royal authority, combined with fiscal and confessional tensions, culminated in the English Revolution (1640–1660) and substantial constitutional realignment. After the Restoration of 1660, the monarchy operated under tighter parliamentary constraints. Persistent religious conflict and foreign dependency during Charles II's reign exposed the fragility of royal power, while James II's Catholic policies provoked opposition that led to the Glorious Revolution of 1688–89 and the assertion of parliamentary supremacy.

The new Anglo-Dutch regime established a modern fiscal-military state, introducing innovative credit systems and bureaucratic governance. This transformation provided the institutional foundations for Britain's eighteenth-century stability and imperial expansion. As Scott (2000) and Sharpe (2013) observe, recurrent crises and negotiated compromises redefined sovereignty, creating a mixed constitution that balanced monarchy and parliament.

Charles II's death in 1685 allowed his brother James II to ascend the throne with the backing of Catholics and Tories, as well as Anglicans. Parliament was crystallising into the two enduring factions—Tories and Whigs—originally terms of abuse: "Tory" from the Irish for "outlaw" and "Whig" from a Scottish word meaning "rebel" or "sour milk" (Uglow 2009: 518).

Table 4.1 Re-inventing Britain from seventeenth-century recurrent crises

Period	Main political processes	Synthetic description
1618–89	England's troubles: Political instability	A century marked by recurrent crises—dynastic conflict, religious division, and shifting forms of governance—that undermined continuity and provoked reform (Scott 2000)
1640–60	Charles I Stuart: The English revolution with civil war, Cromwell, and radical imagination	"A political rebellion sparked off by religious passion" culminating in regicide, republican experiment, and military rule (Ashley 1987)
1660–1702	Restoration and constitutional monarchy	"Rebranding rule with restoration and revolution monarchy," as monarchy and parliament negotiated a new balance of power (Sharpe 2013)
1660–65	Charles II: First restoration	The Stuart Restoration was reinstated in May 1660. Marked by unresolved religious divisions among Anglicans, Catholics, and dissenters, which undermined initial reconciliation efforts
1681–85	Charles II: Second restoration	Increasing royal dependence on French subsidies turned Charles into "the pensioner of the French King" (Shama 2001)
1685–88	James II: Anti-popery tensions	The high church, Anglicans, and dissenters briefly united against the spectre of a renewed Catholic dynasty
1688–94	William III: The glorious revolution and third restoration	William's cautious yet decisive intervention reshaped sovereignty, consolidating Protestant succession and parliamentary legitimacy (Shama 2001)
1695–1702	Anglo-Dutch state-building	A bureaucratic, militarized, and fiscally innovative state emerged—Parliament-dependent yet resilient in foreign policy

Source: Our original processing

James II's reign confronted entrenched religious divisions. His 1687 *Declaration of Indulgence* sought to repeal penal laws against Catholics and dissenting Protestants. As Harris (2006: 211) notes, the King declared that while he preferred universal Catholicism, "conscience should not be forced," since persecution harmed trade and depopulated nations. Yet, despite assurances regarding the Church and property rights, distrust persisted. Harris (2006: 195) clarifies James's dual objective:

> James not only wanted to ensure that his co-religionists had the ability to practice their religion peaceably but also to create an environment that would encourage his Protestant subjects to convert.

His attempt at toleration was politically premature. Many perceived it as an instrument of Catholic advancement, threatening Protestant hegemony. In a culture shaped by censorship and confessional rivalry, even proposals for liberty of conscience appeared subversive (Thomas 1969: 6–7; Treadwell 2002). As Robertson (2009: 1) emphasises, seventeenth-century England was engaged in "an unremitting struggle among Crown, Parliament and people for sovereignty and the right to define 'liberty and property'," a conflict fought through language and representation.

Consequently, the Test Act was paradoxically regarded by Anglicans, Catholics, and dissenters alike "as a bulwark against the threats to English independence" (Ogg 1961: 315). The Tory party, rooted in the lower clergy and landed gentry, was "devoted to the Church of England; but ... the High-Church party, in their detestation of Protestant Dissent, were reputed to be more sympathetic to Catholicism than to Protestantism" (*Ibid.*: 316).

The pervasive insecurity of the period was vividly captured by Macaulay (1848: 550):

> Every time that the power passed from one party to the other, there was a proscription and a massacre, thinly disguised under the forms of judicial procedure. ... Papist or Protestant, Tory or Whig, Priest or Alderman, all was one to those greedy and savage natures, provided only there was money to earn or blood to shed.

The Glorious Revolution replaced James II with William and Mary, entrenching constitutional monarchy, Protestant succession, and parliamentary ascendancy. The period also fostered intellectual and social transformation, marked by the growth of scientific empiricism, the influence of the Royal Society, and the emergence of women in public and literary life (De Beer 1970; Knights 2015).

This climate proved receptive to Fontenelle's *Entretiens sur la pluralité des mondes*. Within 2 years of its French publication, three English versions appeared—Sir William Domville's *Conversations on the Plurality of Worlds* (Dublin, 1687), John Glanvill's (London, 1688), and Aphra Behn's (London, 1688). Their near-contemporaneity with the Revolution reveals how political and religious ferment encouraged engagement with continental science and philosophy. Fontenelle's Copernican dialogues, once censored in France, now circulated in England, where debates on cosmology, theology, and authority intertwined with questions of liberty and knowledge (Hooykaas 1972; Hunter 1992).

The ideological context of late Stuart England profoundly shaped these translations. Each translator interpreted *Entretiens* through distinctive religious, social, and political lenses. Consequently, the English versions functioned as cultural mediations rather than mere renderings, reflecting England's transition from confessional absolutism toward Enlightenment rationality. The years surrounding 1688 thus form both the historical and intellectual matrix from which Fontenelle's early English reception emerged—a moment when politics, religion, and science converged to redefine the boundaries of translation, authorship, and belief.

4.3 Social and Intellectual Culture in Seventeenth-Century England

Seventeenth-century England was marked by religious upheaval, political instability, and intellectual renewal. The English Reformation, with its emphasis on predestination and scriptural authority, generated intolerance and civil conflict. Yet, paradoxically, it laid the foundations for later liberal values, such as constitutionalism and intellectual freedom (Simpson 2019). Protestant societies, shaped by "worldly asceticism" (Weber 1904–5/1930), cultivated frugality, entrepreneurship, and moral discipline—an ethic that, as Tawney (1922/1926) argued, connected religious conviction to economic behaviour and opposed traditional aristocratic ideals.

Against Weber and Tawney, Trevor-Roper (1967/2001) argued that the role of religion in shaping modern Europe has often been overstated. He recognised Weber's idea of "the calling" as necessary for capitalism but it was not exclusive to Protestantism. For example, Venetian merchants maintained independence from ecclesiastical authority, and entrepreneurs from Northern Italy moved to Northern Europe, where they demonstrated initiative and ambition. Ironically, England's early confessional rigidity ultimately encouraged liberal ideals, such as free will and toleration, unintentionally (Miller 2015; Simpson 2019). The Protestant insistence on personal interpretation of Scripture fractured ecclesiastical authority and fostered habits of independent thought that proved vital to the development of later intellectual freedom.

As Simpson (2019) observes, English liberalism did not arise directly from Protestant reform but rather emerged as a reaction against evangelical extremism, shaped by protracted theological and political conflicts. Thinkers such as John Locke, whose "Letter Concerning Toleration" (1689) was published anonymously, built upon this complex legacy. The Restoration period exemplifies the complex interplay between politics, religion, and intellectual life. After Charles II died in 1685, James II's accession aroused both hope and apprehension. Protestant fears of Catholic resurgence were heightened by censorship and surveillance, which, as Patterson (1984), Dutton (2000), and McKenzie (2002) note, linked literary expression to political loyalty. Translation thus became a cautious cultural practice requiring delicate negotiation.

This rejection of the concept of historical determinism is not a new phenomenon. Cambridge historian Herbert Butterfield (1931) exposed the "Whig interpretation of history"—the anachronistic reading of the past through modern values. He maintained that "the chief aim of the historian is the elucidation of the *unlikeness* between past and present and his chief function is to act in this way as the mediator between previous generations and our own" *(ibid.*: 87, emphasis added). This view implied that historians must explain, rather than judge, the past and that their mediation between epochs necessarily entails subjectivity, a challenge shared by the sciences (Butterfield 1949/1957; McIntyre 2011; Stapleton 2008, 2012: 690).

The rediscovery of Behn's work owes much to early twentieth-century scholars, such as Montague Summers (1930, 1933), and to later advocates, including Vita Sackville-West (1927) and Virginia Woolf (1929). Yet, feminist scholarship of the 1970s and 1980s often portrayed Behn primarily as a proto-feminist dramatist who depicted gendered power struggles (Pearsons 1988: 152), while others, such as Rogers (1982: 58, 98), questioned overtly feminist interpretations.

Within this last interpretative framework, the varied historiographical "re-readings" of Aphra Behn can be reassessed. Christa Knellwolf (2001), titled *Women Translators, Gender and the Cultural Context of the Scientific Revolution*, examined women's contributions as translators during an age of transformation shaped by Baconian empiricism. She argued that any historiography of science must consider how gender and national stereotypes condition constructions of knowledge (*ibid.*: 85). Similarly, Roberta Falcone (2004: 6, 9, 10, 11), citing Kavenik (1991: 177) and Hutner's *Rereading Aphra Behn* (1993), highlighted the distortions of certain nationalist or feminist readings, observing that each era has tended to confine Behn to a single role. Although feminist criticism revived her reputation, it also risked limiting her historical complexity.

Scientific and theological debate intensified this climate. The Copernican heliocentric model, elaborated by Kepler and Galileo, challenged scriptural cosmology rooted in Ptolemaic geocentrism. Advocates of heliocentrism faced charges of heresy in a milieu where church authorities closely policed unorthodox ideas. Stein (2014) demonstrates that the theological implications of Copernicanism in Restoration England reflected existing political divisions: the Tory party upheld Anglican orthodoxy, while the Whigs tended toward interpretative flexibility. Even within Tory ranks, High Church members were sometimes accused of Catholic sympathies (Ogg 1961: 315, Spurr 1992). Thus, cosmological debate became a proxy for larger conflicts over authority and belief.

In this contested environment, William Domville, John Glanvill, and Aphra Behn undertook English translations of Fontenelle's *Entretiens sur la pluralité des mondes* (1686), each navigating the challenge of presenting Copernican ideas to an English readership. Their rhetorical strategies reveal efforts to mediate between scientific innovation and religious orthodoxy. Behn's *Translator's Preface* explicitly addressed scriptural passages—Joshua commanding the sun to stand still and the Psalm describing it as a bridegroom—to reconcile biblical language with heliocentrism. Engaging Jesuit scholarship, she positioned herself at the intersection of faith and reason, demonstrating how translators served as cultural mediators between theology and natural philosophy.

Fontenelle's text itself reflects the transitional character of late seventeenth-century science. Although he embraced heliocentrism, he rejected Newton's theory of universal gravitation, favouring instead Descartes's mechanistic vortices. This model, in which celestial bodies move within whirlpools of subtle matter, appeared less metaphysical than Newton's notion of attraction acting through a vacuum. Fontenelle's dialogues thus combined boldness in rejecting geocentrism with caution toward Newton. His elegant conversational style transformed scientific exposition into social discourse, popularising speculative cosmology far beyond learned circles. Unlike Galileo's *Dialogues* (1632), *Entretiens* consciously addressed a general, inclusive audience, thereby initiating a new sociability in scientific writing.

By framing scientific issues in accessible dialogue, Fontenelle connected cosmology to culture. In England, his work appealed to readers eager to integrate science into polite conversation. As Mason (1953: 30) observed, the collapse of hierarchical cosmology marked a fundamental intellectual shift:

> The leit-motif of the medieval view of the world, to which both the Reformers and the early modern scientists had taken exception, was the concept of hierarchy. ... The Calvinists in

> theology and the astronomers in science reacted against this conception that the universe was hierarchically ordered. (ibid., emphasis added)

The erosion of cosmic hierarchy resonated across theology, politics, and society, undermining both metaphysical and social order (Westfall 1958). Fontenelle's dialogues epitomised this transformation, bridging the Scientific Revolution and the Enlightenment through a language of reasoned sociability.

As Kuhn (1962), Zaret (1989), and Stein (2014) have shown, the intellectual and social upheavals of the late seventeenth century were inseparable: rejecting divinely ordained hierarchy opened pathways to Enlightenment thought and the proto-industrial revolution. The English translations of Fontenelle's *Entretiens* by Domville, Glanvill, and Behn thus constituted not merely linguistic acts but strategic cultural interventions that negotiated authority, faith, and the emerging science and technology.

As summarised in Table 4.2, late seventeenth-century England was a world of paradoxes: intolerance bred tolerance, unrest fostered constitutionalism, and suspicion of dissent encouraged inquiry. Liberalism evolved less from dogma than from the effort to contain fanaticism. Through conversation, translation, and popular science, ideas of reason and moderation entered the social fabric. Within this dynamic framework, Fontenelle's *Entretiens*—and its English mediators—epitomise how literature, science, and translation contributed to the intellectual temper of the age.

4.4 The Scientific Revolution in the Age of Proto-Enlightenment

Francis Bacon (1561–1626) stands as one of the pre-eminent figures of early Enlightenment thought and is often called the "herald of modern science." Although not a practising scientist, his advocacy for the empirical method and his programme for the systematic reform of knowledge profoundly influenced the Scientific Revolution and subsequent Enlightenment philosophy (Heimann 1979; Martin 1992; Peltonen 1996; Shapin 1994, 1996; Stern 2014; Dear 2019). In *The Advancement of Learning*, *Novum Organum*, and *New Atlantis*, Bacon advocated for a comprehensive overhaul of natural inquiry, replacing tradition and speculative deduction with inductive reasoning. In *Novum Organum,* he proposed generalisation through *systematic observation*, opposing the Aristotelian reliance on syllogistic deduction (Blair 2003: 400).

Table 4.3 outlines Bacon's epistemological reform and main philosophical ideas. The "Idols of the Mind" warned against psychological and linguistic distortions that obstruct objectivity. He thus transformed epistemology by grounding knowledge in empirical experience and collaborative experimentation, shaping the ethos of the Royal Society and the methodological culture that inspired Boyle, Hooke, and Newton. His institutional legacy anticipated modern scientific research communities, defining the transition from medieval scholasticism to empirical modernity.

Table 4.2 From the illiberal roots to liberalism of "popular science" in Reformation England

Dimension	Key insight
Paradoxical origins of liberal culture	The English Reformation, despite intolerance and iconoclasm, unintentionally laid the groundwork for liberalism, toleration, and constitutionalism (Simpson 2019)
Political-religious context	Under James II's reign, efforts to expand religious toleration and the Declaration of Indulgence (1687) provoked fears of Catholic resurgence, creating a climate of censorship and suspicion that shaped intellectual and literary activity
Science and theology entangled	Copernican heliocentrism and natural philosophy challenged biblical cosmology, forcing writers and translators to negotiate accusations of heresy or heterodoxy
Role of Fontenelle (1686)	By presenting cosmology through elegant dialogues, Fontenelle popularised scientific speculation within polite society, bridging learned discourse and social conversation
Function of translation	Domville, Glanvill, and Behn acted as cultural mediators between theology, politics, and emerging science. Behn's *preface*, in particular, highlights both erudition and the risks of confronting scriptural authority

Source: Our original processing

Table 4.3 Francis Bacon (1561–1626) and the foundations of Scientific Revolution

Key Insights	Synthetic description
Epistemological reform	Bacon transformed the criteria for knowledge by substituting the *deductive* reasoning associated with scholasticism with an *inductive* approach rooted in systematic observation and empirical experience, thus establishing the foundational framework for modern empirical science
Critique of the "idols of the mind"	Bacon's examination of *idola mentis* highlighted the psychological and linguistic distortions that impede objective investigation, foreshadowing subsequent theories related to cognitive bias and epistemic limitations
Institutional and methodological legacy	Bacon's concept of organised collaborative research led to the founding of the Royal Society and has influenced modern scientific institutions
Goal of practical knowledge	Becon's method aimed to generate practical knowledge and inventions to benefit humanity
Enduring influence	While later thinkers balanced induction and deduction, Bacon's methodological rigour, emphasis on epistemological reform, and collaborative approach to knowledge had a profound influence on the ethos of the seventeenth-century scientific revolution

Source: Our original processing

Yet, as Hesse (1970: 373) observes, Bacon remained somewhat detached from the contemporary developments of Gilbert, Kepler, and Harvey, and he never accepted the Copernican heliocentric system or the mathematical foundations of physics, criticising Kepler's geometrical formalism (Grant 2007: 280). Nevertheless, his philosophical reformism established the conceptual preconditions for modern science.

Building on the intellectual momentum generated by Bacon, seventeenth-century Europe witnessed an unprecedented transformation in the understanding of nature. Drawing on the discoveries of Copernicus, Kepler, Galileo, and Descartes, Fontenelle developed a rational cosmology that translated complex astronomical theories into language accessible to educated readers. His approach embodied the balance between speculative reasoning and the emerging requirement for empirical validation. Institutions such as the *Académie des Sciences* and the Royal Society institutionalised observation and experimentation, creating a collaborative infrastructure that consolidated the new scientific ethos.

Table 4.4 displays the major contributions of the age—from Copernicus's heliocentrism to Newton's gravitation—which redefined humanity's place in the cosmos. Copernicus displaced Earth from the centre of the universe, while Kepler mathematically demonstrated that the planets travel in elliptical orbits, moving with variable velocities and inversely with their distance from the sun (Blair 2003: 400; Stephenson 1987).

Galileo's *Sidereus Nuncius* (1610) and *Dialogues Concerning the Two Chief World Systems* (1632) extended these discoveries through telescopic observation. By revealing the moons of Jupiter, the mountains of the Moon, and sunspots, Galileo destroyed the Aristotelian image of celestial perfection and opened new conceptions of cosmic disconcerting vastness—*"the instant realisation of countless stars beyond the visible sky,"* as later noted in contemporary accounts. Although his *Dialogue*s avoided explicit theology, its defence of heliocentrism led to the Inquisition's trial of 1633 and his subsequent confinement.

René Descartes (1596–1650) offered a contrasting synthesis of philosophy and science. In the *Principia Philosophiae* (1644), he envisaged a mechanistic, matter-filled universe governed by vortices of subtle substance and universal laws (Ariew 1999; Cottingham 2006; Nadler et al. 2019). In a different perspective, Isaac Newton (1642–1727) would later reconcile terrestrial and celestial phenomena under a single mathematical framework in the *Philosophiae Naturalis Principia Mathematica* (1687), uniting the contributions of Copernicus, Kepler, Galileo, and Descartes (Iliffe and Smith 2016). Newton's law of universal gravitation—*attractio inter gravia*—offered a coherent system based on observation and mathematical representation, consolidating the methodological synthesis that became emblematic of the Enlightenment's scientific spirit (e.g., MacDougal 2012).

Yet the Newtonian synthesis was neither immediate nor uncontested. Descartes had rejected the notion of forces acting across empty space, proposing instead his vortex cosmology. The late seventeenth century was therefore characterised by ongoing debate between Cartesian mechanism and Newtonian gravitation—between a universe of material vortices and one structured by mathematically

Table 4.4 Major figures in the seventeenth-century scientific revolution

Natural philosopher	Main work	Key contribution
Nicolaus Copernicus (1473–1543)	*De revolutionibus orbium coelestium* (*On the Revolutions of the Celestial Spheres*, 1543)	Formulating the heliocentric theory, placing the sun rather than the earth at the Centre of the planetary system
Johannes Kepler (1571–1630)	*Astronomia Nova* (1609); *Harmonices Mundi* (1619); *Epitome Astronomiae Copernicanae* (1618–1621)	Refining and mathematically demonstrating the Copernican model through his three laws of planetary motion, describing elliptical orbits and variable velocities. (Blair 2003: 400; Stephenson 1987)
Galileo Galilei (1564–1642)	*Sidereus Nuncius* (1610) *Dialogo sopra i due massimi sistemi del mondo* (*Dialogue Concerning the Two Chief World Systems*, 1632)	Providing telescopic observations and experimental evidence supporting heliocentrism, articulated the methodological foundations of modern physics (Drake 1978)
René Descartes (1596–1650)	*Principia Philosophiae* (*Principles of Philosophy*, 1644)	Proposing the vortex theory, and sought to explain celestial mechanics through a mechanistic, matter-filled universe governed by mathematical laws
Isaac Newton (1642–1727)	*Philosophiae Naturalis Principia Mathematica* (*Mathematical Principles of Natural Philosophy*, 1687)	Formulating the law of universal gravitation and the three laws of motion, establishing a unified mathematical framework for terrestrial and celestial phenomena

Source: Our original processing

defined attraction. Both perspectives continued to shape discourse well into the eighteenth century (Watson 1966; Domski 2019; Bussotti and Lotti 2022).

William Wotton and John Dryden regarded this transformation as the true rebirth of Western intellect after the medieval period (Crombie and Michael Hoskin 1970: 70; Hall 1961; Boas 1962). But, as Hall (1961: 54) remarked, the limitations of early instrumentation and mathematical technique impeded verification:

> Kepler at the beginning of the century had strained the resources of conventional geometry in his struggle to determine the true shape of a planetary orbit, yet the problems involved in setting out a physical theory of planetary motions in mathematical form were far more severe. Descartes had not attempted it; he had asserted that the planets were borne around the Sun in an ethereal vortex, without examining mathematically the conditions of such motion. (Newton undertook this, and [mathematically] proved that a vortex could not impart to the planets their observed velocities.)

The gradual displacement of Cartesian cosmology by Newtonian physics was accompanied by persistent resistance. As already stressed, Fontenelle himself remained sceptical of gravitation acting at a distance in the *vacuum*, preferring the Cartesian model of vortices. In the *General Scholium* to the *Principia* (1713), Newton acknowledged the limits of his own system, famously declaring that he would not feign hypotheses—*"hypotheses non fingo"*—since the ultimate cause of gravity remained unknown.

This epistemological tension between description and causation endures in the history of science. René Thom (1972: 8; Gillies and Giorello 1993: 340) summarised the controversy:

> At the end of the seventeenth century, a controversy raged between the supporters of Descartes' and Newton's physics. Descartes, with his vortices and projected atoms, *explained everything but calculated nothing*; Newton, with his law of gravitation ($1/r^2$), *calculated everything but explained nothing*. (Emphasis added)

Margherita Hack (2002: v), in her introduction to the Italian translation of Fontenelle's *Entretiens* (1686), revisited this unresolved problem:

> In the mechanical explanation of vortices proposed by Descartes, Fontenelle instead identified the natural cause which was not provided by Newtonian theory, and would find an explanation only in the second decade of the twentieth century with Einstein's theory of general relativity. [Our translation.]

Einstein's general relativity indeed reinterpreted gravity as spacetime curvature, addressing the causal framework Newton lacked while echoing the earlier dialectic between mechanism and mathematics. The persistence of such a foundational question illustrates how the seventeenth-century debates between explanation and quantification continue to resonate in modern physics (Rowe et al. 2018).

The Scientific Revolution thus represented far more than a sequence of discoveries; it redefined epistemology itself (Lancaster 1979; Stein 2014). By uniting observation, experiment, and mathematics, it transformed the intellectual culture of Europe. The interplay between Cartesian deduction and Newtonian empiricism, as well as between speculative philosophy and practical science, established the conditions for Enlightenment rationality. As Crombie and Hoskin (1970: 61–62) observed, Fontenelle epitomised the delicate equilibrium of imagination and reason, reconciling the rationalist heritage of Descartes with the empirical ethos of the Royal Society. This equilibrium marked the dawn of the modern scientific worldview.

4.5 A Plurality of Worlds from Ancient to Modern Literature

Long before the Scientific Revolution, ancient philosophers such as the Pythagoreans, Thales, and Epicurus speculated about the existence of an infinite universe populated by countless worlds. Their theories challenged the traditional conception of a closed cosmos and prefigured later cosmological models. The early Ionian school advanced the notion of a uniform and infinite universe—a precursor to the modern "Cosmological Principle," which assumes the equivalence of all regions of space. As Pierre Connes (2020) observes, these mechanical explanations closely anticipated Descartes' rational cosmology (see also McColley 1932, 1936; Dick 1980, 1982).[1]

[1] On the history of astronomic knowledge from the ancient to modern times, see also, e.g. Hoskin 2003; McLeod 2016; Habing 2018.

The idea of multiple inhabited worlds, deeply rooted in ancient cosmological monism, persisted through centuries of intellectual repression and revival. Its durability reflects a continuing fascination with the possibility of other worlds, as shown even in modern discussions such as Sarah Scoles's "We Probably Are Not Alone" (*Scientific American*, September 2025), which traces the lineage of this concept from antiquity to Fontenelle's *Entretiens sur la pluralité des mondes*.

The relationship between the Copernican theory and the plurality of worlds is at the centre of the scientific revolution. The controversy over the existence of extraterrestrial intelligent life began at the beginning of the seventeenth century, when the Copernican theory started to gain acceptance and provided a physical framework for the existence of Earth-like worlds inside and outside the solar system.

The Copernican theory was decisive in providing a physical framework for such speculations by situating the Earth among other planetary bodies. As Dick (1980) notes, advocates of extraterrestrial life—including Bruno, Kepler, Wilkins, Fontenelle, and Huygens—were typically adherents of the Copernican model, while opponents of heliocentrism often rejected the notion of other worlds. Thus, belief in a plural cosmos was closely linked to the intellectual emancipation initiated by Copernicus.

The fascination with extraterrestrial life extended beyond science into literature. Misinterpretations of Martian "canals" in 1877, for example, inspired works such as H. G. Wells's *The War of the Worlds*, though later disproved by NASA's *Mariner 4* mission (1965). Fontenelle's *Entretiens* thus stands within a continuous tradition of cosmological speculation uniting philosophy, science, and imaginative literature.[2]

In her *Translator's Preface* to the 1688 English edition, Aphra Behn addressed the tension between Fontenelle's literary charm and philosophical intent:

> I am sorry, I must write what some may understand to be satire against him [Fontenelle]. The design of the author is to treat of this part of natural philosophy in a more familiar way than any other hath done […] I must tell you freely he hath failed in his design; for endeavouring to render this part of natural philosophy familiar, he hath turned it into ridicule; he hath pushed his wild notions of the plurality of worlds to the height of extravagancy, that he most certainly will confound those readers who have no judgement or wit to distinguish between what is truly solid (or, at least, probable) and what is trifling and airy: […] And for his Lady Marquise, he makes her say a great many very silly things, though sometimes she makes observations so learned, that the greatest philosophers in Europe could make no better.

[2] This conviction continues to stimulate academic debate and publishing, as attested by a wide array of studies (Sagan 1966, 1973; Tipler 1981; Brin 1983; Jones 1985; Crowe 1988, 2008, 2018; Zuckerman and Hart 1995; Daston and Park 1998; Jakosky 1998; Webb 2002; Brake 2006; Briot 2013; Coustenis and Encrenaz 2013; Drake 2013; Drake and Sobel 1992; Jheeta 2013; Prantzos 2013; Rospars et al. 2013; Loeb 2014; Gray 2015; Ćirković 2018; Martin 2018; Schulze-Makuch and Irwin 2018; Forgan 2019; Connes 2020; Roush 2020; Smith 2021; Bennet et al. 2022; Playford et al. 2024). Parallel to this scholarly literature, popular works continue to address themes akin to those of Fontenelle's dialogues, including Sagan and deGrasse Tyson's *Cosmos* (2013), Michaud's *Contact with Alien Civilizations* (2006), Cabrol's *Secret Life of the Universe: Searching for the Origins and Frontiers of Life* (2023), and Kaltenegger's *Alien Earths: The Search for Life in the Cosmos* (2024).

Behn's commentary captures a central paradox of Fontenelle's work: the very wit that made *Entretiens* accessible risked trivialising its philosophical substance. Yet it was precisely this fusion of literary elegance and scientific curiosity that popularised cosmology for Enlightenment audiences, transforming speculative inquiry into cultural discourse.[3]

Among the English works that likely influenced Behn were John Wilkins's *A Discovery of a New World* (1638/1684) and *A Discourse Concerning a New World and Another Planet* (1640), which anticipated Fontenelle's theme and even his English title. As Shapiro (1969: 2) observes,

> Wilkins [...] seems to have played a key role in each of the movements to reform and liberalize English intellectual life. [...] His popularizations of science were among the most widely read scientific works of the day in England. [...] During and after the Civil War, Wilkins was England's single most influential and effective organizer and purveyor of the scientific culture.

Wilkins's influence extended back to classical sources, such as Plutarch's *De Facie in Orbe Lunae*, one of the earliest works to consider the Moon a potentially habitable world. Similarly, Lucian of Samosata's *True History*—often regarded as the first example of science fiction—described voyages to the Moon and encounters with extraterrestrial beings. This theme recurs in diverse literary traditions, including Japan's *Tale of the Bamboo Cutter*, the Arabic *Adventures of Bulukiya*, Astolfo's lunar journey in Ariosto's *Orlando Furioso*, and Cyrano de Bergerac's *The States and Empires of the Moon*—the latest of which influenced Fontenelle's synthesis of philosophy and narrative imagination.

In the early modern era, Giordano Bruno's *On the Infinite Universe and Worlds* (1584) extended Copernican cosmology by postulating an infinite universe populated by an innumerable number of inhabited planets. His vision of a plural cosmos, grounded in both philosophy and faith in cosmic uniformity, challenged orthodox theology and ultimately led to his condemnation and execution in 1600. Nevertheless, his cosmological pluralism exerted enduring influence, particularly in England, where it intersected with emerging rationalist thought.

Later writers, including Kepler (*Somnium*), Henry More (*Democritus Platonissans*), Milton (*Paradise Lost*), and Huygens (*Cosmotheoros*), expanded on these ideas, merging metaphysical speculation with empirical observation. Collectively, their works created the intellectual foundation upon which Fontenelle's *Entretiens* was built. By blending scientific reasoning with literary dialogue, Fontenelle mediated between ancient speculation and modern empiricism, transforming cosmological thought into a form accessible to the broader culture of the Enlightenment.

Thus, the idea of a "plurality of worlds" traces a continuous trajectory from antiquity through early modern science to the proto-Enlightenment. Its persistence reveals the human impulse to reconcile imaginative wonder with rational

---

[3] For insights on how planet hunting affects observers' psychology and sparks cross-cultural imagination, see Sheehan (2010), *A Passion for the Planets. Envisioning Other Worlds, from the Pleistocene to the Age of Telescope.*

explanation—a dialectic that Fontenelle and his translations brought to the forefront of Europe's intellectual consciousness.

4.6 The Fontenelle's Moment

Bernard Le Bovier de Fontenelle (1657–1757), born in Rouen, was a leading French intellectual of the early Enlightenment, renowned for making scientific ideas accessible to a broad audience. His *Entretiens sur la pluralité des mondes* (1686) stands as a landmark in the popularisation of natural philosophy. Elected to the *Académie des Sciences* in 1691 and later its perpetual secretary, Fontenelle bridged the cultural transition from Descartes to Voltaire, becoming a central figure in the dialogue between literature and science (Bromley 1970: 32).

Although inspired by earlier works, *Entretiens* distinguished itself through its lucid explanation of heliocentrism and Cartesianism. By choosing a dialogic form between a philosopher and a Marquise, Fontenelle expanded the reach of scientific discourse, allowing women to participate in intellectual conversation at a time when such inclusion was rare. His refined style transformed cosmology into an exercise in wit and elegance rather than abstract speculation.

Helge Jordheim (2019) described this cultural influence as the "Fontenellian moment," borrowing from Pocock's (1975) "Machiavellian moment." The term designates a century-long epoch in which questions of cosmic structure, the plurality of worlds, and humanity's place in the universe occupied a central role in European intellectual life. Fontenelle's rhetorical and conceptual emphasis on "plurality" reshaped Enlightenment anthropology, reimagining the universe as an open, populated system rather than an Earth-centred hierarchy. His notion of plurality was not only numerical but epistemological—an invitation to intellectual diversity and critical comparison across possible worlds.

Jordheim's comparative analysis of *Entretiens* translations into English, German, and Danish shows how the text became a prism through which evolving cosmologies and conceptions of humanity were refracted. Fontenelle's work thus destabilised both theological orthodoxy and metaphysical certainties, promoting instead a rational and imaginative openness that anticipated Enlightenment cosmopolitanism.[4]

At the time, hypotheses about the structure and habitability of other worlds gained momentum alongside improvements in telescopic observation. Fontenelle's adherence to Cartesian vortex theory (Aiton 1972; Ferlin and Chabot 2020), his scepticism toward Newtonian gravitation, and his accessible style all contributed to a broader cultural transformation. *Entretiens* not only popularised cosmology but reshaped the epistemic conditions under which such ideas could circulate.

[4] Section 4.7.2 below discusses Giovanni Lista's (2024) comparative study on how national cultures have influenced translations of *Entretiens*. Instead, the present study examines the impact of local cultures specifically on the English versions of *Entretiens*.

Fontenelle's thought was deeply rooted in Cartesian natural philosophy. His use of *tourbillons* ("vortices") directly adapted Descartes's mechanical cosmology, where celestial phenomena were explained by the swirling motions of matter in a "liquid sky." As Descartes wrote in *Principia Philosophiae* (1644: 69–72):

> It is to be assumed that not only the matter of the Sun and the fixed stars, but the whole sky is liquid. [...] The celestial material in which all the planets are located rotates steadily, much like a vortex, with the Sun at its centre.

Fontenelle's (1752) *Théorie des tourbillons cartésiens avec des réflexions sur l'attraction,* composed at the author's age of ninety-five, revisited these ideas in a more rigorous tone:

> A book where the most sublime subject was treated with such grace and such elegant clarity that both learned and ignorant people were equally charmed by it [...]. It is the fruit of a profound meditation and a marvellous sagacity [...]. (*ibid.*: iii–iv)

Yet he remained sceptical of Newton's "attraction at a distance," rejecting *"a quality he does not define at all"* (*ibid.*: xii). His cautious Cartesianism reflected an intellectual prudence characteristic of late seventeenth-century France, where mechanistic explanations still rivalled mathematical abstraction.

Fontenelle is also credited with originating the modern concept of scientific progress. Špelda (2024), in *The Origin of the Idea of Scientific Progress: Bernard de Fontenelle and His Contemporaries*, argues that Fontenelle's notion of *esprit humain* framed human knowledge as cumulative and developmental. This epistemological model viewed science as advancing irreversibly from myth toward universal law, with progress defined by liberation from ignorance and anthropocentrism. Marsak (1959) had earlier observed that Fontenelle's vision of progress was dual: positively, the steady acquisition of knowledge; negatively, the emancipation from superstition.

This conception is already evident in *Entretiens*, which unfolds across a preface and six nightly dialogues between a philosopher and the Marquise de G., a figure modelled on Marquise de la Mésangère. The sequence transitions from the Earth's rotation and the Moon's habitability to the nature of other planets, and the heliocentric model is explained through Cartesian vortices. The Marquise, initially portrayed as scientifically naïve, becomes an engaged interlocutor whose insight grows throughout the conversation. Her wit and curiosity embody Fontenelle's pedagogical ideal: reasoned inquiry as a shared human enterprise transcending gender and class.

Through this conversational structure, Fontenelle not only disseminated cosmological knowledge but also staged the Enlightenment's new social vision of science as dialogue. The *Fontenellian moment* therefore, signifies more than a phase of cosmological speculation—it marks the expansion of intellectual participation and the emergence of the public sphere in scientific debate. By reconciling imagination with reason, *Entretiens* transformed the scientific revolution into a cultural one, making Fontenelle a pivotal mediator between Cartesian philosophy and the Enlightenment ideal of universal rationality.

4.7 *Entretiens* Made English in a Changing Europe

Bernard le Bovier de Fontenelle's *Entretiens sur la pluralité des mondes* was conceived as a graceful and accessible exposition of revolutionary scientific ideas. By weaving together lucid scientific explanation with wit, charm, and narrative sophistication, his dialogical strategy enabled abstract theories, above all, heliocentrism, the plurality of worlds, and Cartesian mechanics, to circulate in cultural and literary spaces beyond the academy. In this respect, *Entretiens* stands as one of the most important models of Enlightenment popularisation.

The immediate reception of *Entretiens* across Europe testifies to its resonance. Within a few years of its French publication in 1686, it was translated into several European languages. England, in particular, proved fertile ground for its dissemination. Between 1687 and 1688, three distinct English versions appeared in rapid succession: Sir William Domville's (1687), John Glanvill's (1688), and Aphra Behn's (1688). Each of them reveals a distinctive stance toward Fontenelle's scientific and philosophical arguments. The translators' choices were conditioned not only by the technical challenges of rendering scientific speculation in English but also by the volatile intellectual, political, and religious climate of late Stuart England.

4.7.1 The Three Early English Translations

Domville's translation, the earliest (1687), is characterised by restraint and caution. His phrasing frequently tends toward understatement, and he omits passages that might have been perceived as too provocative. This circumspection suggests an intention to neutralise Fontenelle's potentially controversial cosmology, adapting it to the sensibilities of English readers still deeply shaped by scriptural authority. His translation represents a strategy of prudence rather than boldness, seeking to accommodate Fontenelle's hypotheses within a more limited intellectual framework.

By contrast, John Glanvill's translation (1688) adopts a more expansive style. Glanvill's tone is notably more confident, and he interpolates clarifications that situate Fontenelle's speculations within contemporary English debates on natural philosophy. His additions resonate with the concerns of the Royal Society and reveal his desire to make Fontenelle's ideas relevant to English scientific culture, already gravitating toward Newtonian paradigms. Glanvill thus not only transmitted Fontenelle's arguments but actively reframed them, creating a hybrid text that mediated between French cosmological speculation and English scientific discourse.

Aphra Behn's version (1688), however, occupies a unique position. Behn, a dramatist and novelist of considerable reputation, brought literary sensibility to the task of translation. She captures Fontenelle's wit and rhythm while subtly reshaping the dialogue to conform to English literary conventions. Writers such as Duffy (1989), Goodfellow (1996), Spearing (1996), Todd (1993, 2000) have noted Behn's departures from the source, which range from omissions to interpretative additions. Yet, it is equally important to attend to her more nuanced shifts, lexical choices, rephrasing, and tone adjustments, which reveal her concern with aligning Fontenelle's arguments with broader cultural discourses of gender, authority, and intellectual agency. Behn's preface is especially striking, declaring her support for the neutrality of Copernican astronomy vis-à-vis the biblical narrative.

4.7.2 Translatorial Presence and Strategies

In all three versions, the "translatorial presence" is evident. Strategies of *explicitation* (adding clarifying details), *simplification* (reducing conceptual complexity), *clarification* (supplementing with explanatory material), and *omission* (removing delicate passages) are recurrent features. These interventions were not merely linguistic but ideological and cultural, reflecting each translator's assessment of what could or should be conveyed to English readers. Translation thus functioned as cultural brokerage, shaping the reception of cosmological speculation in ways conditioned by political prudence, theological caution, and literary tradition.

Domville's omissions reflect caution; Glanvill's interpolations indicate active intellectual engagement; Behn's literary reworkings reveal both stylistic instinct and cultural negotiation. Taken together, these strategies demonstrate how translation was embedded in the intellectual conflicts of late Stuart England.

4.7.3 Scholarly Perspectives

Earlier scholarship has focused disproportionately on Behn's translation, given her literary stature and the boldness of her interventions. Scholars, including Goodfellow (1996), Todd (1993, 2000), Cottegnies (2003, 2004, 2024), Schnell (2004), Ferguson (2008), Achinstein (2019), Gill (2020), and Mills (2025) have documented her divergences, noting how Behn reshaped Fontenelle's text in light of her cultural positions. Yet subtler interventions in all three translations are equally revealing. Domville's strategic omissions speak volumes about caution in a fraught religious context; Glanvill's clarifications show a translator deeply engaged with contemporary English science. Each translator's voice thus illuminates broader patterns in the reception and domestication of continental scientific thought.

4.7.4 A Transnational Dimension

The English translations must also be understood within the broader European context. Giovanni Lista (2024), in his study *On Translating Knowledge in the Enlightenment: The Case of Fontenelle's Plurality of Worlds*, highlights the interconnectedness of translations of Fontenelle's *Entretiens* across languages and contexts. Analysing English, Italian, and German versions published between 1687 and 1788, Lista identifies a spectrum of interpretative choices shaped by diverse intellectual traditions and local conditions. He observes that translations frequently moderated Fontenelle's materialism to avoid theological censure, sometimes balancing his "heretical" hypotheses with biblical narratives.

This tendency is evident in the Italian and German versions, which explicitly engage with the Cartesian–Newtonian controversy (Lissa 1971, 1973; Hall 1961: 63–65; Crombie and Hoskin 1970: 49–50; Dear 2019: 151–169). The German and Italian translations of *Entretiens*, respectively, by Johann Christoph Gottsched (1726) and Bernardino Vestrini (1751), reflected the existing critiques of the Cartesian concept of vortices. These examples underscore how translation served as a transnational forum for negotiating cosmology, theology, and philosophy.

In contrast, the early English translations, emerging decades earlier, show fewer signs of systematic scientific scepticism. Domville and Glanvill avoided overtly polemical commentary, while Behn's preface, though bold, focused more on asserting the compatibility of Copernican astronomy with biblical neutrality than on engaging in detailed scientific discussions. Nevertheless, Behn's stance reveals a translator prepared to adopt a forthright intellectual position, making her contribution exceptional in the English context at that time.

4.7.5 *Translation as Cultural Mediation*

Taken together, the three English translations of *Entretiens* appear as a cultural act rather than mere linguistic transfer. They demonstrate how ideas travelled across linguistic and national boundaries, acquiring new meanings in the process. The English translators functioned as mediators, negotiating between innovation and tradition, between cosmological speculation and theological caution. Their choices both reflected and shaped the intellectual climate of the British Isles during a moment of transition.

Domville embodied caution and compromise, Glanvill represented scholarly engagement and expansion, and Behn combined literary flair with interpretative boldness. Read side by side, their versions offer insight into how Enlightenment science was refracted through translation, and how translation itself became a mode of intellectual participation in the scientific revolution.

Each of those early English translations of Fontenelle's *Entretiens* demonstrates how translation functions not merely as a conduit but as a crucible of a particular cultural transformation. In late Stuart England, an era of political upheaval, religious contention, and scientific innovation, Domville, Glanvill, and Behn interpreted, reshaped, and reframed Fontenelle's cosmology in distinct ways. Their translations reveal the pressures and possibilities of transmitting continental science into an English milieu deeply marked by theological sensitivities and the emerging rationality of the Enlightenment.

Beyond England, the wider European trajectory of *Entretiens* translations demonstrates the multiplicity of ways in which scientific speculation was accommodated, contested, or reimagined. The "Fontenellian moment" was thus not confined to France but unfolded transnationally, as translators across Europe engaged with the plurality of worlds and the plurality of interpretations it invited.

In this sense, the extant critical literature recognises the translations of *Entretiens* as appearing in Europe not as derivative shadows of the French original, but as active, authorial works that both mirrored and shaped the hosting cultural contexts. Translation here emerges as an intellectual act of co-authorship, an enterprise in which language, philosophy, science, and politics converged to redefine humanity's place in the universe. The three early English translations of *Entretiens* are revisited here to assess how the ST has been differently accommodated in the target culture. In this perspective, further relevant personal information about the translators is provided in the following sections.

4.7.6 Sir William Domville

Sir William Domville (1643–1698) (hereafter the younger William Domville), a barrister and political figure active in Ireland, served as Attorney General under Charles II and remained loyal to the monarchy throughout the English Civil War and the Restoration. He was a staunch protestant, although always tolerant towards dissidents, Catholics, and political opponents. His family came from a dynasty dating back to Hugh Domville, who lived at the time of William the Conqueror (1017–1087), and William Domville (or Domvile) (1565–1624) of Lymn, Cheshire.

His father, William (1609–1689), was an Irish politician, barrister and Constitutional writer who served as Attorney General for Ireland under the reign of Charles II (1660–1685) and wrote an unpublished disquisition in 1660 arguing for the independence of the Irish Parliament under the rule of the English Crown. This work starts from the fact that Henry II (1133–1189), King of England from 1154, acquired Ireland through the voluntary submission of the Irish rather than by forcible conquest. His son-in-law, William Molyneux, later made extensive use of that disquisition in *"The Case of Ireland"* (1698), which was widely regarded as the most important Irish political work published until the end of the eighteenth century.

The younger William and his brother Launcelot followed their father by joining Lincoln's Inn in 1660 and 1668, though Launcelot died in 1673. In 1664, William was granted the reversion of Clerk of the Crown and Hanaper, a post once held by his grandfather, Gilbert Domville. He was knighted by Ormond in 1684, and his brother Thomas received the same recognition from James II in 1687.

The younger William Domville produced the first English translation of Fontenelle's work at the request of his brother-in-law William Molyneux and published it in Dublin in 1687 as *A Discourse of the Plurality of Worlds*. Though innovative, the translation had a limited impact due to both its geographical publication context and the political sensitivities of the time.

Domville's translation was completed within 1 year in 1687, before the Glorious Revolution of 1688–89, and reflects the cautious intellectual atmosphere of James II's reign. In the *Translator's preface*, Domville compares his work to Cicero's effort to present Greek philosophy in Latin, aiming to make natural philosophy accessible and engaging for both scholars and general readers. He introduces a fictional female student to enhance relatability and blends real philosophical arguments with imaginative elements to create an enjoyable experience. Addressing potential religious objections to the idea of other inhabited worlds, he argues for the diversity of life forms. He acknowledges that while his work may not satisfy everyone, public feedback will determine its value.

In keeping with the religious conservatism of the period, Domville preserved Fontenelle's philosophical content while avoiding controversial theological interpretations. His approach was primarily literal and restrained, aiming for clarity and fidelity to the original, without venturing into speculative commentary. The translation's modest tone and avoidance of overt religious or political engagement suggest an attempt to render the text acceptable to both Anglican and Catholic audiences.

He published his translation in Dublin, using only his initials and title, W.D., Knight, reflecting the original text's anonymity, with the indication of the source text as "written in French by the Most ingenious Author of *The Dialogues of the Dead*, printed by Andr. Crook and Sam. Helsham for William Norman, Bookbinder to His Grace the Duke of Ormond, in 1687".

He died in 1698, just 9 years after his father, and was buried at St. Patrick's Cathedral.

4.7.7 John Glanvill

John Glanvill (c.1664–1735), a scholar, poet, and translator, produced his version of *Entretiens* as *A Plurality of Worlds* in 1688, the very year of the Glorious Revolution. A former student at Trinity College, Oxford, who later became a barrister at Lincoln's Inn, he had a reputation for eccentricity and eclecticism. He translated several classical texts and participated actively in the literary and intellectual circles of Restoration London. Glanvill translated Seneca and Horace, wrote poetry, and participated in philosophical discussions.

His translation was one of his most significant works, making Fontenelle's ideas on cosmic pluralism accessible to English readers. Glanvill's translation is more interpretative than Domville's, characterised by paraphrasing and occasional amplification of the original. His rendering integrates theological reflection into scientific discourse, reflecting a desire to reconcile natural philosophy with Christian belief.

In his *Translator's Preface*, Glanvill explains that the work combines philosophical reasoning with imaginative storytelling to explore the concept of inhabited worlds beyond Earth, aiming to engage readers like a novel without requiring prior knowledge. It clarifies that the inhabitants described are not claimed to be human and addresses potential religious concerns by distinguishing these beings from human descendants, emphasising a blend of fact and fiction to stimulate both reason and imagination.

Unlike Domville's version, which maintains a cautious tone, Glanvill's translation engages more actively with the cosmological implications of heliocentrism and implicitly endorses a synthesis of science and providential theology. In doing so, Glanvill helped shape English readers' reception of Fontenelle's ideas at a time when science was increasingly perceived as compatible with religious inquiry.

He remained unmarried and left his wealth, including an estate in Cornwall, to his nephew upon his death in 1735.

4.7.8 Aphra Behn

Aphra Behn (1640–1689) was among the first English women to live by her pen. Born in Canterbury, possibly among Huguenot refugees, she likely acquired fluency in French early on (McMurran 2005: 5). Her eventful life encompassed travel to Suriname, espionage for Charles II under the code name "Astrea," imprisonment for debt, and active participation in the literary and intellectual circles of Restoration London (Spender 1992: 17; Todd 2000: 5–6). Without aristocratic support, Behn declared in her *Sir Patient Fancy* preface (1678/1996: 2) that she wrote to earn her livelihood. Mary Ann O'Donnell (1989) observes, "Behn chose for herself untraditional a role as she could: professional writer. She also chose a second untraditional role, especially in her prologues, epilogues, and dedications, as unabashed Tory and faithful supporter of the Stuart kings and their circle".

Behn's career as a translator reveals a strong authorial self-awareness. She contributed as a translator to *Ovid's Epistles* edited by Dryden (1680), which he publicly praised (Duffy 1989: 199), and translated part of Cowley's *Of Plants* (1689), identifying herself explicitly as translator. Her literary production—encompassing drama, poetry, fiction, and translation—demonstrates both intellectual ambition and resilience in an era of limited opportunities for women. Following the Popish Plot (1678), censorship reduced theatrical activity (Schnell 2004: 351); yet, she continued to write, approaching translation as both a necessity and a vocation. As Goodfellow (1996: 230) notes, her translations constituted "a social statement," while Robinson (1995: 153) observed that she pursued them with the same audacity found in her plays.

Her most famous translation, *A Discovery of New Worlds* (1688), adapts Fontenelle's *Entretiens sur la pluralité des mondes* (1686) and echoes the title of John Wilkins's *A Discovery of a New World* (1638/1684). The title page boldly declares: "From the French. Made English by Mrs. A. Behn," which appears as a rare assertion of female authorship in scientific translation. Behn's accompanying notice—"To which is prefixed a PREFACE, by way of ESSAY on Translated PROSE; wherein the Arguments of Father *Tacquet*, and others, against the System of *Copernicus* (as the Motion of the Earth) are likewise considered, and answered:

Wholly new"—advertises her engagement with the philosophical and theological controversies surrounding Copernican cosmology.

In her *Translator's Preface*, Behn critiques Fontenelle for omitting references to God and directly confronts the theological dilemmas raised by heliocentrism. Without embracing heterodoxy, she distinguishes scriptural revelation from scientific explanation, asserting that the Bible was written to guide faith, not astronomy. She refutes Jesuit Father André Tacquet's objections to heliocentrism and interprets biblical passages allegorically. In this, she aligns herself with Wilkins and other Protestant thinkers who sought reconciliation between Scripture and emerging science (Rossetter 2019).

Behn's stance reflects the intellectual maturity of post-Restoration England. As Mason (1953: 41) observed, by the late seventeenth century, "the Bible and the works of the ancient and medieval philosophers were no longer taken as authoritative upon matters relating to the structure of the world." When Newton's *Principia* (1687) appeared, English theologians, prepared by Wilkins's and Behn's generation, offered little resistance to its heliocentrism. Mason (1953: 41) also observed:

> After the period of the Civil Wars and the Commonwealth, the Bible and the works of the ancient and medieval philosophers were no longer taken as authoritative upon matters relating to the structure of the world in England. Even the makers of popular almanacs generally adopted the Copernican system of the world and critics of science took pains to deny, for fear of ridicule, that they believed in the medieval world system. When Newton's *Principia* appeared in 1687, it encountered little religious opposition in England, for Wilkins and the men of his generation had borne the brunt of the Anglican resistance to science and had made apparent the elements common to the new science and the new religion.

Behn's *Preface* notably mirrors Wilkins's argument in *A Discovery of a World* (1640/1684), where he claims: "there is not any Argument from the words of Scriptures, Principles of Nature, or observations in Astronomy, which can sufficiently evidence the Earth to be in the centre of the Vniverse" (ibid.: Prop. VI). The parallelism between the two texts—in title, structure, and purpose—demonstrates Behn's awareness. Steiner (1975), Buesa Gómez (2003), and Dimitriu (2009) affirm that her *Preface* represents an act of intellectual authorship; Duffy (1989: 280–81) sees it as mediation between Fontenelle's ideas and England's theological debates.

Cottegnies (2024: 46) has recently argued that Behn's negotiation of science and faith resembled the criticised Fontenelle's prudence on religion: in such a critique, Behn's approach would be as fraught as Fontenelle's silence, but evidence suggests otherwise. As already stated, by the late seventeenth century, it had become increasingly acceptable to question the official interpretation of the Vulgate Bible and to discuss cosmology. However, these topics remained subjects of ongoing debate. Hence, the risks she faced were much less severe than implied in that critique. By the 1680s, questioning scriptural literalism was increasingly tolerated, allowing Behn to strike a balance between rationalism and piety. Her translation thus exemplifies the Restoration synthesis of faith and reason, as well as the new confidence in women's intellectual agency.[5] As a matter of fact, Behn navigated between rationalism and faith *without serious censure*, allowing her to engage with new ideas while upholding her beliefs. The success of her translation reflects contemporary interest in reconciling reason and revelation. However, she still faced the risk of plagiarism accusations.

Behn's literary reputation was marred by accusations of libertinism and plagiarism. In Restoration England, imitation and adaptation were integral to authorship, and charges of plagiarism often masked gender or political bias. In fact, in the late seventeenth century, the accusation of plagiarism needed to be contextualised within a literary culture where imitation, borrowing, and adaptation were standard practices. Her adaptation of Killigrew's *Thomaso* (1664) for *The Rover* (1677) exemplifies creative transformation rather than theft (Link 1968: 98, Hughes 2004).

Persistent accusations prompted her to defend herself in *The Rover*'s postscript (Spender 1982: 39; Vander Motten 2013). Behn's case illustrates well both the shifting semantics of "plagiarism" and the cultural asymmetries of that period. Classical debates had long distinguished between acceptable borrowing and culpable theft, and this distinction continued to inform Restoration criticism. As Nicoll (1923), Kewes (1998) and Todd (2000: 186) note, literary borrowing was commonly praised as learned imitation in Restoration drama, though Behn's gender rendered her vulnerable to moralised censure.

Behn's dual identity as translator and author is manifest in her dedication to *A Discovery of New Worlds*. With humility and confidence, she concedes her limited scientific training yet asserts independent judgment. But also in this context, her citation in the *Translation Preface* of "the two texts (of Psalm 19 and Joshua 10) [which] are as much for Copernicus as against him" are clearly "borrowed", along with the title, from Wilkins (1640/1684) without recognising or even mentioning him. Her translation corrects misprints, recalculates data, and includes explanatory notes—acts of interpretive engagement that make the work pedagogical rather than derivative, but not without imprecisions, errors, and misinterpretations visible even to her contemporaries. As a translator, she aims to mediate between science and faith, between French rationalism and English empiricism in a manner and to an extent that are considered in detail in the present study.

Aphra Behn can be acknowledged as a mediator of scientific culture, not just a pioneering writer. Her *A Discovery of New Worlds* blended cosmology, theology, and literature, while treating translation as a form of co-authorship. Along with Domville and Glanvill, Behn helped introduce Fontenelle's pluralism to the English Enlightenment, embodying the intellectual audacity that defined their age.

[5] The Anglican Alexander Ross (1591–1654) replied with *The New Planet no Planet* (1646), after his *Commentum de Terrae Motu* (1634), in favour of the literal interpretation of the Scriptures and against the Copernican system and Wilkins' works.

4.8 Further Remarks

The age of scientific discovery fundamentally altered humanity's understanding of the cosmos, envisioning a universe of multiple populated worlds. As noted in recent scholarship (e.g., Jordheim and Sandmo 2019), Fontenelle played a pivotal role in disseminating new physical and astronomical ideas during a period of rapid epistemological transformation. First published in Paris in 1686, *Entretiens* achieved immediate international acclaim, was translated into several languages, and appeared in numerous editions throughout Fontenelle's lifetime. Though not the earliest text to speculate on extraterrestrial life, *Entretiens* was instrumental in popularising the idea during the Enlightenment. It challenged anthropocentric worldviews by relocating Earth from the cosmic centre to one planet among many and advocated for a contextual and relativised understanding of humanity's place in the universe.

By proposing that Earth was not unique but rather one of many potentially inhabited worlds governed by the same physical laws, Fontenelle undermined traditional theological and cosmological assumptions. This conceptual shift, decentralising Earth and rejecting the doctrine of celestial perfection, profoundly influenced Enlightenment thought and continues to resonate in modern scientific and philosophical discussions. European readers found the idea of planetary plurality captivating, and it became a powerful metaphor for emerging global, scientific, and anthropological paradigms.

Fontenelle and his translators were careful to clarify that "worlds" refers not solely to Earth but to other planets as well. In the original French, the term "Terre" (a proper noun) gradually gave way to "terre" (a common noun), indicating a broader, more universal application. Similarly, stars are described as "worlds" because of their capacity to emit light and heat, each presiding over its own planetary system. The Marquise's evolving response in the dialogues, from astonishment to intellectual curiosity, mirrors the reader's progressive engagement with these ideas.

In English translations, the term "worlds" acquired particular resonance within imperial and colonial discourse, appealing to a British audience attuned to exploration and expansion. In contrast, German and Danish translators often avoided the plural form, perhaps to sidestep its theological or moral implications. This variation illustrates how translation not only mediates linguistic content but also reconfigures conceptual frameworks in accordance with local intellectual and ideological climates.

The second edition of Behn's translation, published posthumously in 1700 as part of the second volume of her collected works, appeared under the expanded title *A Theory or System of Several New Inhabited Worlds Lately Discovered and Pleasantly Described, in Five Nights' Conversations with Madam the Marchioness of...* The inclusion of the word "system" gestures not only to the Copernican model but also to a broader Enlightenment tendency to organise knowledge rationally and methodically, in contrast to the teleological certainties of scholastic and Aristotelian thought.

As noted in the *Encyclopédie*, a system was understood as "the arrangement of the different elements of an art or a science in an order that makes them mutually dependent." This emphasis on internal coherence and secular explanation distinguished Enlightenment systems from religious or mythological cosmologies. Cliff Siskin (2010) has suggested that "system" functioned as both a conceptual and literary genre that encapsulated the Enlightenment's epistemological ambitions.

Examining how Fontenelle's translators responded to the concept of "plurality" and "system" offers valuable insight into the historical evolution of cosmological thinking. While the idea of multiple worlds gradually waned in the nineteenth century, eclipsed by anthropocentric paradigms and disciplinary specialisation, it has re-emerged in contemporary discourse on globalisation, astrobiology, and climate change. The philosophical and rhetorical frameworks advanced by Fontenelle and refracted through his translators remain relevant as we continue to grapple with the plurality of planetary futures.

References

Primary Sources

Behn, Aphra (1688) TT3: *A Discovery of New Worlds*. From French. Made English by Mrs. A. Behn. To which is prefixed a Preface, by way of essay on translated prose; wherein the arguments of Father Tacquet, and others, against the System of Coprnicus (as to the Motion of the Earth) are likewise considered, and answere: Wholly new. London, printes for William Canning, at his Shop in the Temple-Cloysters.

Domville, William (1687) TT1: *A Discourse of the Plurality of Worlds*, written in French by the most ingenious Author of the *Dialogues of the Dead*, and translated into English by Sir W.D. Knight. Dublin: Printed by Andr. Crook and Sam. Helsham for William Norman bookbinder to His Grace the Duke of Ormond.

Fontenelle, Bernard le Bovier de Fontenelle (1686) ST: *Entretiens sur la pluralité des mondes*. Paris: Veuve Blageart. Registered on Livre de la Communauté des Libraires & Imprimeurs de Paris, on 22 January 1686. Printed on 8 March 1686

Glanvill, J. (1688) TT2: *A Plurality of Worlds*, Written in French by the Author of the *Dialogues of the Dead*; Translated into English by Mr. Glanvill. London: printed for R. Bentley and S. Magnes.

Secondary Sources

Achinstein, Sharon. 2019. New World Behn: Toleration, Geography, and the Question of Humanity. In *Imagining Religious Toleration: A Literary History of an Idea, 1600–1830*, ed. D. Alvarez and A. Conway, 35–57. Toronto: University of Toronto Press.

Aiton, E. J. 1972. *The Vortex Theory of Planetary Motion*. London/Macdonald/New York: American Elsevier.

Ashley, Maurice. 1987. *Charles I and Oliver Cromwell: A Study in Contrasts and Comparisons*. Malton, U.K.: Methuen Publishing.

Ariew, Roger. 1999. *Descartes and the Last Scholastics*. Ithaca: Cornell University Press.

Behn, Aphra. 1678/1996. *Sir Patient Fancy*. In *The Works of Aphra Behn*, ed. J. Todd, vol. 6, 1–82. London: Routledge.

Bennet, Jeffrey, Seth Shostak, Nicholas Schneider, and Meredith MacGregor. 2022. *Life in the Universe*. 5th ed. Princeton/Oxford: Princeton University Press.

Blair, Ann. 2003. Natural Philosophy. In *The Cambridge History of Science, Vol. 3 Early Modern Science*, 365–410. Cambridge, UK: Cambridge University Press.

Boas, Marie. 1962. *The Scientific Renaissance. 1450–1630*. London: Collins.

Brake, Mark. 2006. On the Plurality of Inhabited Worlds: A Brief History of Extraterrestrialism. *International Journal of Astrobiology* 5 (2): 99–107.

Brin, Glen David. 1983. The Great Silence. The Controversy Concerning Extraterrestrial Intelligent Life. *Quarterly Journal of the Royal Astronomical Society* 24 (3): 283–309.

Briot, Danielle. 2013. Elements for the History of a Long Quest: Search for Life in the Universe. *International Journal of Astrobiology* 12 (3): 254–258.

Bromley, John Selwyn. 1970. Introduction. In *The New Cambridge Modern History. Vol. VI: The Rise of Great Britain and Russia 1688–1725*, ed. J. S. Bromley, 1–36. Cambridge, UK: Cambridge University Press.

Buesa Gómez, María Carmen. 2003. The Preface as a Genre in English Translations in the 17th Century. *Estudios Humanísticos. Filología* 25:185–196.

Bussotti, Paolo, and Brunello Lotti. 2022. *Cosmology in the Early Modern Age: A Web of Ideas*. Cham: Springer.

Butterfield, Herbert. 1931. *The Whig Interpretation of History*. New York: WW Norton and Company.

Butterfield, Herbert. 1949/1957. *The Origins of Modern Science 1300–1800*. New York: G. Bells and Sons.

Cabrol, Nathalie A. 2023. *The Secret Life of the Universe: An Astrobiologist's Search for the Origins and Frontiers of Life*. New York: Simon & Schuster.

Ćirković, Milan M. 2018. *The Great Silence: Science and Philosophy of Fermi's Paradox*. Oxford: Oxford University Press.

Connes, Pierre. 2020. *History of the Plurality of Worlds: The Myths of Extraterrestrials Through the Ages*. Cham: Springer.

Cottegnies, Line. 2003. The Translator as Critics: Aphra Behn's Translation of Fontenelle's *A Discovery of New Worlds* (1688). *Restoration: Studies in English Literary Culture, 1660–1700* 27 (1): 23–38.

Cottegnies, Line. 2004. Aphra Behn's French Translations. In *The Cambridge Companion to Aphra Behn*, ed. Derek Hughes and Janet Todd, 221–234. Cambridge, UK: Cambridge University Press.

Cottegnies, Line. 2024. Aphra Behn's Use of *Translation*: Mediation, Adaptation, and Emulation in a Cross-Channel Perspective. *Sederi* 34 (2): 31–52.

Cottingham, John. 2006. *The Cambridge Companion to Descartes*. Cambridge, UK: Cambridge University Press.

Coustenis, Athena, and Thérèse Encrenaz. 2013. *Life beyond Earth. The Search for Habitable Worlds in the Universe*. Cambridge, UK: Cambridge University Press.

Crombie, A. C., and Michael Hoskin. 1970. The Scientific Movement and the Diffusion of Scientific Ideas, 1688–1751. In *The New Cambridge Modern History. Vol. VI: The Rise of Great Britain and Russia 1688–1725*, ed. J. S. Bromley, 37–71. Cambridge, UK: Cambridge University Press.

Crowe, Michel J. 1988. *The Extraterrestrial Life Debate 1750–1900: The Idea of a Plurality of Worlds from Kant to Lowell*. Cambridge, UK: Cambridge University Press.

Crowe, Michel J. 2008. *The Extraterrestrial Life Debate, Antiquity to 1915: A Source Book*. Notre Dame: University of Notre Dame Press.

Crowe, Michael J. 2018. William and John Herschel's Quest for Extraterrestrial Intelligent Life. In *The Scientific Legacy of William Herschel*, ed. C. J. Cunningham, 239–274. Cham: Springer.

Daston, L., and K. Park. 1998. *Wonders and the Order of Nature 1150–1750*. New York: Zone Books.

De Beer, E. S. 1970. The English Revolution. In *the New Cambridge Modern History. Vol. VI: The Rise of Great Britain and Russia 1688–1725*, ed. J. S. Bromley, 193–222. Cambridge, UK: Cambridge University Press.

Dear, Peter. 2019. *Revolutionizing the Sciences: European Knowledge in Transition, 1500–1700*. 3rd ed. Princeton/Oxford: Princeton University Press.

Dick, Steve J. 1980. The Origins of the Extraterrestrial Life Debate and Its Relation to the Scientific Revolution. *Journal of the History of Ideas* 41 (1): 3–27.

Dick, Steve J. 1982. *Plurality of Worlds: The Origin of the Extraterrestrial Life Debate from Democritus to Kant*. Cambridge, UK: Cambridge University Press.

Dimitriu, Rodica. 2009. Translator's Prefaces as Documentary Sources for Translation Studies. *Perspectives: Studies in Translation Theory and Practice* 17 (3): 193–206.

Domski, Mary. 2019. Imagination, Metaphysics, Mathematics. Descartes' Arguments for the Vortex Hypothesis. *Synthese* 196:3505–3526.

Drake, Stillman. 1978. *Galileo at Work: His Scientific Biography*. Chicago: Chicago University Press.

Drake, Frank. 2013. Reflections on the Equation. *International Journal of Astrobiology* 12 (3): 173–176.

Drake, Frank, and Dava Sobel. 1992. *Is Anyone Out There? The Scientific Search for Extraterrestrial Intelligence*. New York: Dalacorte Press.

Dryden, John (ed. by). 1680. *Ovid's Epistles, Translated by Several Hands*. London: Jacob Tonson.

Duffy, Maureen. 1989. *The Passionate Shepherdess: Aphra Behn 1640–89*. London: Methuen London.

Dutton, Richard. 2000. *Licensing, Censorship and Authorship in Early Modern England*. Houndmills/New York: Palgrave Macmillan/St. Martin's Press.

Falcone, Roberta. 2004. Aphra Behn Dietro le Quinte: Pensare, Recitare, Scrivere [Aphra Behn behind the Scenes: Thinking, Acting, Writing]. In *Aphra Behn. L'infrazione del Canone* [Aphra Behan: Breaking the Canon] Naples e Rome: Edizioni Scientifiche Italiane.

Ferguson, Margaret. 2008. With All Due Reverence and Respect to the Word of God: Aphra Behn as Skeptical Reader of the Bible and Critical Translator of Fontenelle. In *Reading Women. Literacy, Authorship, and Culture in the Atlantic World, 1500–1800*, ed. H. Brayman Hackel and C. E. Kelly, 199–216. Philadelphia: University of Pennsylvania Press.

Ferlin, Fabrice, and Hugues Chabot. 2020. Vortex Theories in the Early Modern Period. In *Encyclopedia of Early Modern Philosophy and the Societies*, ed. D. Jalobeanu and C.T. Wolfe, 1–6. Cham: Springer.

Forgan, Duncan. 2019. *Solving Fermi's Paradox*. Cambridge, UK: Cambridge University Press.

Gill, Catie. 2020. The Bible and its Exegesis in Aphra Behn's "an Essay on Translated Prose" (1688). *Women's Writing* 27 (3): 310–324.

Gillies, Donald and Giulia Giorello. 1993. *Philosophy of Science in the Twentieth Century. Four Central Themes*. Oxford, UK and Cambridge, MA: Blackwell.

Goodfellow, Sarah. 1996. Such Masculine Strokes: Aphra Behn as Translator of *A Discovery of New Worlds*. *Albion: A Quarterly Journal Concerned with British Studies* 28 (2): 229–250.

Gottsched, Johann Christoph. 1726. *Herrn Bernhards von Fontenelle Gespräche von Mehr als einer Welt: zwischen einem Fräuenzimmer und einem Gelehrten*. [Mr. Bernhard de Fontenelle's Conversations of More Than His World: Between a Lady and a Scholar.] Leipzig, Germany.

Grant, Edward. 2007. *A History of Natural Philosophy. From Ancient World to the Nineteenth Century*. Cambridge, UK/New York: Cambridge University Press.

Gray, Robert H. 2015. The Fermi Paradox Is Neither Fermi's Nor a Paradox. *Astrobiology* 15 (3): 195–199.

Habing, Harm. 2018. *The Birth of Modern Astronomy*. Cham: Springer.

Hack, Margherita. 2002. Introduzione. In *Trattenimenti su' la pluralità de' Mondi* di Monsieur De Fontenelle. Trans. Bernardino Vestrini, printed in Arezzo (Italy), 1751. Republished in Florence: Nuova MSC.

Hall, A. R. 1961. The Scientific Movement. In *The New Cambridge Modern History, Volume V: The Ascendancy of France: 1648–88*, ed. F. L. Carsten, 47–72. Cambridge, UK: Cambridge University Press.

Harris, Tim. 2006. *Revolution. The Great Crisis of the British Monarchy, 1685–1720*. London: Allen Lane.

Heimann, Peter M. 1979. The Scientific Revolution. In *The New Cambridge Modern History. XIII Companion Volume*, ed. P. Burke, 248–270. Cambridge, UK: Cambridge University Press.

Hesse, Mary. 1970. Bacon, Francis. In *Dictionary of Scientific Biography*, vol. 1. New York: Charles Schtibner's Sons.

Hooykaas, R. 1972. *Religion and the Rise of Modern Science*. Edinburgh/London: Scottish Academic.

Hoskin, Michael. 2003. *The History of Astronomy. A Very Short Introduction*. Oxford: Oxford University Press.

Hughes, Derek. 2004. Aphra Behn and the Restoration Theatre. In *The Cambridge Companion to Aphra Behn*, ed. D. Hughes and J. Todd, 29–45. Cambridge, UK: Cambridge University Press.

Hunter, Michael. 1992. Latitudinarianism and the "Ideology" of the Early Royal Society: Thomas Sprat's History of the Royal Society (1667) Reconsidered. In *Philosophy, Science and Religion in England 1640–1700*, 199–229. Cambridge, UK: Cambridge University Press.

Hutner, Heidi. 1993. *Rereading Aphra Behn: History, Theory, and Criticism*. Charlottesville: University of Virginia Press.

Iliffe, Rob, and George E. Smith. 2016. *The Cambridge Companion to Newton*. 2nd ed. Cambridge, UK: Cambridge University Press.

Jakosky, Bruce. 1998. *The Search for Life on Other Planets*. Cambridge, UK: Cambridge University Press.

Jheeta, Sohan. 2013. Final Frontiers: The Hunt for Life Elsewhere in the Universe. *Astrophysics and Space Science* 348 (1): 1–10.

Jones, Eric M. 1985. "Where Is Everybody?": An Account of Fermi's Question. In *WP no. LA-10311 MS*. Los Alamos: Los Alamos National Laboratory.

Jordheim, Helge. 2019. The Fontenellian Moment. In *Conceptualising the World. An Exploration across Disciplines*, ed. H. Jordheim and E. Sandmo, 339–355. New York/Oxford: Berghahn.

Jordheim, Helge, and Erling Sandmo. 2019. Introduction. The World as Concept and Object of Knowledge. In *Conceptualising the World. An Exploration across Disciplines*, ed. H. Jordheim and E. Sandmo. New York/Oxford: Berghahn.

Kaltenegger, Lisa. 2024. *Alien Earths. The Search for Life in the Cosmos*. New York: St. Martin's Press.

Kavenik, Frances M. 1991. Aphra Behn: The Playwright as 'Breeches Part'. In *Curtain Calls: British and American Women and the Theater, 1660–1820*, ed. Mary Anne Schofield and Cecilia Macheski, 177–192. Athens: Ohio University Press.

Kewes, Paulina. 1998. *Authorship and Appropriation. Writing for the Stage in England, 1660–1710*. Oxford: Oxford University Press.

Knellwolf, Christa. 2001. Women Translators, Gender and Cultural Context of the Scientific Revolution. In *Translation and Nation. Towards a Cultural Politics of Englishness*, ed. R. Ellis and L. Oakley-Brown, 85–119. Clevedon: Multilingual Matters.

Knights, Mark. 2015. The Long-Term Consequences of the English Revolution: State Formation, Political Culture, and Ideology. In *The Oxford Handbook of the English Revolution*, ed. M. J. Braddick, 518–534. Oxford: Oxford University Press.

Kuhn, Thomas. 1962. *The Structure of Scientific Revolutions*. Chicago: Chicago University Press.

Lancaster, Henry Oliver. 1979. *Expectations of Life: A Study in the Demography, Statistics, and History of World Mortality*. New York: Springer-Verlag.

Link, Frederick M. 1968. *Aphra Behn*. New York: Twayne.

Lissa, Giuseppe. 1971. *Cartesianesimo e anticartesianesimo in Fontenelle*. Naples: Morano.

Lissa, Giuseppe. 1973. *Fontenelle tra scetticismo e nuova critica*. Naples: Morano.

Lista, Giovanni. 2024. On Translating Knowledge in the Enlightenment: The Case of Fontenelle's Plurality of Worlds. *Journal of the History of Ideas*. https://www.jhiblog.org/2024/07/15/on-translating-knowledge-in-the-enlightenment-the-case-of-fontenelles-plurality-of-worlds/.

Loeb, Abraham. 2014. The Habitable Epoch of the Early Universe. *International Journal of Astrobiology* 13 (4): 337–339. (Preprint: *arXiv* WP no. 1312.0613).

Macaulay, Thomas Babington. 1848. *History of England from the Accession of James the Second*. London: Longman.

MacDougal, Douglas W. 2012. *Newton's Gravity. An Introductory Guide to the Mechanics of the Universe*. New York: Springer.

Marsak, Leonard Mendes. 1959. Bernard de Fontenelle: The Idea of Science in the French Enlightenment. *Transactions of the American Philosophical Society*, NS 49: pt. 7.0065-9746.

Martin, Julian. 1992. *Francis Bacon, and the Reform of Natural Philosophy*. Cambridge, UK: Cambridge University Press.

Martin, Anthony R. 2018. The Origin of the "Fermi Paradox". *Journal of the British Interplanetary Society* 71 (6): 200–206.

Mason, S. F. 1953. Science and Religion in 17th-Century England. *Past and Present* 3:28–44.

McColley, Grant. 1932. The Theory of a Plurality of Worlds as a Factor in Milton's Attitude toward the Copernican Hypothesis. *Modern Language Notes* 47 (5): 319–325.

McColley, Grant. 1936. The Seventeenth-Century Doctrine of a Plurality of Worlds. *Annals of Science* 1 (4): 385–430.

McIntyre, Kenneth B. 2011. *Herbert Butterfield: History, Providence, and Skeptical Politics*. Wilmington: ISIS Books.

McKenzie, D. F. 2002. Printing and Publishing 1557–1700: Constraints on the London Book Trades. In *The Cambridge History of the Book in Britain*, ed. J. Barnard and D. F. McKenzie, vol. 4, 553–567. Cambridge, UK: Cambridge University Press.

McLeod, Alexus. 2016. *Astronomy in the Ancient World. Early and Modern Views on Celestial Events*. Cham: Springer.

McMurran, Mary Helen. 2005. Aphra Behn from Both Sides: Translation in the Atlantic World. *Studies in Eighteenth-Century Culture* 34:1–23.

Michaud, Michael. 2006. *Contact with Alien Civilizations: Our Hopes and Fears about Encountering Extraterrestrials*. Göttingen: Copernicus Publications.

Miller, John. 1973. *Popery and Politics in England, 1660–1688*. Cambridge, UK: Cambridge University Press.

Miller, John. 2003. Politics in Restoration England. In *A Companion to Stuart Britain*, ed. B. Coward, 416–435. Oxford/Malden: Blackwell.

Miller, John. 2015. The Long-Term Consequences of the English Revolution: Economic and Social Development. In *The Oxford Handbook of the English Revolution*, ed. M. J. Braddick, 501–517. Oxford: Oxford University Press.

Mills, Amelia. 2025. Overcoming Barriers to Educated Discourse: A *Discovery of New Worlds* (1688), Translation, and Aphra Behn's "Passionate Thirst of Knowledge of the Mind". *Women's Writing* 32 (2): 195–209.

Mullan, J. 2008. *Anonymity: A Secret History of English Literature*. Princeton: Princeton University Press.

Nadler, Steven, Tad M. Schmaltz, and Delphine Antoine-Mahut, eds. 2019. *The Oxford Handbook of Descartes and Cartesianism*. Oxford: Oxford University Press.

Nicoll, Allardyce. 1923. *A History of Restoration Drama, 1660–1700*. Cambridge, UK: Cambridge University Press.

O'Donnell, Mary Ann. 1989. Tory Wit and Unconventional Woman. Aphra Behn. In *Women Writers of the Seventeenth Century*, ed. K. M. Wilson and F. J. Warnke, 341–374. Athens/Georgia/London: University of Georgia Press.
Ogg, David. 1961. Britain after the Restoration. In *the New Cambridge Modern History, Vol. V. The Ascendancy of France: 1648–88*, ed. F. L. Carsten, 301–329. Cambridge, UK: Cambridge University Press.
Patterson, Annabel. 1984. *Censorship and Interpretation: The Conditions of Writing and Reading in Early Modern England*. Madison: University of Wisconsin Press.
Pearsons, Jacqueline. 1988. *The Prostitute Muse: Images of Women and Women Dramatis 1642–1737*. London: Harvester.
Peltonen, Markuu, ed. 1996. *The Cambridge Companion to Bacon*. Cambridge, UK: Cambridge University Press.
Playford, Richard, Stephen Bullivant, and Janet Siefert. 2024. *God and Astrobiology*. Cambridge, UK: Cambridge University Press.
Pocock, J. G. A. 1975. *The Machiavellian Moment: Florentine Political Thought and the Atlantic Republican Tradition*. Princeton: Princeton University Press.
Prantzos, Nikos. 2013. A Joint Analysis of the Drake Equation and the Fermi Paradox. *International Journal of Astrobiology* 12 (3): 246–253.
Robertson, Randy. 2009. *Censorship and Conflict in Seventeenth-Century England. The Subtle Art of Division*. University Park: The Pennsylvania State University Press.
Rogers, Katherine. 1982. *Feminism in Eighteenth-Century England*. Urbana: University of Illinois Press.
Rospars, Jean-Pierre, Florence Raulin-Cerceau, and Rocco Mancinelli. 2013. Guest Editorial of the Special Issue on the Drake Equation. *International Journal of Astrobiology* 12 (3): 171–172.
Rossetter, Thomas. 2019. *The Theorist: Thomas Burnet and his Sacred History of the Earth*. Ph.D. Thesis. Durham: Department of Philosophy. Durham University.
Roush, Wade. 2020. *Extraterrestrials*. Cambridge, MA: The MIT Press.
Rowe, David E., Tilman Sauer, and Scott A. Walter, eds. 2018. *Beyond Einstein: Perspectives on Geometry, Gravitation, and Cosmology in the Twentieth Century*. New York: Springer.
Sackville-West, Vita. 1927. *Aphra Behn: The Incomparable Astrea*. London: Gerard Howe.
Sagan, Carl E. 1966. *Intelligent Life in the Universe*. San Francisco, CA: Holden–Day.
Sagan, Carl E. 1973. *Communication with Extraterrestrial Intelligence*. Cambridge, MA: The MIT Press.
Sagan, Carl E., and Neil deGrasse Tyson. 2013. *Cosmos*. New York: The Random House.
Schnell, Lisa. 2004. Aphra Behn, Fontenelle's *A Discovery of New Worlds* (1688). In *Reading Early Modern Women: An Anthology of Texts in Manuscript and Print, 1500–1700*, ed. H. Ostovich and E. Sauer, 350–351. New York: Routledge.
Schulze-Makuch, Dirk, and Louis N. Irwin. 2018. *Life in the Universe*. Springer.
Scott, Jonathan. 2000. *England's Troubles: Seventeenth-Century English Political Instability in European Context*. Cambridge, UK: Cambridge University Press.
Shama, Simon. 2001. *A History of Britain. Vol. 2: The British Wars, 1603–1776*. London: BBC Worldwide.
Shapin, Steven. 1994. *A Social History of Truth: Civility and Science in Seventeenth-Century England*. Chicago: Chicago University Press.
Shapin, Steven. 1996. *The Scientific Revolution*. Chicago: Chicago University Press.
Shapiro, Barbara June. 1969. *John Wilkins 1614–1672. An Intellectual Biography*. Berkeley/Los Angeles: University of California Press.
Sharpe, Kevin. 2013. *Rebranding Rule: The Restoration and Revolution Monarchy, 1660–1714*. New Haven and London: Yale University Press.
Sheehan, William. 2010. *A Passion for the Planets. Envisioning Other Worlds, from the Pleistocene to the Age of the Telescope*. New York: Springer.
Simpson, James. 2019. *Permanent Revolution: The Reformation and the Illiberal Roots of Liberalism*. Cambridge, MA: Harvard University Press.

Siskin, Cliff. 2010. Mediated Enlightenment: The System of the World. In *This Is Enlightenment*, ed. C. Siskin and W. Warner, 164–172. Chicago: University of Chicago Press.

Smith, Graeme H. 2021. Jules Verne's Formulation of the Fermi Question. *Research Notes of the American Astronomical Society.* 5 (252): 252.

Spearing, Elizabeth. 1996. Aphra Behn: The Politics of Translation. In *Aphra Behn Studies*, ed. Janet Todd, 154–177. Cambridge, UK: Cambridge University Press.

Špelda, Daniel. 2024. *The Origin of the Idea of Scientific Progress: Bernard de Fontenelle and His Contemporaries*. Cham: Springer.

Spender, Dale. 1982. *Woman of Ideas and What Men Have Done to Them: From Aphra Behn to Adrienne Rich*. London: Routledge.

Spender, Dale. 1992. Introduction: A Vindication of the Writing Women. In *Living by the Pen: Early British Women Writers*, ed. D. Spender, 1–35. New York/London: Columbia University, Teachers College Press.

Spurr, John. 1992. *The Restoration of the Church of England 1646–1689*. New Haven: Yale University Press.

Stapleton, Julia. 2008. Review: Modernism, the English Past, and Christianity: Herbert Butterfield and the Study of History. *The Historical Journal* 51 (2): 547–557.

Stapleton, Julia. 2012. Book Review: Kenneth B. McIntyre. *Herbert Butterfield: History, Providence, and Skeptical Politics*. Wilmington, DE: ISIS Books. *The Review of Politics* 74 (4): 689–692.

Stein, Claudia. 2014. The Scientific Revolution. In *The European World 1500–1800*, ed. B. Kümin, 204–213. London/New York: Routledge.

Steiner, Thomas R. 1975. *English Translation Theory 1650–1800*. Assen: Van Gorcum.

Stephenson, Bruce. 1987. *Kepler's Physical Astronomy*. Heidelberg/New York: Springer.

Stern, Christina. 2014. Enlightenment ideals in our present? Our future. *Clio's Psyche* 21 (4): 295–298.

Tawney, Richard Henry. 1922/1926. *Religion and the Rise of Capitalism. A Historical Study*. London: John Murray.

Thom, René. 1972. *Stabilité Structurelle et morphogénèse. Essay D'une théorie géneral Des modèles*. Paris: InterEditions. Trans. D. H. Fowler, *Structural Stability and Morphogenesis: An Outline of a General Theory of Models*. Reading, MA: W.A. Benjamin. 1975.

Thomas, Donald. 1969. *A Long Time Burning. The History of Literary Censorship in England*. London: Routledge.

Tipler, F. J. 1981. A Brief History of the Extraterrestrial Intelligence Concept. *Quarterly Journal of the Royal Astronomical Society* 22:133–145.

Todd, Janet. 1993. *The Works of Aphra Behn, vol. 4*. London: Pickering and Chatto.

Todd, Janet. 2000. *The Secret Life of Aphra Behn*. 2nd ed. London: Pandora.

Treadwell, Michael. 2002. The Stationers and the Printing Act at the End of the Seventeenth Century. In *The Cambridge History of the Book in Britain, Vol. 4*, ed. J. Barnard and D. F. McKenzie, 755–778. Cambridge, UK: Cambridge University Press.

Trevor-Roper, Hugh. 2001. *The Crisis of the Seventeenth-Century Religion, the Reformation and Social Change*. Indianapolis: Liberty Fund.

Uglow, Jenny. 2009. *A Gambling Man: Charles II and the Restoration, 1660–1670*. London: Faber and Faber.

Vander Motten, J. P. 2013. Recycling the Exile: Thomaso, the Rover and the Critics. In *Thomas Killigrew and the Seventeenth-Century English Stage*, ed. Philip Major, 133–150. Abington/Oxon: Ashgate.

Vestrini, Bernardino. 1751. *Trattamenti su la pluralita' de' mondi di Monsieur de Fontenelle*. Arezzo, Italy. (Anonymously published and attributed to Bernardini Vestrini by Gaetano Melzi, 1852: 166).

Watson, R. A. 1966. *The Downfall of Cartesianism, 1673–1712. A Study of Epistemological Issues in Late 17th-Century Cartesianism*. The Hague: Martinus Nijhoff.

Webb, Stephen. 2002. *If the Universe Is Teeming with Aliens... Where Is Everybody?* New York: Springer.
Weber, Max. 1904–5. Die Protestantische Ethik Und der Geist Des Kapitalismus. Published as a Two-Part Article in *Archiv für Sozialwissenschaft Und Sozialpolitik*. (English Trans. Talcott Parsons, *The Protestant Ethic and the Spirit of Capitalism*. Allen and Unwin, 1930).
Westfall, Richard S. 1958. *Science and Religion in Seventeenth-Century England*. Ann Arbor: University of Michigan Press.
Wilkins, John. 1638/1684. *A Discovery of a New World*, 4th edn. London: Printed by T.M. & F.A. for John Gillibrand at the Golden-Ball in St. Paul's Church Yard.
Wilkins, John. 1640. *A Discourse Concerning a New World & Another Planet in 2 Books*. London: William Marshall, engraver. Printed by John Norton and R. Hearne for John Maynard.
Woolf, Virginia. 1929. *A Room of One's Own*. London: The Hogarth Press.
Zaret, David. 1989. Religion and the Rise of Liberal-Democratic Ideology in 17th-Century England. *American Sociological Review* 54 (2): 163–179.
Zuckerman, Ben, and Michael H. Hart. 1995. *Extraterrestrials – Where Are They?* 2nd ed. Cambridge: Cambridge University Press.

Chapter 5
Empirical Results

Will an emerald, gold, ivory, purple, lyre, a stylus, a small flower, and a sapling lose value if they are not praised?

Marcus Aurelius (121–180 AD)

5.1 Introduction

In this chapter, we conduct a comparative analysis of stylistic features between the source text (ST) and its early English translations (TTs) at macro, meso-, and micro-levels, utilising the approach of corpus translation studies (CTS) enhanced with generative AI (GenAI). We apply literary stylistic methodologies to explore Fontenelle's *Entretiens sur la pluralité des mondes* alongside its seventeenth-century English (re)translations. Section 5.2 presents the empirical results of distant reading at the macro level, while Sect. 5.3 investigates the quantitative outcomes of meso-level analysis focusing on specific stylistic features. Section 5.4 offers qualitative insights gained through close-reading procedures, thereby integrating micro-level evidence. The final sections synthesise the findings, discussing translation as a creative act that generates new cultural value and assessing the stylistic divergences among the different TTs. Through this multi-layered approach, GenAI enhances interpretative accuracy and methodological rigour within CTS under human supervision.

We situate our approach within the broader methodological dialogue of digital humanities, drawing on the established distinction between distant and close reading (Moretti 2000, 2013, 2022; Jockers 2014; Mellinger and Hanson 2017). By combining macro-indicators with fine-grained micro-analyses, we gain a comprehensive perspective on stylistic variation across translations. Such an integrated method, still relatively novel in literary translation studies, proves indispensable for evaluating how English renderings diverge stylistically from their French source (Boot 2009; Jones 2020 [2009]; Zanettin 2013). We utilise automated annotation, alignment, and search functions to identify recurring patterns and translation norms (Cipriani 2020, 2023; Zwischenberger 2020). GenAI further empowers these

A. M. Cipriani, F. Milana, *AI-Powered Corpus Translation Studies at Work*,
New Frontiers in Translation Studies,
https://doi.org/10.1007/978-981-95-5933-6_5

processes by supporting interpretative annotation and enhancing the identification of subtle stylistic shifts (e.g., Xu and Huang 2025). This dual strategy enables us to understand both conformity and deviation in early English translations, thereby positioning the AI-powered CTS as a tool for reassessing the history of literary translation.

5.2 Macro Reading

Quantitative approaches in digital humanities have increasingly provided scholars with tools to examine texts at a macro-level, allowing for broad comparative insights that were previously unattainable through manual reading alone. This form of distant reading, to use Moretti's influential term, complements meso- and close-reading practices by drawing attention to large-scale tendencies and recurrent patterns across entire texts. In the present study of Fontenelle's *Entretiens* and its early English translations, macro reading offers a particularly valuable perspective. It enables the identification of structural and stylistic consistencies and divergences across the French source text (ST) and the three examined target texts (TT1 by Domville, TT2 by Glanvill, and TT3 by Behn).

5.2.1 Descriptive Indicators: TTC, TTR, ALF, and Word Clouds

One of the most informative quantitative indicators in translation analysis is the type-token curve (TTC) and type-token ratio (TTR), which measure lexical diversity by calculating, respectively, the number and proportion of unique word types relative to the text size measured as the total number of tokens. In the comparative analysis, Fig. 5.1 illustrates the TTC representing the progression of the number of word types used as the text size advances. The cumulative model employed in our custom-made *Corpus Processor* program enables precise tracing of when the introduction of new lexical items slows down, thereby highlighting sections of the text where lexical innovation or narrative shifts occur.

The comparative use of metrics such as type-token ratios (TTR) in Fig. 5.2, average lexical frequency (ALF) in word occurrence patterns (Fig. 5.3), and repetition rates (Fig. 5.4) provides further insights into the translators' different approaches to rendering Fontenelle's work. These measures reveal tendencies toward simplification, explicitation, addition, or domestication, which are well-established translation norms in Descriptive Translation Studies (DTS). They also allow us to visualise key differences through graphs and word clouds (as those shown in Fig. 5.5), thereby linking numerical evidence to interpretive claims. Importantly, these quantitative methods are not meant to supplant close philological and literary scrutiny but to

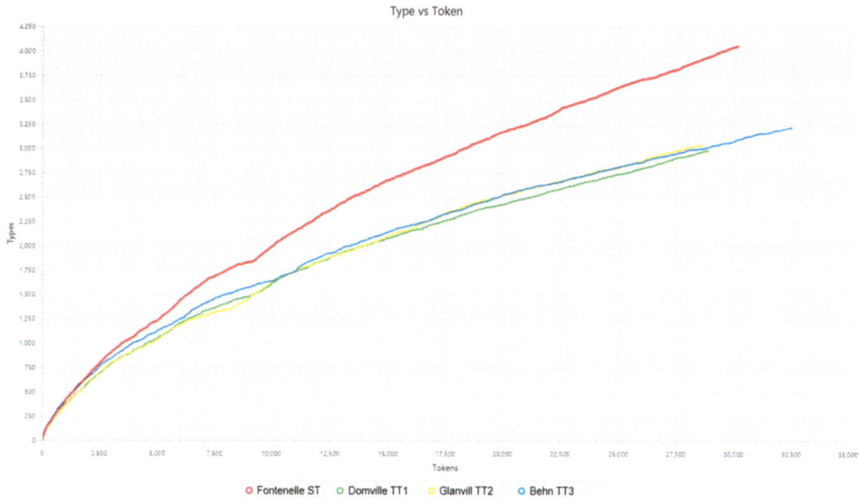

Fig. 5.1 *Type-token curve* (with stopwords). *Note*: The pronounced downward inflection observed in the continuous TTC at approximately 9000 tokens provides a clear indication of a shift in stylistic and lexical patterns, signifying the transition from the conclusion of the second night to the commencement of the third night. This change cannot be captured so clearly with the discrete TTR computation, e.g. every 1000 words or more, by extant commercial software. *Source*: Our original computations

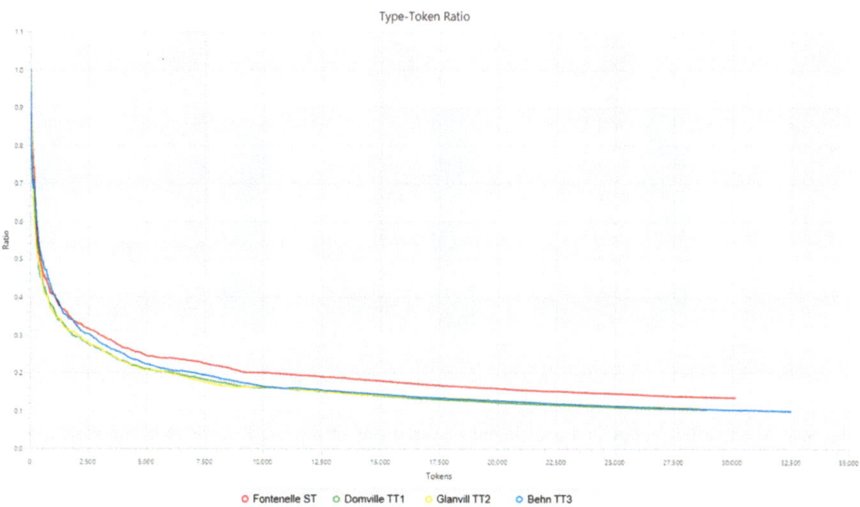

Fig. 5.2 The complete and continuous *Type-token ratio* over the compared whole texts (with stopwords). *Note*: The TTR is recalculated every time the computer program Corpus Processor reads an additional word while going through the text. Compared to any fixed token along a vertical line, TTR assumes the meaning of a standardized type-token ratio. *Source*: Our original computations

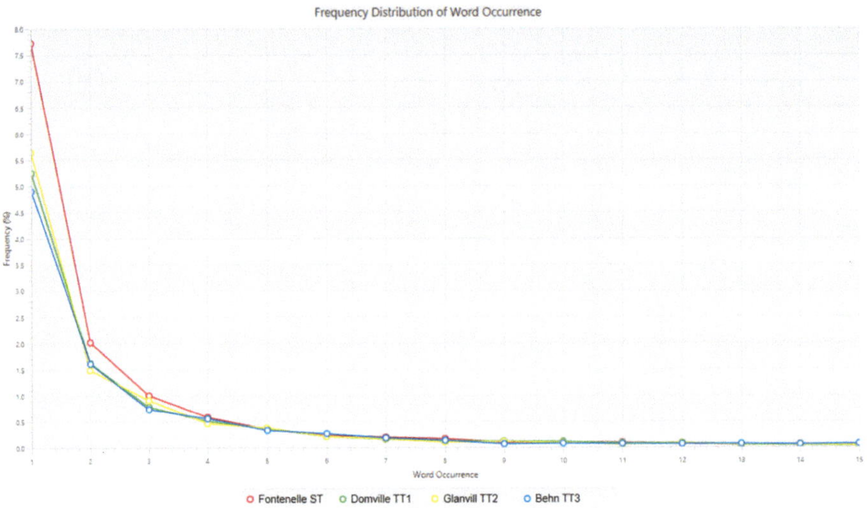

Fig. 5.3 Relative frequency distribution of word occurrences (in percentage). *Source*: Our original computations

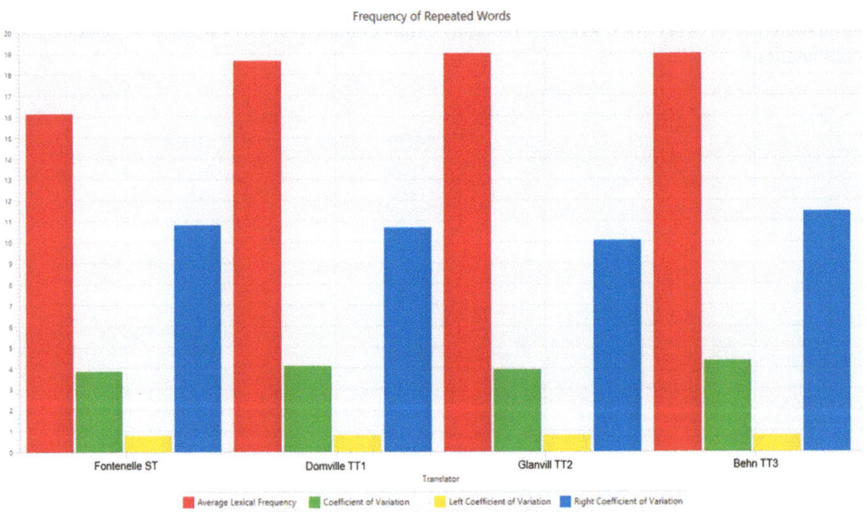

Fig. 5.4 Average frequency and coefficient of variations of repeated words (without stopwords). *Source*: Our original computations

guide it by pointing to areas where shifts or anomalies occur. The results presented here thus serve both as evidence in their own right and as a roadmap for more nuanced textual and cultural interpretation.

The results indicate that Domville's TT1 and Glanvill's TT2 are broadly similar in terms of length, while Behn's TT3 is notably longer, by approximately 14%. This lengthening cannot be ascribed simply to interlingual expansion, for the original

Fig. 5.5 Word clouds for the first three English translations of Fontanelle's *Entretiens* generated by the custom-made *Corpus Processor* software. *Source*: Our original computations

French text is situated between these extremes. Instead, it reflects Behn's distinctive stylistic register, which is more expansive and personalised than her contemporaries. The higher TTR observed in the early chapters of TT3 points to enriching her vocabulary, creating a translation that reads as literarily inventive. By contrast, Domville TT1's consistently lower TTR suggests a more cautious, even restrained strategy, perhaps aimed at clarity and concision at the expense of stylistic variety. Glanvill TT2, for his part, falls between these two extremes, with a TTR that is comparable to Domville TT1's but with occasional peaks that reflect moments of lexical experimentation.

A particularly revealing feature is the observed downward shift at approximately 9000 tokens in the source text, between the close of the "Second Night" and the beginning of the "Third Night". This marks a narrative transition in Fontenelle's dialogue: the Marquise and her interlocutor move from lighter, conversational exchanges to more extended scientific explanations that require specialised terminology. The custom-made *Corpus Processor* software (see Chap. 3) highlights this turning point by showing a marked increase in new word types, thereby signalling the introduction of a different register. Unlike other commercial software, such as *Wordsmith Tools* or *WMatrix*, the custom-built program allows for fine-grained, cumulative monitoring of lexical shifts, thereby identifying stylistic transitions with remarkable precision (Cipriani 2023: 48–62).

Another dimension of macro analysis concerns lexical frequency and repetition. The French ST has a lower ALF (2.3%) compared with the three English TTs, which average around 3.1%. This means that words recur more frequently in translations, a finding that aligns with the tendency of translations to favour clarity through repetition, thereby minimising ambiguity. The difference is even more evident in repetition rates: in the ST, approximately 16% of words are repeated, while in the TTs the figure rises to 19%. Such quantitative evidence corresponds with the well-documented norm of simplification in translation practice. However, variation exists among the translators. Behn's TT3 exhibits the highest rate of repetition, consistent with her expansive narrative style, while Glanvill's TT2 shows slightly lower repetition than Domville's TT1, reflecting his occasional lexical adventurousness.

Behn's TT3 demonstrates fidelity to the scientific terminology of the French ST, preserving terms such as "tourbillons" in their original form rather than replacing them with the English "vortices," as Domville TT1 and Glanvill TT2 do. This translational decision suggests a conscious attempt to foreground the technical authority of Fontenelle's cosmology while also exoticising the text for an English readership. It aligns with a strategy of foreignisation, where linguistic otherness is preserved. By contrast, Glanvill TT2 systematically domesticates key terms: he downgrades the "marquise" to the inferior "countess" title and prefers "people" to "inhabitants." Such choices adapt the text to English cultural expectations but simultaneously reduce its foreign specificity. Domville TT1 tends to remain closer to the French lexicon than Glanvill TT2, yet without the bold scientific retention seen in Behn TT3.

Taken together, these macro indicators provide not only descriptive statistics but also a basis for interpretive judgment. Domville TT1's translation emerges as cautious and somewhat plain, prioritising accessibility but limiting stylistic variety. Glanvill TT2, with his notable cuts or rewriting, appears more inclined to reshape the text for English readers, domesticating cultural and social references in line with late seventeenth-century Anglicising tendencies. Behn TT3, in contrast, produces a translation that is both longer and lexically richer, displaying a strong narrative voice and preserving key elements of French scientific discourse.

5.2.2 The Typical Features of Literary Translation

Corpus-based translation studies (CTS) have long investigated recurrent features and translation universals, since Baker's (1993) seminal article (Curry and McEnery 2025). This study introduces generative AI for rapid, thorough, and precise annotation of these features. As covered in Chap. 3, due to the variability of generative AI outputs, three systems (ChatGPT-4.1, Claude-3.7-Sonnet, and Gemini-2.5-Pro) were used to identify, annotate, and explain occurrences of typical literary translation features. Each GenAI also produces TEI-compliant XML files, aligning source texts, manually annotated translations, and AI-annotated versions with explanations in interactive comparison tables.

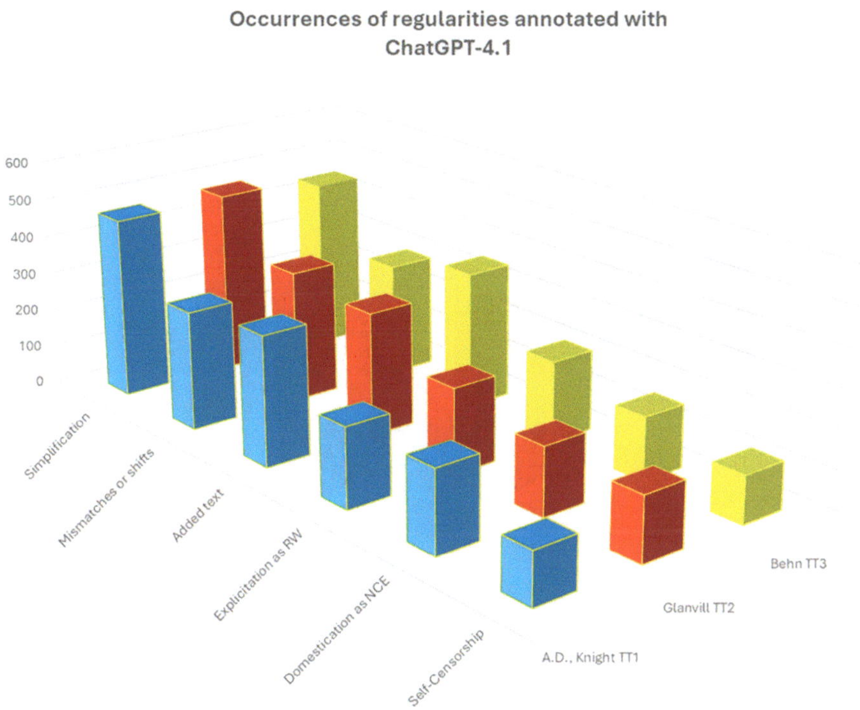

Fig. 5.6 Number of occurrences of the six universal characteristics of literary translation identified by ChatGPT-4.1 in the three early English versions of Fontenelle's *Entretiens*. *Source*: Our original computations

The user-defined encoding for this study refers to the "regularities of behaviour" or norms (Toury 2012: 10).[1] Specifically, the study identifies "mismatches or shifts," self-censorship, simplification, explicitation, text addition, and domestication, as defined and discussed in previous translation studies as well as in Chaps. 1 and 3 above.

A summary of the occurrence numbers identified by Gen AI systems for specific features in each of the three English translations is presented in Figs. 5.6, 5.7, 5.8. The data indicate a consistent pattern, with "simplification" showing the highest frequency, followed by "mismatches or shifts", "added text", "explicitation", "domestication", and "self-censorship," in descending order of occurrence numbers.

Secondly, Gemini identified a higher number of occurrences compared to the other two GenAI systems. Claude identified the lowest number of occurrences in all cases. Despite these differences in performance, each of the three approaches used to integrate their reasoning offers practical value, particularly regarding the relative

[1] While some critics have questioned whether these features are truly universal, their common occurrence in literary translations suggests they should often be viewed as probabilistic characters (*Ibidem*: 226).

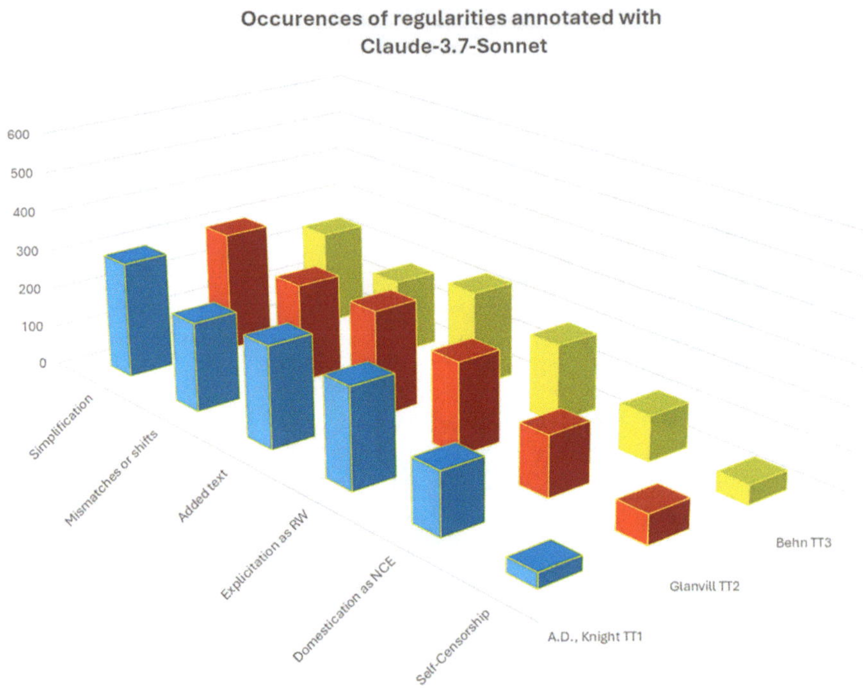

Fig. 5.7 Number of occurrences of the six universal characteristics of literary translation identified by Claude 3.7 Sonnet in the three early English versions of Fontenelle's *Entretiens. Source*: Our original computations

significance of various typical features, which do not always align in ranking or interpretation. For instance, Gemini ranks "mismatches or shifts" lower than "Added text" in Glanvill TT2, while it aligns with the other two systems by ranking the former higher than the latter in Domville TT1 and Behn TT3. Additionally, Gemini indicates that "Simplification," "Added text," and "Explicitation" are among the most frequently observed features. Further discussion of the relevance and meaning of each occurrence is provided in the micro-reading sections below and explored in greater detail in this chapter.

5.3 Close Reading: Qualitative Analysis at the Micro Level

5.3.1 Simplification

This section presents examples of lexical simplification (LS) in translation, such as the use of general terms and sentence shortening to reduce the average sentence length (Lind 2007: 3). The first LS example appears at the novel's beginning, where

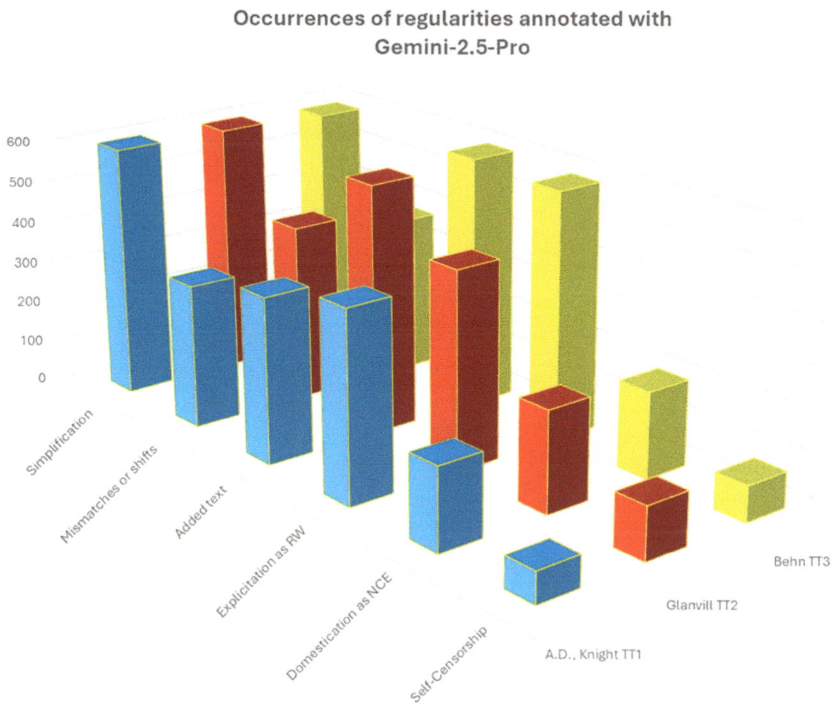

Fig. 5.8 Number of occurrences of the six universal characteristics of literary translation identified by Gemini 2.5 Pro in the three early English versions of Fontenelle's *Entretiens*. *Source*: Our original computations

the protagonist describes a meeting between Monsieur and the Marquise in a park to discuss Earth's orbit around the Sun (Table 5.1).

The register of the French original text is formal, addressing 'Monsieur,' but Domville TT1 uses simpler, direct language and reduces vivid imagery. *"Un blanc fort vif"* is rendered as "a lively white" in English, reducing the original's vividness. Glanvill TT2 streamlines the scene by omitting reflections and simplifying descriptions, which decreases narrative complexity. The translator keeps the first French sentence but omits the next (*'Je sens, Monsieur… nécessairement'*), which lessens both narrative complexity and reader engagement. Behn TT3 combines and simplifies sentences for clarity, also omitting ornate phrasing and 'Monsieur'.

5.3.1.1 Variations and Similarities Between the TTS

Glanvill TT2 is the briefest translation, at 46 words, almost half the length of Domville TT1's 87 words. Behn TT3 is the longest at 94 words, exceeding the original French's 90 words. All three are semantically faithful with unique styles, and each mentions "the Air", which is absent from the source.

Table 5.1 Segmented text with language "simplification" in translation

ST and TTs	Extracted text	Generative AI	AI-generated Explanation
Fontenelle ST	*Nous allâmes donc un Soir aprés Soupé, nous promener dans le Parc.* ***Il faisoit un frais délicieux, qui nous récompensoit d'une journée fort chaude que nous avions essuyée. Je sens, Monsieur, que je vais vous faire une Description, mais il n'ya a pas moyen de vous l'épargner, la chose m'y porte necessairement.*** *La Lune estoit levée il y avoit peut-estre une heure. & ses rayons qui ne venoient à nous qu'entre les branches des arbres, faisoient un agreable mélange d'un blanc fort vif, avec tout ce verd qui paroissait noir.* [So, one evening after supper we went for a walk in the park. **It was delightful cool, which rewarded us for a very hot day we had endured. I feel, Sir, that I am going to give you a description, but there is no way to spare you, the thing necessarily leads me to it.** The moon had risen perhaps an hour ago, and its rays, which only came to us between the branches of the trees, made a pleasant mixture of a very bright white, with all this green which appeared black.]		

ST and TTs	Extracted text	Generative AI	AI-generated Explanation
Domville TT1	'Twas then in the Evening, after Supper, that we took a walk into the Park; **the Air was delicate and fresh, which made amends for the heat of the day. I find I am falling into a Description, and I cannot well avoid it, the Subject leads me naturally to it.** The Moon was about an hour high, and her beams, which came to us through the branches of the trees, made a pleasing mixture of a lively white, with all that green which then appeared black.	ChatGPT-4.1	The translator omits the formal address '*Monsieur*' and shortens the sentence by fusing clauses, resulting in a structure that is more direct and accessible.
		Clause-3.7-Sonnet	The French original uses a more formal and elaborate phrasing with the direct address '*Monsieur*' and a somewhat apologetic tone. The English translation **simplifies** this by removing the address and using more straightforward language with less formality. The French text uses more intensive and vivid descriptive language with '*un blanc fort vif*' (a very bright white), while the English translation **simplifies** this to 'a lively white', reducing some of the vividness of the original description.
		Gemini-2.5-Pro	The formal French address "*Monsieur*" is omitted, reducing formality. The somewhat abstract phrase "*la chose m'y porte necessairement*" (the thing carries me there necessarily) is **simplified** to the more direct and common English "the Subject leads me naturally to it."
Glanvill TT2	We went one Evening after Supper, to walk in the Park**, the Air was extremely refreshing, because that day had been very hot;** the Moon had been up about an hour, and **as she shone between the Trees, made an agreeable mixture of Light and Darkness.**	ChatGPT-4.1	The translation **omits** the narrator's explicit self-referential admission of impending description and **compresses** a lengthy, atmospheric depiction of the scene.
		Claude-3.7-Sonnet	The evocative and detailed description of the moonlight in French has been considerably **simplified**. The translator **omits** the rich detail about the '*blanc fort vif*' (very bright white) mixing with the green that appeared black.
		Gemini-2.5-Pro	The English translation renders the first French sentence but completely **omits** the second sentence ('*Je sens, Monsieur... necessairement.*'). This **omitted** sentence contains the narrator's meta-commentary and direct address to an implied reader ('*Monsieur*'), **simplifying** the narrative style by removing a self-conscious authorial interjection and making the introduction more direct.

(continued)

Table 5.1 (continued)

ST and TTs	Extracted text	Generative AI	AI-generated Explanation
Behn TT3	We went one Evening after Supper to walk in the Park, **the Air was cool and refreshing, which made us sufficient amends for the excessive heat of the Day, and of which I find I shall be obliged to make you a Description, which I cannot well avoid, the fineness of it leading me so necessarily to it.** The Moon was about an hour high, and her beams, which came to us through the branches of the trees, made a pleasing mixture of a lively white, with all that green which then appeared black.	ChatGPT-4.1	The English condenses and **simplifies** two sentences into one, using plainer phrasing and **omitting** the reference to the addressee as '*Monsieur*', making it more immediately accessible.
		Claude-3.7-Sonnet	The translator has **simplified** the formal, somewhat self-conscious phrasing of the original. The French version includes the address '*Monsieur*' and uses a more elaborate expression, while the English version streamlines this into more direct language.
		Gemini-2.5-Pro	No annotation.

Source: Our original processing

The French phrase "*il faisoit un frais délicieux*" ("it was deliciously cool") is translated as

Domville TT1's "**the Air** was delicate and fresh",
Glanvill TT2's "**the Air** was extremely refreshing",
Behn TT3's "**the Air** was cool and refreshing".

The original French phrase "*qui nous récompensoit d'une journée fort chaude que nous avions essuyée*" ("which rewarded us for a very hot day we had endured") appears in translation as

Domville TT1's "which made **amends for** the heat of the day",
Granvill TT2's "because that day had been very hot",
Behn TT3's "which made us sufficient **amends for** the excessive heat of the Day".

Additionally, the French ST "*je vais vous faire une Description, mais il n'ya a pas moyen de vous l'épargner*" ["I am going to give you a description, but there is no way to spare you"] is rendered with

Domville TT1's "**I find** I am falling into a Description, and **I cannot well avoid it**"
Behn TT3's "**I find** I shall be obliged to make you a Description, which **I cannot well avoid**".
Ganvill TT2, instead, does not translate this phrase.

These examples illustrate both differences and similarities, particularly between Domville TT1 and Behn TT3, suggesting that retranslations may have connections to earlier translations (Pym 1998: 82; Tahir Gürçağlar 2020/2009: 487).

5.3.1.2 The Translator's Presence

Domville TT1 adopts a more assertive tone than the French ST. For instance, "*La Lune estoit levée il y avoit* ***peut-estre*** *une heure*" ("The moon had risen **perhaps** an hour ago") is translated with less uncertainty.

Domville TT1's "The Moon was **about** an hour high"
Glanvill TT2's "the Moon had been up **about** an hour"
Behn's TT3's "The Moon was **about** an hour high"

where the translator's "voice" (Hermans 1996: 27), "thumbprint" (Baker 2000: 244), or "visibility" (Venuti 2008/1995: 267–268) creates a narration often clearer than the original.

Moreover, the original "*ses rayons [de la Lune] qui ne venoient à nous qu'entre les branches des arbres, faisoient un agreable mélange d'un blanc fort vif, avec tout ce verd qui paroissait noir*" ("its rays, which only came to us between the branches of the trees, created a mixture of very bright white and green that appeared black") is rendered with

Domville TT1's "her [the Moon's] beams, which came to us through the branches of the trees, made a pleasing mixture of a lively white, with all that green which then appeared black".

Glanvill TT2's "she [the Moon] shone between the Trees, made an agreeable mixture of Light and Darkness.

Behn TT3's "her [the Moon's] beams, which came to us through the branches of the trees, made a pleasing mixture of a lively white, with all that green which then appeared black."

Domville (1687) TT1 and Glanvill (1688) TT2 exhibit a distinct translator's "presence" (Cipriani 2022), whereas Behn (1688) TT3 is virtually identical to TT1 from the previous year.

5.3.1.3 Historical and Cultural Considerations

The length differences between Domville TT1 and Glanvill TT2's English translations and the original French highlight their distinct socio-cultural backgrounds. Domville TT1 employs a clear, elegant style influenced by his social background, the Anglo-Irish Protestant elite's preference for intellectual yet restrained expressions, as illustrated in Table 5.1.

Glanvill TT2 employs clear, utilitarian prose in line with the principles of the Royal Society and the English Protestant emphasis on rationality during periods of political upheaval. His style reflects the Society's call for concise scientific language, as described by Thomas Sprat (1667), aligning with the cultural shift toward accessible, rational writing during the Glorious Revolution.

Behn's TT3 closely mirrors Domville's TT1 and the source text's lyricism. Unlike Domville, Behn treats poetic metaphor as vital for conveying scientific awe, reflecting her political and literary context. Her use of "the fineness of it" introduces a specifically English, courtly tone. As a royalist dramatist, Behn valued the rhetorical sophistication of the French court and was receptive to continental literary styles.

5.3.2 Mismatches or Shifts and Mistakes

A frequent feature in translation is *implicit manipulation* that leads to "mismatches or shifts" (Toury 2012: 291, House 2015, 2016; Munday 2016: 146–149). In the three early English translations of Fontenelle's *Entretiens*, for example, Behn's TT3 incorrectly confuses Cato of Utica (born, 95 BC; Died 46 AD) with Cato the Censor (Born 234 BC; Died 149 BC): *i.e.*, the ST "[Page 287] [...] *qui eussent trouvé* ***Caton d'Utique*** *trop badin & trop folâtre*" is translated in Behn TT3 as "[Page 128] [...] wou'd have look'd upon the grave **Cato the Censor**, as too wild and youthful for their Conversation."

Another Behn's mismatch is her avoidance of direct translation of "*grand Pape*" in ST "[Page 124] [...] *Tout le Poëme est dédié à un* ***Cardinal***, *& un* ***grand Pape*** *l'à honoré d'une approbation éclatante que l'on voit au-devant de quelques Editions*." Behn TT3 translates this into "The whole Poem is dedicated to a **great Church-man** and **another great Church-man** has honour'd it with a signal Approbation; which one may perceive by the several Editions." As noted in AI Claude's comment (see Table 5.2), Behn TT3 **deliberately downplays Catholic ecclesiastical hierarchy in Protestant England.** By contrast, both Domville TT1 and Glanvill TT2 translate "***grand Pape***" into "**great Pope**".

A third mismatch in Behn TT3 is confusing Earth with Mercury when discussing planets near the firmament in Fontenelle's ST. The ST's "[Page 226] *Pur les autre Planètes, comme ells sont* ***au-delà de la Terre*** *vers le Firmament, ils les voyent plus petites que nous ne les voyons*" is translated by Behn TT3 into "[Page 101] [...] As for the other Planets, since they are remov'd **further than Mercury**, towards the Firmament, his inhabitants must see them less than they appear to us". That is, regarding the other planets, as they are positioned further from Mercury and closer to the firmament, their inhabitants would perceive these planets as smaller than we observe them.

5.3.2.1 Variations and Similarities Between the TTS

Significant variations can be found in the last two examples. The French text reported in Table 5.2 "*J'avoüe qu'il eust mieux fait de n'y pas mêler Saint Jean, dont le nom est si digne de respect; mais enfin c'est une licence Poëtique, qui peut* ***seulement passer pour un peu trop gaye***." ("I confess that he would have done better not to mix in Saint John, whose name is so worthy of respect; but after all it is a poetic license, which **can only pass for a little too gay.**") is rendered with.

Domville TT1: I confess, he had done better not to have introduc'd St. John, a Name worthy of Veneration, but 'tis a Poetical Licence, **that may pass for only too much Gayty.**

Glanvill TT2: I must confess he had better have let alone St. John, whose Name is so worthy of Respect, but 'tis a Poetical License, and **must be allow'd**.

Behn TT3: I own, I ought not to meddle with St. John, whose Name is so worthy of Respect: But since there is a Poetical Licence, **and Liberty of Conscience, it ought to pass as a Gayety**.

In the translation by Domville TT1, the English **translation shifts** this by placing "**only**" before **"too much Gayty"**, which intensifies the criticism of the poetic license. As noted by the AI Claude's comment on this choice, This subtle change could reflect the **translator's more critical stance toward religious irreverence in a period of religious tension in England.** Instead, as noted by the AI Gemini's comment**,** Glanville TT2's **"must be allow'd"** neutralises the critique, presenting it as a simple acceptance and thereby **altering Fontenelle's nuanced tone**. Finally,

Table 5.2 Segmented text with "mismatches or shifts" in translation

ST and TTs	**Extracted text**	Gen AI	AI-generated comments
Fontenelle ST	*Je vous parle d'une des plus agréables folies de l'Arioste, & je suis seur que vous serez bien-aise de la sçavoir. J'avoüe qu'il eust mieux fait de n'y pas mêler Saint Jean, dont le nom est si digne de respect; mais enfin c'est une licence Poëtique, qui peut* ***seulement passer pour un peu trop gaye****. Tout le Poëme est dédié à un* ***Cardinal****, & un* ***grand Pape*** *l'a honoré d'une* ***approbation éclatante*** *que l'on voit au devant de quelques Editions.* [I am speaking to you of one of the most agreeable follies of Ariosto, and I am sure that you will be glad to know it. I confess that he would have done better not to mix in Saint John, whose name is so worthy of respect; but after all it is a poetic license, which **can only pass for a little too gay.** The whole poem is dedicated to **a cardinal**, and **a great pope** has honoured it with a **resounding approbation** that one sees at the front of some editions.]		
Domville TT1	'tis one of the most pleasant follys of Ariosio, and I am sure you will be well pleas'd to hear it. I confess, he had done better not to have introduc'd St. Iohn, a Name worthy of Veneration, but 'tis a Poetical Licence, that may pass for **only too much Gayty.** The whole Poem is dedicated to a Cardinal, and **a great Pope** has honour'd it with a **glorious Approbation**, which is to be seen before some Editions.	ChatGPT-4.1	No annotation
		Claude-3.7-Sonnet	The French text uses '*seulement*' (only) to qualify '*passer pour un peu trop gaye*' (pass for a bit too merry/gay), suggesting the license is merely **a bit too playful.** The English **translation shifts** this by placing 'only' before 'too much Gayty', which intensifies the criticism of the poetic license. This subtle change could reflect the **translator's more critical stance toward religious irreverence in a period of religious tension in England.**
		Gemini-2.5-Pro	The French term "*éclatante*" (meaning striking, brilliant, resounding) describes the manifest and evident nature of the Pope's approval. The English translation "**glorious Approbation**" elevates this by introducing strong connotations of splendor, magnificence, and even divine favor, which are not the primary senses of "*éclatante*." In the highly charged religious and political atmosphere of 1687 England, where King James II's Catholic leanings and Declaration of Indulgence caused significant Protestant anxiety about a resurgence of Catholic power, this choice of word subtly manipulates the reader's perception. It presents the **Papal endorsement in a more majestic and venerable light** than a more direct translation like "striking" or "brilliant" would convey. This **shift in tone and connotation** could be seen as an attempt to lend greater weight or a more positive framing to Catholic cultural authority during a period when such authority was deeply contested, thereby indirectly influencing the reader's understanding.

Glanvill TT2	I am going to tell you one of the agreeable Follies of Ariosto, and I am confident you will be well pleas'd to hear it: I must confess he had better have l*et al*one St. John, whose Name is so worthy of Respect, but 'tis a Poetical License, and **must be allow'd**. The Poem is dedicated to a Cardinal, and **a great Pope** hath honour'd it with **his Approbation**, which is prefix'd to several of the Editions.	ChatGPT-4.1	No annotation
		Claude-3.7-Sonnet	No annotation
		Gemini-2.5-Pro	Fontenelle's phrase '*un peu trop gaye*' (a little too lighthearted/irreverent) subtly criticizes Ariosto's poetic license in using St. John's name. The translation 'must be allow'd' neutralizes this critique, presenting it as a simple acceptance and thereby **altering Fontenelle's nuanced tone.**
Behn TT3	What I shall tell you now, is one of the most pleasant Fooleries in all Ariosto; and I am satisfy'd, 'twill not displease you to know it. I own, I ought not to meddle with St. Iohn, whose Name is so worthy of Respect: But since there is a Poetical Licence, and **Liberty of Conscience**, it **ought to pass as a Gayety**. The whole Poem is dedicated to a great Church-man, and **another great Church-man** has honour'd it with a **signal Approbation**; which one may perceive by the several Editions.	ChatGPT-4.1	The French text states the poem is 'dedicated to a Cardinal, & **a great Pape**,' directly naming both a figure of high clergy and the Pope; **the translation changes this to** 'a great Church-man, and **another great Church-man**,' thereby muting both the specific Catholic context and Papal approval—likely for Protestant readers' sensibilities.
		Claude-3.7-Sonnet	The translation alters the original by adding **'Liberty of Conscience'** which was not in the source text. This addition introduces a politically charged concept during a time of religious tension in England under James II, who had issued the Declaration of Indulgence. Additionally, **the translation changes 'Cardinal' to the more general 'great Church-man' and alters 'un grand Pape' (a great Pope) to 'another great Church-man,' deliberately downplaying Catholic ecclesiastical hierarchy in Protestant England.**
		Gemini-2.5-Pro	The translation introduces the phrase "**and Liberty of Conscience,**" which is absent in the original French. This addition is highly significant given the English historical context of 1687, particularly **James II's Declaration of Indulgence (also known as the Declaration for Liberty of Conscience**). By inserting this contemporary and politically charged phrase, the translator anachronistically links Ariosto's poetic license to a contentious political principle of the translator's time, subtly manipulating the reader's perception by framing the discussion within current English political debates. **The translation replaces the specific Catholic hierarchical terms "Cardinal" and "grand Pape" (great Pope) with the more general "great Church-man" and "another great Church-man."** In the context of Protestant England in 1687, marked by anti-Catholic sentiments, this alteration serves to neutralize the overt Catholic references in Fontenelle's text. This change **manipulates** the reader's perception by **downplaying the Catholic Church's connection to the poem**, potentially making the text more palatable to a Protestant audience or avoiding religious controversy.

Source: Our original processing.

Behn's translation introduces the phrase **"Liberty of Conscience",** not present in the original French, which references England's 1687 Declaration of Indulgence.

5.3.2.2 The Translator's Presence

The translator's visibility is clear. The Irish Protestant Domville TT1, by suggesting "the license is merely a bit too playful", is more critical towards religious irreverence; the Anglican Glanvill TT2 neutralises the critique of the irreverent literary choice by toning it down and presenting it as "a bit too playful". The royalist and equidistant Behn TT3 makes the text more palatable to a heterogeneous audience or avoids religious controversy by declaring that the choice "ought to pass as a Gayety".

5.3.2.3 Historical and Cultural Considerations

Political and religious contexts influenced the translators' choices here, as shown by the Catholic Church' ban on the French source text. The distinct backgrounds of the three translators resulted in notable differences in meaning and tone across their versions.

The religious and political context of 1687 England, shaped by King James II's Catholic ties and his Declaration of Indulgence, likely influenced translation choices. For example, Domville TT1 uses grand language for Papal endorsement, shifting tone and connotation, possibly to reshape perceptions of Catholic authority. In contrast, Behn TT3 downplays Catholic references thus avoiding potential tensions with a Protestant audience.

5.3.3 Added Text

In her Preface, Behn (1688) declares, "I was necessitated to add a little in some places [of the text], otherwise the book could not have been understood". She also criticises some of the author's speculations: "if he had let alone his learned Men, *Philosophical Transactions*, and Telescopes in the Planet Jupiter, and his Inhabitants not only there, but in all the fixed Stars, and even in the Milky-Way, and only stuck to the greatness of the Universe, he had deserved much more Praise" (Behn 1688: *Translator's Preface*). Such criticism was strikingly bold for a translator, far exceeding the conventional limits of her role. In her commentary, Behn even claims to have corrected several of the author's mistakes. For instance, in the Second Night, she clarifies the reference to "Inhabitants" by conjecturing that they are "hardly Men, but rather a kind of Brutes in human shape" (*ibid.*: 61), and by identifying "some newly-discovered lands" unequivocally as "the new discovered world of America" (*ibid.*: 61). Moreover, Behn (1688: 89) translates Fontenelle's (1686: 198–199) passage in the Third Night:

> Venus tourne sur elle-mesme, & autour du Soleil **comme la Lune**
> [Venus turns on itself, and around the Sun like the Moon]

into

> Venus turns around the Sun on its Axis, **as the Moon** does around the Earth

thus, providing immediate clarification that Venus rotates on its own axis, as the Moon orbits the Earth.

Behn's intervention here has been widely discussed. Some scholars observe that she not only translates faithfully but also amends what they regard as an error in the source text, namely, the mistaken implication that the Moon turns directly around the Sun (Cottegnies 2003: 31–32; 2004: 227; 2024: 47; Mills 2025: 203–204). These scholars interpret Behn's addition as corrective, presenting it as an insertion of accurate astronomical information: "Venus turns round the Sun on her own Axis, **as the moon does round the earth**."

Cottegnies (2003: 31–32), for example, describes Behn as a translator apologetically: "Her attention never flags, and she uses all the resources of common sense to serve the text she translates. In fact, she very rarely makes mistakes, and sometimes, as it happens, she even corrects mistakes in the original text, as when Fontenelle describes Venus as 'turning on itself and around the sun, **like the moon**', Behn corrects the text with the right information […] Although she is by no means a scientist and often shies away from technical details, she is constantly on the alert, and her enthusiasm for the subject and for the dialogues always shows through." (Emphasis added.)

Yet, the reading of Fontenelle's complete phrase reveals that his formulation was elliptical rather than erroneous by stressing that "we discover, with the telescopes, that Venus turning on itself and around the sun, **like the Moon [waxes and wanes**]" (reported in Table 5.2 below), while elsewhere in the *Entretiens* he clearly specifies that *the Moon revolves around the Earth, and only indirectly around the Sun by following the Earth in its orbital movement around it.* Consider the following:

> *Tout tourne présentement autour du Soleil […] Enfin […] il ne luy est demeuré que la Lune qui tourne encore autour d'elle.* (Fontenelle 1686: 48)
> [Everything now revolves around the Sun […] Finally, of all this celestial crew with which this little Earth was accompanied and surrounded, only the Moon remains, **which still revolves around it.**]

And even more explicitly:

> ***La Lune tourne autour de la Terre***, *& ne l'abandonne point* […] *si elle tourne autour du Soleil, ce n'est que pour ne point quitter la Terre* (*Ibid.*: 50–52).
> [**The Moon turns around the Earth** and does not abandon it; […] **if it turns around the Sun, it is only so as not to leave the Earth**.]

Further clarifications appear when he observes that the Moon rotates on its axis in the same period as it orbits the Earth (*Ibid.*: 100), and when he draws an analogy with Jupiter's satellites (*Ibid.*: 243).

Behn's rendering, therefore, seems less a correction of a scientific error than an explicitation of Fontenelle's elliptical phrasing. Her translation itself of the extended passage makes this clear:

> Venus turns round the Sun on her own Axis, as the Moon **does round the Earth**; and by the means of Telescopes, we discover that Venus **waxes and wanes, being sometimes altogether enlightened, and sometimes darkened according to her different Positions** in respect to the Earth. (Behn 1688: 89)

This strategy aligns with what translation studies describe as explicitation, a recognised universal of translation practice (Even-Zohar 1978/2012; Toury 1978/2012; Baker 1993: 243; Robinson 2002: 180–183; Munday 2016: 92).

Todd (2000: 398–399) apologetically emphasises that, despite Behn's irony and parody, her engagement was serious. However, Todd recognises that she was not primarily concerned with scientific precision, and therefore left Cartesian vortices (*turbillions*) and the emerging concept of gravity proposed much before Newton competing with each other and largely unexplored, instead engaging with broader intellectual history, particularly the destabilisation of religious dogma by new systems of thought. Her critical stance echoes that of Lucretius and Hobbes in their attacks on pedantry and superstition.

The observation that faults Behn for ignoring Newton's *Principia* (1687) seems, however, somewhat anachronistic, but not so much, however, if other previous authors are considered. At the time, Newton's work had just been published, was inaccessible to most non-specialists and almost certainly unknown to both Fontenelle (1686) and his earliest translators.[2]

Behn herself candidly admitted her lack of competence in cosmology: "I shall not venture upon the astronomical part but leave that to the mathematicians" (Behn's "*Translator's Preface*", 1688), thus clarifying why she did not enter critically into this argument.

5.3.3.1 Variations and Similarities Between the TTs

The ST "*Venus tourne sur elle-mesme, & autour du Soleil comme la Lune, on découvre avec les Lunettes d'approche, que Venus aussi-bien que la Lune, est tantost en Croissant, tantost en Décours, tantost pleine selon les diverses situations où elle est à l'égard de la Terre.*" [Venus turns on itself, and around the Sun **like the Moon; we discover with the telescopes, that Venus as well as the Moon is sometimes in Crescent, sometimes in Waning, sometimes full according to the various situations in which it is with respect to the Earth**] is translated with slight variations as follows:

---

[2] Although gravity is often linked to Newton, earlier scientists like Copernicus, Kepler, Galileo, and Hooke also discussed the concept. Copernicus (1543), in *De revolutionibus orbium coelestium*, identified gravity as essential to his model of the universe, suggesting that even celestial bodies possess this property. Kepler (1609), in *Astronomia Nova* and previously in 1602, prefigured several Newtonian gravitation concepts (mutual attraction between objects based on mass, tidal explanation). Galileo (1632), in *Dialogues*, provided observational and physical evidence (e.g. tides and falling bodies) necessary for formalizing gravitational theory. Newton (1687) ultimately provided the mathematical foundation for universal gravitation, building on these prior insights and using Kepler's laws (syntheses of Newton's system and later contributions on gravity include Laplace 1796, Poisson 1813, Dick 1980, Misner et al. 2017).

Domville (TT1): "Venus turns about her self and about the Sun, as the Moon doth; and it is found by the Telescope that **Venus, as well as the Moon, has her Increases and Decreases, and is full, according to her diverse situation in respect of the Earth**."
Glanvill (TT2): "Venus turns upon her self, and round the Sun, as well as the Moon; they likewise discover by their Telescopes, that Venus like the Moon, (**if I may speak after the same manner**) is sometimes new, sometimes full, and sometimes in the wain, according to the diverse situations she is in, in respect of the Earth**is sometimes new, sometimes full, and sometimes in the wain, according to the diverse situations she is in, in respect of the Earth**."
Behn (TT3): "Venus turns round the Sun on her own Axis, as the Moon does **round the Earth**; and by the means of Telescopes, we discover that **Venus waxes and wanes, being sometimes altogether enlightened, and sometimes darkened** according to her different Positions in respect to the Earth."

5.3.3.2 The Translator's Presence

No added text for explicitation is present in Domville TT1, who adopts a literal rendering; Glanvill TT2 introduces an informal aside ("if I may speak after the same manner"); and Behn TT3 employs explicitation, clarifying the orbital relation and thereby asserting a more authoritative presence as translator.

5.3.3.3 Historical and Cultural Considerations

These variations must be contextualised. Behn's translation choices, often incorrectly perceived as corrections, reflect not only her interpretative freedom but also her cultural positioning. In late seventeenth-century England, debates about cosmology were intertwined with questions of intellectual authority, religion, and politics. Fontenelle, a declared Copernican, knew well that the Moon orbits the Earth and only secondarily the Sun. His formulations, e.g. "*ce n'est que pour ne point quitter la Terre*" (*Ibid.*: 52) ["it is only so as not to leave the Earth"], make this explicit. Behn's explicitation should therefore be read less as a scientific correction than as a rhetorical gesture aligning the translation with contemporary expectations of clarity and authority (Table 5.3).

5.3.4 Explicitation

One of the most frequently discussed tendencies in translation studies is explicitation, which refers to the process by which implicit information in the source text is rendered more explicit in the target text. Explicitation has often been described as a universal feature of translation. However, in literary translation, its role is particularly significant because it interacts with stylistic choices, cultural expectations, and

Table 5.3 Segmented text with "added text" in translation

ST and TTs		Gen AI	AI-generated comments
Fontenelle ST	*Venus tourne sur elle-mesme, & autour du Soleil comme la Lune, on découvre avec les Lunettes d'approche, que Venus aussi-bien que la Lune, est tantost en Croissant, tantost en Décours, tantost pleine selon les diverses situations où elle est à l'égard de la Terre.* [Venus turns on itself, and around the Sun like the Moon, we discover with the telescopes, that Venus as well as the Moon, is sometimes in Crescent, sometimes in Waning, sometimes full according to the various situations in which it is with respect to the Earth.]		
Domville TT1	Venus turns about her self and about the Sun, as the Moon doth; and it is found by the Telescope that Venus, as well as the Moon, has her Increases and Decreases, and is full, according to her diverse situation in respect of the Earth.	ChatGPT-4.1	No annotation
		Claude-3.7-Sonnet	No annotation
		Gemini-2.5-Pro	No annotation
Glanvill TT2	Venus turns upon her self, and round the Sun, as well as the Moon; they likewise discover by their Telescopes, that Venus like the Moon, **(if I may speak after the same manner)** is sometimes new, sometimes full, and sometimes in the wain, according to the diverse situations she is in, in respect of the Earth.	ChatGPT-4.1	**(if I may speak after the same manner)' is inserted by the translator** to bring an informal, conversational tone explaining that he is drawing a parallel between the phases of Venus and those of the Moon. This is not present in the source.
		Claude-3.7-Sonnet	No annotation
		Gemini-2.5-Pro	**The translator inserts a parenthetical meta-comment** from the narrator, a polite aside about the phrasing used, which is not present in the original French text.

(continued)

Table 5.3 (continued)

ST and TTs		Gen AI	AI-generated comments
Behn TT3	Venus turns round the Sun on her own Axis, **as the Moon does round the Earth;** and by the means of Telescopes, we discover that Venus **waxes and wanes**, being sometimes altogether enlightened, and sometimes darkened according to her different Positions in respect to the Earth.	ChatGPT-4.1	The translation makes explicit two scientific mechanisms: 'Venus turns round the Sun on her own Axis, **as the Moon** does round the Earth; and by the means of Telescopes, we discover that Venus **waxes and wanes**, being sometimes altogether enlightened, and sometimes darkened according to her different Positions in respect to the Earth.' The clarification and didactic extension are **normalization additions for naturalness and specificity.**
		Claude-3.7-Sonnet	No annotation
		Gemini-2.5-Pro	The source states Venus revolves 'like the Moon' ('comme la Lune'). **The translator added 'round the Earth'** to clarify the Moon's specific motion being used for comparison, making the analogy **more explicit**.

Source: Our original processing

interpretative strategies.[3] The passage considered in Table 5.4 provides an illustrative case of explicitation in semantics. Here, Domville TT1 makes explicit the spatial distance between the Earth and the celestial matter, while Glanvill TT2 and Behn TT3 amplify and clarify the vastness and fluidity of this celestial matter, which were only implicit in Fontenelle's original text.

5.3.4.1 Variations and Similarities among the Translations

Fontenelle's source text reads:

> "*Tout* **ce** *grand amas de matiere celeste, qui est depuis le Soleil jusqu'aux Etoiles fixes, tourne en rond, & emportant avec soy les Planetes,* [...]"
> [All **this** great mass of celestial matter, which is from the Sun to the fixed Stars, turns in circles, and carrying the Planets with it]

The three early English translators render this passage as follows:

Domville TT1: "All **that** great mass of celestial matter from the Sun to the fixed Stars turns round and carrying the Planets with it,"
Glanvill TT2: "**this** great Mass, **or Ocean** of Celestial Matter, which flows as far as from the Sun to the fix'd Stars, turns round, and bears the Planets along with it,"
Behn TT3: "all **that vast Ocean**, and Mass of Celestial **Substance**, which is between the Sun, and the Sphere of the fixed Stars, turns round,"

A close examination of these renderings reveals both the subtle shifts of meaning introduced by explicitation and the distinctive stylistic signatures of each translator.

Domville's TT1 departs from the demonstrative "***ce***" [**this**] of the ST and replaces it with "**that**," thereby making explicit the sense of distance between the terrestrial observer and the cosmic expanse. This lexical choice subtly alters the deictic orientation of the sentence, situating the celestial matter as a remote object rather than one that is immediately graspable.

Glanvill's TT2, on the other hand, retains "**this**" but supplements the image with the metaphorical expression "**Ocean** of Celestial Matter." By adding the metaphor of the ocean, Glanvill TT2 expands Fontenelle's relatively restrained description into a more vivid, imaginative, and explanatory picture. His addition serves not only to emphasise the vastness of space but also to foreground the idea of motion, liquidity, and flow, which makes the Cartesian theory of vortices more tangible to an English readership.

Behn's TT3 occupies an intermediary position, merging elements from both predecessors. She introduces "**that vast Ocean**, and Mass of Celestial **Substance**", thus adopting Domville's TT1 distancing "**that**" while simultaneously retaining Glanvill's TT2 metaphorical "**Ocean**." Her rendering demonstrates a tendency to balance and negotiate between two available models, while also adding her own

[3] See, e.g., Vanderauwera (1985: 97–98), Klaudy (1998), Saldanha (2008), Munday (2016: 92) for various types of explicitations and Zhang (2025) on this feature in corpus-based translation studies.

Table 5.4 Segmented text with "explicitation" in translation

ST and TTs	Extracted text	Gen AI	AI-generated comments
Fontenelle ST	*Tout ce grand amas de matiere celeste, qui est depuis le Soleil jusqu'aux Etoiles fixes, tourne en rond, & emportant avec soy les Planetes, les fait tourner toutes en un mesme sens autour du Soleil, qui occupe le centre.* [All this great mass of celestial matter, which is from the Sun to the fixed Stars, turns in circles, and carrying the Planets with it, makes them all turn in the same direction around the Sun, which occupies the center.]		
Domville TT1	All **that** great mass of celestial matter from the Sun to the fixed Stars turns round and carrying the Planets with it, **makes them turn all uniformly about the Sun**, which possesses the Center [...]	ChatGPT-4.1	No annotation
		Claude-3.7-Sonnet	The French *'de ce grand amas de matiere celeste'* (this great mass of celestial matter) has been translated as 'of **that** celestial matter', where the translator has changed the demonstrative from 'this' to 'that', **making explicit a spatial distance** that was only implicit in the original, suggesting the celestial matter is something distant or separate from the speakers
		Gemini-2.5-Pro	No annotation
Glanvill TT2	this great Mass, **or Ocean** of Celestial Matter, which flows as far as from the Sun to the fix'd Stars, turns round, and bears the Planets along with it, making them all turn after the same manner round the Sun, who possesses the Centre, [...]	ChatGPT-4.1	The phrase or Ocean of Celestial Matter, which flows as far as' **explicates** the metaphorical sense of *'grand amas de matiere celeste'*, clarifying the **vastness and fluidity** of the celestial matter, which was only implicit in the source. The English rendering introduces the image of an 'Ocean', **supplying the reader with a vivid mental model absent from the French**
		Claude-3.7-Sonnet	No annotation
		Gemini-2.5-Pro	No annotation

(continued)

Table 5.4 (continued)

ST and TTs	Extracted text	Gen AI	AI-generated comments
Behn TT3	all that **vast Ocean**, and Mass of Celestial Substance, which is between the Sun, and the Sphere of the fixed Stars, turns round, and carries with it the Planets one way, **from East to West**, round the Sun, [...]	ChatGPT-4.1	The translation specifies 'carries with it the Planets one way, **from East to West**, round the Sun, which is plac'd in the Centre' while the French only mentions *'les fait tourner toutes en un mesme sens autour du Soleil, qui occupe le centre.'* **The addition of 'from East to West'** and the **explanation about the Sun's specific position add clarification not strictly present in the French.**
		Claude-3.7-Sonnet	No annotation
		Gemini-2.5-Pro	The French *'grand amas de matiere celeste'* (great mass of celestial matter) is translated as 'vast Ocean, and Mass of Celestial Substance.' **The addition of 'Ocean' explicitly uses a metaphor to clarify the fluid, expansive, and immense nature of the celestial matter**, which is only implied by *'grand amas.'*

Source: Our original processing

lexical nuance: "Substance" instead of "Matter." This substitution contributes a metaphysical resonance that aligns with contemporary debates about substance, essence, and materiality. Furthermore, Behn supplements the movement of the celestial mass with an explicit clarification that it turns round, and carries with it the Planets one way, "**from East to West,**" round the Sun, a specification absent from the ST but consistent with the astronomical conventions of the time.

5.3.4.2 Scientific and Philosophical Context

It is important to note that Fontenelle, along with his English translators, was adhering to the Cartesian hypothesis of vortices (*tourbillons*) as the primary explanation for planetary motion. According to this theory, the planets are borne along in their orbits by whirlpools of subtle, physical matter that circulate the Sun. While this model had exerted considerable influence in the mid-seventeenth century, by the time Fontenelle published the *Entretiens* (1686), other Copernicans had already expressed their criticism about the inadequacy of the vortex hypothesis, particularly its incompatibility with the observed elliptical orbits of the planets.[4] Newtonian mechanics also eliminated the necessity of positing the existence of vast amounts of celestial matter.

The metaphor of vortices offered an accessible and imaginative way to communicate complex cosmological ideas to a non-specialist audience. The English translators, in turn, engaged with this imagery in accordance with the expectations of their own readerships. By introducing metaphors such as "Ocean" or by clarifying movement and spatial relations, they were aligning Fontenelle's cosmology with the stylistic and intellectual sensibilities of late seventeenth-century England.

5.3.4.3 The Translator's Presence

This example demonstrates, with particular clarity, how the presence of the translator becomes visible through explicitation. Domville's TT1 intervention is minimal but significant: a single lexical choice ("that") subtly reconfigures the relationship between observer and cosmos. Glanvill TT2, characteristically expansive, enriches the text with metaphorical imagery and rhythmic elaboration. Behn TT3, by contrast, appears to oscillate between imitation and synthesis, borrowing from both Domville and Glanvill while reshaping their renderings into a hybrid solution of her own.

The different strategies highlight the translators' distinct literary *personae*. Domville TT1 favours restraint and clarity; Glanvill TT2 indulges in rhetorical flourish; Behn TT3 practices negotiation, producing a text that is at once faithful and adaptive. Explicitation thus functions not only as a linguistic adjustment but also as a marker of translatorial agency and style.

5.3.4.4 Sociocultural Influences

As has often been observed, explicitations of this kind are typically non-obligatory: they are not required by the structures of the target language but emerge from cultural, stylistic, and pragmatic considerations. Munday (2016: 92, 184) emphasises that explicitation is closely tied to sociocultural factors that shape linguistic choice in translation, particularly in literary contexts.

Seventeenth-century English prose, particularly in the realm of natural philosophy, exhibited a strong tendency toward clarity, order, and explicitness. Philosophical and scientific writing of the period often favoured transparent exposition, intended

[4] Newton noted that Descartes overlooked elliptical, non-circular morions, such as those of planets, the Moon, and Jovian satellites, already described by Borrelli (1666). For early discussions, refer to Newton's *De Motu Corporum* (1684) *and his 1681 letter to* Crompton for Flamsteed (Turnbull 1960: 361, and Whiteside 1991: 21, fn. 58).

to educate readers and persuade them of the rationality of new cosmological systems. The translations of Fontenelle reflect not merely individual preference but also the broader stylistic ethos of Restoration and early Enlightenment England.

The explicitation strategies deployed by Domville TT1, Glanvill TT2, and Behn TT3 can therefore be interpreted as part of a cultural adaptation process. By expanding or clarifying Fontenelle's images, the translators were accommodating the expectations of English readers for "neat and clear" accounts of natural philosophy. In doing so, they contributed to the dissemination of cosmological ideas at a time when England was negotiating between Cartesian heritage and Newtonian innovation.

5.3.4.5 Conclusion

This case study illustrates the complex interplay between implicitness and explicitness in the translation of scientific and literary texts. Explicitation here is not a mechanical process but a culturally inflected and stylistically charged intervention. Each translator responds differently to Fontenelle's imagery: Domville TT1 emphasises spatial remoteness, Glanvill TT2 magnifies cosmic fluidity, and Behn TT3 synthesises both approaches while introducing her own refinements. The result is a set of translations that, while sharing a common source, diverge in subtle but telling ways.

Ultimately, explicitation in these texts demonstrates how translation mediates between scientific discourse, literary style, and cultural expectation. It reveals the translator not as an invisible conduit but as an active interpreter, whose choices reflect broader intellectual and cultural currents. This perspective not only enriches our understanding of Domville, Glanvill, and Behn as translators but also situates their work within the shifting landscape of seventeenth-century science, philosophy, and literature.

5.3.5 Domestication

The concept of **domestication** is central to discussions of translation strategy, particularly since it was prominently theorised by Venuti (1998), who traced it back to Schleiermacher's (1813) foundational reflections on translation in his 1813 lecture *On the Different Methods of Translating* (republished in Venuti 2012: 43–63). Schleiermacher distinguished between two opposing strategies: one that moves the reader toward the author, preserving the foreignness of the original, and another that moves the author toward the reader, thereby adapting the foreign to the familiar. Venuti reformulated this dichotomy in terms of *foreignization* and *domestication*. The latter, as Venuti (2008: 15) observes with a degree of criticism, involves "an ethnocentric reduction of the foreign text to receiving cultural values," whereby the translator erases the alterity of the source culture to produce a text that conforms to the expectations of the target readership (see also Munday 2016: 225–227).

Domestication thus refers to the process by which cultural, geographical, or linguistic references in the source text (ST) are adjusted, replaced, or recontextualised in the target text (TT) to appear natural, familiar, and immediately intelligible to the receiving audience. It is a strategy with deep historical roots, particularly in the seventeenth and eighteenth centuries, when translation was often conceived not merely as a linguistic transfer, but as a cultural act of adaptation. As the present case study demonstrates, the three early translations of *Entretiens* exhibit varying degrees and types of domestication.

First Example: Paris and Saint-Denis
Fontenelle's original text reads:

> Fontenelle ST: "[Page 90] [...] *Supposons qu'il n'y ait jamais eu nul commerce entre **Paris** & **Saint-Denis**, & qu'un Bourgeois de Paris, qui ne sera jamais sorty de sa Ville, soit sur les Tours de **Notre Dame**, & voye **Saint-Denis** de loin; on luy demandera s'il croit que **Saint Denis** soit habité comme **Paris**.*
>
> [Let us suppose that there has never been any trade between **Paris & Saint Denis**, & that a Bourgeois of Paris, who will never have left his City, is on the Tower of **Notre Dame**, & sees **Saint Denis** from afar; he will be asked if he believes that **Saint-Denis** is inhabited like **Paris.**]

The translations provide three distinct solutions:

Domville TT1: [page 22] [...] Let us suppose that there was never any Commerce between **Paris** and **St. Denis** (a Town about three miles from Paris) and that a Burgess of Paris, who never stirr'd out of the Town, should from the top of **Notre Dame** see **Saint Denis** at a distance, the question is put him, whether he believes that Saint Denis is inhabited as Paris is.
Glanvill TT2: [...] Suppose there had never been any Communication between **London** and **Greenwich,** and a **Cockney**, who was never beyond the **Walls of London,** saw **Greenwich** from the top of the Pyramid; you ask him if he believes **Greenwich is inhabited as London is**?
Behn TT3: [...] Suppose then, there had never been any Commerce between **Paris & Saint Denis**, and that a **Citizen of Paris**, who had never been out of that City shou'd go up to the top of the **Steeple of our Lady**, and shou'd view St. Denis at a distance, and one shou'd ask him if he believ'd St. Denis to be inhabited [...].

In this example, only Glanvill TT2 adopts a clear domesticating strategy**.** Instead of retaining the French geographical references, he replaces *Paris* with *London*, *Saint-Denis* with *Greenwich*, and *Bourgeois de Paris* with *Cockney*. This substitution effectively transplants the scene from a French to an English cultural landscape, transforming Fontenelle's allegorical thought experiment into one immediately accessible to a London readership.

By contrast, Domville TT1 maintains the French place names but inserts an explanatory note, *"a Town about three miles from Paris"*, which provides clarification without replacing the foreign references. His solution is closer to a foreignising strategy with slight explicitation. Behn TT3 likewise preserves the French setting, declaring explicitly in her Preface: *"I have laid the scene at Paris, where the original was writ."* Her refusal to domesticate in this case suggests an ideological commitment to maintaining the French cultural frame, though she does not articulate her reasons further.

This divergence illustrates the varying attitudes toward cultural adaptation among translators: Glanvill emphasises accessibility and immediacy, while Domville and Behn respect the foreign scene, albeit in different registers.

Second Example: The Chariot and Charles's Wain

Another revealing instance of domestication arises in Fontenelle's astronomical description:

Fontenelle ST: [Page 29] […] ***Le Chariot**, par example, que vous voyez qui est formé de ces [Page 30] sept Etoiles, a toujours été fait comme il est".*

[The **Chariot**, for example, that you see which is formed of these seven Stars, has always been made as it is]

This becomes:

Domville TT1: "**The Waign**, for example, which you see is form'd of those seven Stars, has been and ever shall be the same it is."

Glanvill TT2: "[Page 12] […] [F]or Example, **Charles's Wain** which is compos'd of those seven Stars, hath been and ever will be as it now is."

Behn TT3**:** "[Page 15] […] As for Example, **Charles's Wain, or the Constellation of the Great Bear**, which you see, and which consists of Seven Stars, has always been, and will still continue the same."

Here, all three translations engage in domestication, albeit to varying degrees. The French *Chariot* is replaced with its English equivalent, *Charles's Wain*, a familiar popular term for the constellation known today as Ursa Major. Domville TT1 abbreviates this to *Waign*; Glanvill TT2 retains *Charles's Wain*; Behn TT3 expands further, adding the scientific designation *Constellation of the Great Bear.*

Behn's choice exemplifies her general preference for clarification and amplification, ensuring that readers encounter not only the culturally familiar term but also the more learned astronomical label. At the same time, the demonstrative *"ces sept Etoiles"* [these seven stars] is transformed into *"Seven Stars,"* with capitalisation suggesting a proper astronomical name. Although the *Seven Stars* has traditionally referred to the Pleiades in Taurus, Behn's capitalisation here appears to serve more as emphasis and domestication than as a precise astronomical identification.

This example highlights how domestication operates not merely through cultural substitution but also through terminological adaptation, whereby translators adjust references to align with the shared cultural and scientific vocabulary of the target audience.

Third Example: Love Songs and Elegies

A further case of domestication concerns a passage about lovers addressing their songs to the night (Table 5.5):

Table 5.5 Segmented text with "domestication" in translation

ST and TTs	Extracted text	Gen AI	AI-generated comments
Fontenelle ST	*Pourquoy les Amants, qui sont bons Juges de ce qui touche, ne s'adressent-ils jamais qu'à la nuit dans toutes les Chansons & toutes les Elegies* ***que je connois****? Il faut bien que la nuit ait leurs remerciemens, luy dis-je. Mais, reprit-elle, elle a aussi toutes leurs plaintes; le jour ne s'attire point leurs confidences; d'où cela vient-il?* [Why do lovers, who are good judges of what touches, only ever address the night in all the songs and elegies **that I know**? The night must have their thanks, I told her. But, she replied, it also has all their complaints; the day does not attract their confidences; where does that come from?]		
Domville TT1	Why is it that Lovers, who are good Judges of what is charming, ever, in all their Songs and Elegys **that I have met with**, address themselves to the Night? 'Tis doubtless, said I; because it most obliges them. But, says she, it has likewise all their Complaints; the Day shares not at all in their Confidence: from whence should this proceed?	ChatGPT-4.1	No annotation
		Claude-3.7-Sonnet	The French source refers to songs and elegies using the first person (*'que je connois'* - 'that I know'), showing the Marquise's personal familiarity with these genres. The English translation changes this to **'that I have met with'**, suggesting a more distant relationship with these cultural forms, **which aligns with English cultural expectations** of a noblewoman's more limited engagement with romantic literature.
		Gemini-2.5-Pro	No annotation

(continued)

Table 5.5 (continued)

ST and TTs	Extracted text	Gen AI	AI-generated comments
Glanvill TT2	why do Lovers in their Songs and Elegies address themselves to the Night? 'Tis the Night, Madam, said I, that crowns their Joys, and therefore deserves their thanks. But 'tis the Night, said she, that hears their Complaints, and how comes it to pass, the day is so little trusted with their secrets?	ChatGPT-4.1	No annotation
		Claude-3.7-Sonnet	No annotation
		Gemini-2.5-Pro	No annotation
Behn TT3	Lovers who are the best Judges of what is pleasing and touching, do always address themselves to the Night, in all their Songs and Elegies? I told her, that they most certainly paid their acknowledgments to the Night; for she was ever most favourable to all their Designs. But, Sir, replied the Marquise, she receives also all their Complaints, **as a true Confident of all their Entrigues**; from whence proceeds that?	ChatGPT-4.1	No annotation
		Claude-3.7-Sonnet	No annotation
		Gemini-2.5-Pro	The English translation adds **"as a true Confident of all their Entrigues,"** a phrase absent in the French. This addition frames the night's role in the context of amorous intrigue, a familiar theme in English literature, thereby **domesticating the original by linking it to target-culture literary conventions.**

Source: Our original processing

Fontenelle ST: "*Pourquoy les Amants, qui sont bons Juges de ce qui touche, ne s'adressent-ils jamais qu'à la nuit dans toutes les Chansons & toutes les Elegies* ***que je connois****? Il faut bien que la nuit ait leurs remerciemens, luy dis-je. Mais, reprit-elle, elle a aussi toutes leurs plaintes; le jour ne s'attire point leurs confidences; d'où cela vient-il?*"

[Why do lovers, who are good judges of what touches, only ever address the night in all the songs and elegies **that I know**? The night must have their thanksgiving, I told her. But, she replied, it also has all their complaints; the day does not attract their confidences; where does that come from?]

The translations are as follows:

Domville TT1: "Why is it that Lovers, who are good Judges of what is charming, ever, in all their Songs and Elegys **that I have met with**, address themselves to the Night? 'Tis doubtless, said I; because it most obliges them. But, says she, it has likewise all their Complaints; the Day shares not at all in their Confidence: from whence should this proceed?"
Glanvill TT2: "Why do Lovers in their Songs and Elegies address themselves to the Night? 'Tis the Night, Madam, said I, that crowns their Joys, and therefore

> deserves their thanks. But 'tis the Night, said she, that hears their Complaints, and how comes it to pass, the day is so little trusted with their secrets?"
> Behn TT3: "Lovers who are the best Judges of what is pleasing and touching, do always address themselves to the Night, in all their Songs and Elegies? I told her, that they most certainly paid their acknowledgments to the Night; for she was ever most favourable to all their Designs. But, Sir, replied the Marquise, she receives also all their Complaints, **as a true Confident of all their Entrigues**; from whence proceeds that?"

The variations here are subtle but significant. Domville TT1 translates ***"que je connois"*** [that I know] as "**that I have met with**," which implies a more distanced engagement with literary culture, perhaps consistent with English expectations of a noblewoman's limited familiarity with songs and elegies. Glanvill TT2 omits the secondary phrase *"qui sont bons Juges de ce qui touche"* altogether, thereby reducing the evaluative dimension of the lovers' judgment. Behn TT3, conversely, renders it expansively as "best Judges of what is pleasing and touching."

The most striking act of domestication is Behn's addition of "**as a true Confident of all their Entrigues**," absent from the French text. This insertion reframes the night as an agent within the culture of amorous intrigue, a theme deeply rooted in English literary conventions of the Restoration stage. Behn, as a playwright and novelist, integrates her own cultural imagination into the translation, thereby domesticating the French text by aligning it with familiar English tropes of secrecy, intrigue, and confession.

5.3.5.1 Translator's Presence and Cultural Context

These three examples illustrate the distinctive translator profiles that emerge in relation to domestication.

> Domville TT1 tends to be more restrained, occasionally explanatory, but generally loyal to the French context. His preference is for formality and distance, consistent with his Dublin context, where continental intellectual imports were framed with cautious fidelity.
> Glanvill TT2 is the most openly domesticating translator, relocating French references into an English landscape and simplifying expressions for immediacy. His approach aligns with a more anglocentric perspective, perhaps reflective of a London readership eager to see itself mirrored in philosophical discourse.
> Behn TT3 demonstrates a hybrid strategy: she preserves French geographical settings but simultaneously introduces cultural domestication through amplifications, clarifications, and added motifs of intrigue. Her literary persona as dramatist and novelist informs her interventions, making her translations resonate with the conventions of English literary culture.

5.3.5.2 Conclusion

The analysis of domestication in these translations of Fontenelle underscores the complexity of translator agency. Domestication is not a uniform or unidirectional strategy, but rather manifests in varying degrees, from Glanvill's overt cultural substitution to Domville's cautious clarification, and Behn's creative reframing. Each act of domestication reflects both stylistic individuality and cultural mediation, illustrating how translators navigated the tension between foreign cosmology and local literary expectations.

Domestication and foreignization were not abstract categories but practical strategies shaped by audience expectations, publishing markets, and the cultural politics of the period. Both fascination with French intellectual culture and ambivalence toward foreign authority marked the Restoration era. Translation thus functioned as both mediation and negotiation, and the strategies employed by Domville, Glanvill, and Behn reflect their differing positions within this spectrum.

5.3.6 *Self-Censorship*

Self-censorship in translation represents one of the most revealing aspects of the translator's agency, especially in politically and religiously sensitive contexts. In the case of the early English translations of Fontenelle's *Entretiens*, instances of omission and modification can be interpreted as deliberate acts of self-censorship, motivated not only by stylistic preference but also by the broader ideological and socio-political environment.

As Lawrence Venuti and other scholars of translation have argued and we have stressed above, a translator is never a neutral intermediary. Instead, translation is always shaped by the cultural and political constraints of its time. Self-censorship is therefore best understood as a form of manipulation in Lefevere's (1985) sense of the term, whereby a translated text is adjusted to accommodate the dominant ideology, avoid political risk, or preserve the translator's personal and professional security (Cipriani 2020).[5] While less frequent than other features, self-censorship in *Entretiens*' translations proves to be of particular interest, as it sheds light on the complex intersection of religion, politics, and literature in Restoration and post-Restoration England.

5.3.6.1 Behn's Preface and Religious Caution

Aphra Behn herself provides a revealing signal of her stance in her Preface to the translation. There, she carefully distances questions of physical matter and natural philosophy from those of religion and theology, attributing the latter exclusively to the authority of the Catholic Church:

[5] See also Munday (2016: 186, 215, 220), Zaixi (2019), and Ping (2024).

> I think it is the Duty of all good Christian to acquiesce in the Opinion and Decrees of the Church of Christ, in whom dwells the Spirit of God, which enlightens us to Matters of Religion and Faith; and as to other things contained in the Holy Scriptures relating to Astronomy, Geometry, Chronology, or other liberal Sciences, we leave those Points to the Opinion of the Learned [Men]. (Behn 1988: Preface)

Behn here delineates a sharp boundary between *faith* and *science*. Matters of theology, she insists, fall under the authority of the Church, whereas learned men may debate astronomy and related sciences. This rhetorical strategy simultaneously affirms her orthodoxy as a "good Christian" while also legitimising her engagement with natural philosophy. A few lines before the end, she concludes her Preface by stating: "I hope my readers will be so just as to think I intend no reflection on religion by this essay; which being no matter of faith, is free for everyone to believe, or not believe, as they please." It signals a pre-emptive act of self-censorship, forestalling accusations of irreligion or heresy.

5.3.6.2 The Omission about the Donation of Constantine

One of the most striking examples of self-censorship occurs in Behn's treatment of Fontenelle's reference to the Donation of Constantine (reported with comments in Table 5.6). In the second night of the *Entretiens*, Fontenelle recalls Ariosto's *Orlando Furioso* (1516), in which the knight Astolfo ascends to the Moon with the help of St. John and a flying horse to recover his lost sanity. Ariosto imagines the Moon as a repository for all things lost on Earth, except for folly, which abounds here. Fontenelle extends this conceit by suggesting that among the things not found on the Moon is the "folly" surrounding Constantine's Donation, a notorious forgery by which the Papacy claimed political authority over Rome and Italy.

Fontenelle's French text reads:

> *Mais l'Arioste ne vous dit cela qu'à l'oreille, tout y est jusqu'à la Donation de Constantin.*
>
> [But Ariosto doesn't tell you but in the ear that everything is there [on the Moon] up to the Donation of Constantine.]

Then, it continues:

> **C'est que les Papes ont prétendu estre Maistres de Rome & de l'Italie en vertu d'une Donation que l'Empereur Constantin leur en avoit faite, & la verité est qu'on ne sçauroit dire ce qu'elle est devenuë.**
>
> [It is that the Popes have pretended to be the Masters of Rome and Italy by a Donation the emperor Constantine made to them, and the truth is that one wouldn't say what it has become]. (*Entretiens* 1686: 128.)

The Donation of Constantine, long exposed as a forgery, had nonetheless served for centuries as the papal justification for temporal power in Italy. Lorenzo Valla's famous fifteenth-century philological critique had demonstrated its spuriousness,

Table 5.6 Segmented text with "self-censorship" in translation

ST and TTs	Extracted text	Generative AI	AI-generated comments
Fontenelle ST	*la Lune est si exacte à recueillir ce qui se perd ici-bas, que tout y est. Mais l'Arioste ne vous dit cela qu'à l'oreille, tout y est jusqu'à la Donation de Constantin.* ***C'est que les Papes ont prétendu estre Maistres de Rome & de l'Italie en vertu d'une Donation que l'Empereur Constantin leur en avoit faite, & la verité est qu'on ne sçauroit dire ce qu'elle est devenuë.*** *Mais devinez de quelle sorte de chose on ne trouve point dans la Lune. De la Folie. Tout ce qu'il y en a jamais eu sur la Terre, s'y est tres-bien conservé* [The Moon is so exact in collecting what is lost here below, that everything is there. But Ariosto doesn't tell you but in the ear that everything is there [on the Moon] up to the Donation of Constantine. **It is that the Popes have pretended to be the Masters of Rome and Italy by a donation the emperor Constantine [the Great] have made to them, and the truth is that one wouldn't say what it has become**. But guess what sort of thing we do not find in the Moon? Madness. Everything that has ever been on Earth has been very well preserved there.]		

ST and TTs	Extracted text	Generative AI	AI-generated comments
Domville TT1	the Moon is so exact in collecting all that is lost here below, that all is to be found there, even to the Donation of Constantine, but this Ariosto tells you in your ear. The thing is, the Popes that have pretended themselves **Masters of Rome and Italy by vertue of a Donation from the Emperour Constantine**, and the truth is, no man knows what's become of it.	ChatGPT-4.1	*Mais l'Arioste ne vous dit cela qu'à l'oreille, tout y est jusqu'à la Donation de Constantin.*' is only alluded in English as 'even to the Donation of Constantine, but this Ariosto tells you in your ear,' omitting the direct satirical connection and irony about papal authority. This omission avoids direct criticism or mockery of religious claims, likely out of sensitivity to the religious climate of late 17th-century England. The explicit phrase '*C'est que les Papes ont prétendu estre Maistres de Rome & de l'Italie en vertu d'une Donation que l'Empereur Constantin leur en avoit faite, & la verité est qu'on ne sçauroit dire ce qu'elle est devenuë.*' includes an ideological explanation of the Donation of Constantine and the papal claim, which is reduced in the translation to 'even to the Donation of Constantine, but this Ariosto tells you in your ear. The thing is, the Popes that have pretended themselves Masters of Rome and Italy by virtue of a Donation from the Emperor Constantine, and the truth is, no man knows what's become of it.' The translation omits the explanatory tone and historical sarcasm about the Papacy's claim and the mysterious disappearance of the document, likely due to the anti-Catholic sensitivities in Protestant England at the time.
		Claude-3.7-Sonnet	The translator has censored part of Fontenelle's critique of the Catholic Church. In the source text, Fontenelle states that 'the Popes have claimed to be Masters of Rome & Italy by virtue of a Donation that Emperor Constantine had made to them' using more definitive language that directly challenges papal authority. The English translation softens this by changing it to 'the Popes that have pretended themselves Masters' and omits the direct statement that Constantine made the donation 'to them' (the Popes), making the claim seem more ambiguous. **This self-censorship likely reflects the religious tensions in late 17th-century England**, where criticising Catholic claims too directly could be politically sensitive during the reign of Catholic King James II, even while translating a work that was otherwise critical of Catholic authority.
		Gemini-2.5-Pro	No annotation

(continued)

Table 5.6 (continued)

ST and TTs	Extracted text	Generative AI	AI-generated comments
Glanvill TT2	the Moon keeps all safe that is lost here below. Yet I must tell you Ariosto doth but whisper it, tho' every thing is there, even to the donation of Constantine, **(i. e.)** the Popes have pretended to be Masters of Rome and Italy by Virtue of a Donation which the Emperor Constantine made **Silvester**; and the truth is, no body knows what is become of it	ChatGPT-4.1	The source explanation of the Donation of Constantine—specifically, *'C'est que les Papes ont prétendu estre Maistres de Rome & de l'Italie en vertu d'une Donation que l'Empereur Constantin leur en avoit faite, & la verité est qu'on ne sçauroit dire ce qu'elle est devenuë'*—is replaced with a less direct English expression: '(i. e.) the Popes have pretended to be Masters of Rome and Italy by Virtue of a Donation which the Emperour Constantine made Silvester; and the truth is, no body knows what is become of it'. Here, the translation removes the more explicit source statement that the Papal claim is based on 'a donation that Constantine made to them' and that its current status is unknown, but the ideological charge remains (that the Donation's truth is obscure and its claim possibly false). **The translation is less blunt but not fully censorious.**
		Claude-3.7-Sonnet	While the basic information about the Donation of Constantine is maintained, the translator added the clarifying parenthetical **'(i.e.)'** and specified the recipient as **'Silvester'**, information not present in the original. This represents **self-censorship through modification rather than omission**, as the translator sought to frame this politically sensitive Catholic claim in a more historical and distanced manner for an English Protestant audience that would have been sceptical of papal authority claims.
		Gemini-2.5-Pro	No annotation
Behn TT3	**in short** the Moon is exact in collecting all that is lost here below, and which are all to be found there, even to the Donation of Constantine. (But Astolpho told me this only in my Ear.) Besides all the Folly that was ever committed upon the Earth is well preserv'd there	ChatGPT-4.1	The phrase explaining *'la Donation de Constantin'* (the Donation of Constantine), with its critical exposition of papal claims to temporal authority in Rome and Italy, is omitted in the translation. In the target, only a tongue-in-cheek mention remains, with no explanation of the underlying religious and political critique**. This is likely due to the translator's self-censorship to avoid controversy regarding the legitimacy of papal secular power, a highly sensitive topic in post-Reformation Protestant England.**
		Claude-3.7-Sonnet	The translator significantly altered the explanation of the Donation of Constantine. The original text directly explains how Popes claimed mastery over Rome and Italy based on this document, adding that the truth is no one knows what became of it (implying it may have been fraudulent). The translation reduces this to a parenthetical comment '(But Astolpho told me this only in my Ear.)', removing the explicit criticism of papal claims to temporal power. **This self-censorship likely reflects the sensitive religious and political climate in England regarding Catholic authority.**
		Gemini-2.5-Pro	The translator omitted Fontenelle's explicit explanation regarding the Donation of Constantine. This passage in the source text detailed how **"les Papes" (the Popes)** utilised this (later proven forged) document to assert temporal authority over Rome and Italy, and it also subtly questioned the document's authenticity or existence. **Omitting this section removes a direct critique of papal historical claims and power, a sensitive topic.** While the "Donation of Constantine" is mentioned, excising the explanatory details involving the Popes sanitises a potentially inflammatory anti-Papal statement.

Source: Our original processing

yet the document continued to be a touchstone in debates about papal authority. By Fontenelle’s time, references to it carried clear anti-clerical overtones.

Behn TT3 omits to translate the above passage. She arguably avoids reproducing in English a potentially inendiary critique of the Catholic Church in the troubled last period of James II Stuart's monarchy. This omission thus represents a clear case of self-censorship, likely motivated by the need to avoid political provocation. As an author dependent on patronage and subject to licensing restrictions, she would have been acutely aware of the dangers of engaging too directly with religious controversy.

The “Donation” is recognised as a forged Roman imperial decree attributed to the fourth-century Roman emperor Constantine the Great, an actual historical fraud committed in the eighth century, by which it was attested that the emperor would have transferred absolute political authority over the Western part of the Roman Empire to the Pope of Rome. In Restoration England, with its volatile mix of Anglican, Catholic, and dissenting factions, openly criticising the Papacy could be politically risky (e.g., Schwahn 1994 [1928]).

5.3.6.3 Comparative Treatment by Domville and Glanvill

The phenomenon is not limited to Behn. Other translators also modulate or silence Fontenelle’s ST provocative remarks (see Table 5.6).

Domville TT1 generally retains more of Fontenelle’s content but occasionally reframes it. His version of the passage about folly in the Moon reads:

> But guess you what sort of thing is to be found in the Moon. Folly. All that has ever been upon the face of the Earth, is there carefully preserv’d.

This rendering is less pointed than Fontenelle’s original, smoothing over the satirical edge.

Glanvill TT2 similarly tones down the critique, though without omitting it entirely:

> but what do you think is not to be found in the Moon? Folly, all that ever was upon the Earth is kept there still.

Glanvill retains the reference to folly but omits the specific allusion to the Donation of Constantine, perhaps out of prudence.

In both cases, the translators moderate Fontenelle’s irreverence. Domville TT1 seems cautious, perhaps reflecting the Irish context of his Dublin edition under Catholic King James II, where open anti-papal satire might have been politically delicate. Glanvill TT2, writing in London, avoids the explicit attack while still maintaining the general satirical conceit.

5.3.6.4 The Translator's Presence

The differences between the three translations illustrate distinct modes of translatorial presence:

Domville TT1 manifests a restrained, slightly distanced tone, reflecting a context in which political prudence was paramount.

Glanvill TT2 engages in what may be called *soft censorship*: he retains the humorous conceit but avoids specific references that could be read as incendiary.

Behn TT3 exemplifies severe self-censorship through outright omission, excising entire passages that might have provoked controversy.

In all cases, the translators' choices reflect not only personal style but also the society's constraints through self-censorship and self-preservation.

5.3.6.5 Historical and Cultural Considerations

Understanding these acts of omission requires situating them within the broader history of censorship in seventeenth-century England. Literature in this period was subject to strict pre-publication licensing, intended primarily to suppress seditious or moral, heretical works. The Stationers' Company Registers, "invested by the Crown with the power and the obligation of operating censorship by examining and licensing books before publication" (Thomas 1969: 9). The emphasis was less on the dignity of literature than on the "recognition of the dangers of literature." (*Ibidem.*) It also served as both a legal mechanism to safeguard against plagiarism and as a historical record of licensed publications. The very existence of licensing systems underscored the perceived threat of printed discourse. However, the mandatory nature and the authority of the Company declined over time, particularly after the Copyright Act was passed in 1695.

The late 1680s were a time of acute political tension. Growing fears of Catholic influence marked the reign of James II (1685–1688). In such a climate, translating and publishing a text that openly mocked papal claims to temporal power could have been construed as politically provocative. The translators likely deemed it prudent to omit such material. In this sense, the translators' acts of self-censorship must be seen not as mere prudery but as strategic negotiations with power. By avoiding explicit anti-papal satire, they ensured that their translations could circulate without jeopardising their reputation or provoking censorship.

5.3.6.6 Conclusive Remarks

From the perspective of translation studies, self-censorship belongs to the broader category of manipulation, as theorised by Lefevere. Translations are constantly manipulated to conform to ideological, poetological, or patronage-related pressures. In the focused case, such manipulation takes the form of omission, which can significantly reshape the ideological tenor of the text.

What is lost in these omissions is precisely the edge of Fontenelle's satire, his willingness to link folly with religious and political institutions. By excising such passages, the translators produce a text more palatable to English readers but also less subversive, less daring, and less reflective of Fontenelle's original intent.

Self-censorship in the English translations of Fontenelle's *Entretiens* exemplifies the translator's delicate balancing act between fidelity and survival. The suppression of references to the Donation of Constantine and papal authority demonstrates how translation operates not in a cultural vacuum but within a matrix of political and religious constraints.

Domville's TT1 caution, Glanvill's TT2 moderation, and Behn's TT3 outright omission reflect different strategies of negotiating these constraints. Together, they reveal how translation in late seventeenth-century England was inextricably linked to questions of censorship, ideology, and cultural politics.

While rarely compared to other translation features, instances of self-censorship are disproportionately illuminating, offering insight into the socio-cultural climate of the time and the pressures under which translators laboured. With Fontenelle, they remind us that the *Entretiens* was not merely a work of popular science but also a text suffused with satire, irony, and cultural critique, elements whose fate in translation depended heavily on the courage, prudence, or expediency of those who rendered it into English.

5.4 Translators as Co-Authors

5.4.1 Introduction

The notion of the translator as co-author has long been debated in translation studies. This section examines the translators' "manipulative" initiatives in their translation of Fontenelle's *Entretiens*, a text that was itself subject to censorship in France and presented sensitive issues. Translation is never a neutral act but is always an intervention.

In her *Translation Preface*, Behn openly comments on the challenges of translating French into English, noting that she found herself more comfortable when translating between English and Italian. She acknowledges that different strategies were required depending on the text and target audience, and in doing so, she anticipates what modern translation studies, following Venuti (2008), would later theorise as domestication and foreignisation. Some of her comments dwell on the typical musicality of the French language. At the same time, one of her most striking reflections is "If one endeavours to make it English standard, it is no Translation. If one follows their Flourishes and Embroideries, it is worse than French Tinsel" (Todd 1993: 72).

Here, Behn identifies the double bind of the translator: either risk producing a text that is no longer a translation but an adaptation, or risk being accused of decorative excess that diminishes the English literary standard. Her reflection anticipates the tension described by Venuti between fluency and foreignness and also resonates with Antoine Berman's analysis of "deforming tendencies" (Berman 1985).

Behn could also be considered a modern translator in anticipating what Theo Hermans later defined as "echoing translating," that is, "translating with dissociative attitude" (Hermans 2007: 83). This occurs when a translator expresses personal views in subtle disapproval of the author, using the translation itself as a site of critical dialogue. As Hermans observes:

> Approaching translation as a complex form of quoting makes it clear that translation matters, socially and historically, not only because it transmits cultural goods but because it transmits them under a certain angle, with evaluation attached. (*Ibidem*; emphasis added)

Thus, Behn's work embodies the translator as co-author, not merely repeating Fontenelle's source text but shaping its reception, sometimes through agreement and reinforcement, at other times through omission, alteration, or dissociation.

5.4.2 *Selenography and Translational Fidelity*

In the *Entretiens*, Fontenelle's dialogue during the Second Night mentions various lunar locations borrowed from the contemporary selenographic maps of Riccioli (1651) and Hevelius (1647) (for a reference to a relatively recent mapping of the Moon, see e.g. Whitaker 2008). The source text reads:

> Il y a une Mer Caspienne, les Monts Porphirites, le Lac Noir.
> [There is a Caspian Sea, the Porphirite Mountains, the Black Lake.]

The three early English translators rendered this passage closely but with subtle variations:

Domville TT1: "There's a Caspian Sea, Porphirian Mountains, a black Lake."
Glanvill TT2: "There is the Caspian Sea, the Black Lake, the Porphirite Mountains."
Behn TT3: "There are too a Caspian Sea, Porphory Hills and the Black Lake."

The translators do not comment on the fact that Fontenelle's description merges two distinct and inconsistent systems of lunar nomenclature. The *Entretiens* combined Hevelius' and Riccioli's toponymy, creating confusion that was only later resolved by subsequent editions of *Entretiens* (from the second edition of 1687 onwards), which standardised Riccioli's terms. Fontenelle himself acknowledged this error, later replacing the earlier names with new ones such as *Palus Somni*, *Mare Imbrium*, *Mare Nectaris*, and *Mare Crisium*.[6]

[6] Vertesi (2007) offers a discussion of why Hevelius's *Selenographia* (1647) was supplanted by Riccioli's as offered in *Almagestum novam* (1651) "in spite of the latter's simplistic pictures and

This case illustrates a significant point about translators as co-authors: all three English translators reproduce the confusion without comment, thereby perpetuating Fontenelle's mistake. Their silence contrasts with Behn's otherwise critical stance on the debate on science and religion. In this instance, she aligns herself with the original text, choosing fidelity even where the source text was flawed. This selective approach demonstrates the translator's discretionary power to intervene or to refrain.

The subsequent passage provides further evidence of this discretion. Fontenelle writes:

> *enfin la Description de la Lune est si exacte, qu'un Sçavant qui s'y trouveroit presentement, ne s'y égareroit non plus que je ferois dans Paris.*
>
> [finally, the Description of the Moon is so exact that a scholar who were there at the moment would not get lost any more than I would in Paris.]

The translators render it as follows:

Domville TT1: "and in fine the Description of the Moon is so exact that should a learned man be now there, he'd no more lose his Way than I should do in the Streets of Paris."

Glanvill TT2: "in short, they have publish'd such exact descriptions of the Moon, that a very Almanack-maker will be no more to seek there, than I am in London."

Behn TT3: "In short, they have fram'd so exact a Description of the Moon, that a learned Man, if he were there, wou'd be in no more danger of losing his Way, than I wou'd be, if I were at Paris."

Here, Glanvill TT2 significantly domesticates the comparison by substituting *London* for *Paris*. Domville TT1 and Behn TT3 retain the Parisian reference. Yet, here Behn's rendering is more idiomatic in English, displaying her capacity to balance fidelity with stylistic refinement.

5.4.3 *Behn as Author of the* Translator's Preface

As a translator, Behn was not only transmitting Fontenelle's ideas but also participating in the philosophical moment of late seventeenth-century England, as noted in the *Translator's Preface* (Schnell 2004: 351), which serves as an essay on translation matters and possible conflicts with religious Scriptures. She positioned herself within contemporary debates on astronomy and cosmology by envisioning the new

promotion of geocentric cosmology" (*Ibid.*: 401). As noted in this discussion, "British astronomers use both nomenclatures side-by-side until the mid-eighteenth century […], but while the *Collegio Romano* continued in astronomical adventures, Hevelius's entire observatory was razed to the ground by fire in 1679 and never fully recovered" (*Ibid.*: 418, fn. 42).

Copernican theory as neutral with respect to the Scriptures as the old Ptolemaic system (Gill 2020: 310).

Behn opposes Jesuit Father Tacquet's criticism of Copernicus, which sought to demonstrate that "this system was expressly against the holy Scriptures". In her translation, she is aware of this intellectual tension. She acknowledges that Copernicanism had been condemned as heretical because it was perceived as contradicting the holy Scriptures. She writes:

> I shall not venture upon astronomical part, but leave that to the mathematicians; but because I know that when this opinion of Copernicus [...] was first heard of in the world, those who neither understood the old system of Ptolemy, nor the new one of Copernicus, said that this new opinion was expressly contrary to the holy Scriptures, and therefore not to be embraced; nay, it was condemned as heretical upon the same account (Behn 1688: 106)

This passage prompts Behn to declare

> we leave those points to the opinion of the learned, who by comparing the several copies, translations, versions, and editions of the Bible, are best able to reconcile any apparent differences; and this with all submission to the canons of general councils and decrees of the church. (*Ibidem.*)

She mimics Wilkins' (1638/1684) style and argument in her *Discovery*, reflecting his view of the Scriptures' neutrality regarding Ptolemaic and Copernican cosmologies. Both authors discuss Joshua 10:12 and Psalm 19:5–6 in the Bible, with Behn contending, much like Wilkins, that these passages can be interpreted as supporting either model. Without directly citing him, she replicates Wilkins' offer of a reconciliatory interpretation between science and scripture.

Similarities between Behn's *A Discovery of New Worlds* (1688) and Wilkins's *A Discovery of a New World* (1684 [1638]), include the Scriptures' silence on the immobility of the Earth,[7] for example in the leading propositions such as:

Proposition V: That the words of Scriptures in their proper and strict construction do not affirm the immobility of the Earth. (Wilkins 1640)

Proposition VIII: That there is no sufficient reason to prove Earth incapable of the motions assigned by Copernicus. (*Ibidem*)

This situation raises the question (anticipated above in Sect. 4.7.8) regarding the originality of the crux of Behn's *Preface*, which states no conflict between the Copernican system and the Scriptures. She reflects her alignment with Fontenelle's rationalism while acknowledging theological perspectives. Her disclaimer (*"as far as a woman's reasoning can go"*) may indicate awareness of the limitations perceived at the time for a woman (meaning here a "human being"?), and a desire to assert intellectual participation. The apparent rephrasing of Wilkins with her own

[7] As Hooykaas (1972: 129) notes, "[h]owever, it must at least be reckoned to his credit that although he [Wilkins] would not admit Scriptural arguments for the old system, equally he would not try to use them for his own purposes [... Moreover] Wilkins was not so apodictic as most Copernicans about the 'truth' of the new system. He said that this system had proved that they are 'many strong Probabilities why the Sun should be in the midst of the world.'" Not dissimilar to this position of Wilkins is that of Behn in *Translator's Preface*.

words, without explicit attribution, introduces a discussion about the complete authenticity in this context, which has been absent so far in an apologetic and gender-dominated literature on Aphra Behn.

5.4.4 Translation as Manipulation

Aphra Behn's interventions in translation situate her within what later scholarship has designated as "Manipulation School." Rather than a teaching school, this label refers to a group of literary translation scholars, including André Lefevere, Susan Bassnett, José Lambert, James S. Holmes, Itamar Even-Zohar, Gideon Toury, and Theo Hermans, who, from the late twentieth century onward, emphasised the centrality of ideology, poetics, and patronage in shaping translation.[8] From this perspective, translation is never a neutral transfer of meaning but always an act of manipulation, consciously or unconsciously determined by cultural and historical conditions. The translated *Entretiens* can thus be seen as a series of manipulations, reflecting both literary sensibility and socio-political awareness.

The strategies of manipulation manifest in several distinct ways. Omission plays a central role: the translators deliberately delete or reframe passages that they judged inappropriate, controversial, or dangerous, such as Fontenelle's references to the Donation of Constantine. Such interventions demonstrate awareness of the risks associated with challenging religious or political orthodoxy in Restoration England, where censorship and moral expectations exerted significant influence.

A second form of manipulation lies in domestication. While Behn does not employ domestication as extensively as John Glanvill, she nonetheless adapts specific cultural references to better suit an English readership. This process reveals sensitivity to audience expectations and the need to make foreign ideas accessible without alienating readers.

Translators also engage in clarification, simplification, and explicitation. They frequently reformulate the source text to facilitate comprehension, adding detail or rephrasing passages that might otherwise remain unclear. Such modifications illustrate pedagogical intent: to render complex philosophical and scientific ideas intelligible to a broader, non-specialist audience.

Self-conscious engagement with translation theory is evident in Behn's *Preface*, where she explicitly acknowledges the significance of contemporary reflections on translation. In particular, she invokes the *Essay on Translated Verse* (1684) by the Earl of Roscommon (1633?–1685), noting that "as for translation of verse, nothing can be added to that incomparable Essay." This statement indicates not only her

[8] Munday (2016: 189–190) describes them in these terms: "The key publication of this group of scholars, known as the *Manipulation School* or Group, was the collection of papers entitled *The Manipulation of Literature: Studies in Literary Translation*, edited by Theo Hermans (1985). [...] Scholars from the late André Lefevere [...] began to consider more closely the role of *ideology* and *patronage* in the system of translated literature" [emphasis added].

familiarity with contemporary debates but also her recognition of translation as a creative and critical act.[9] Lefevere (1992, Chap. 7) similarly cites Roscommon's remark on "Holy Garbage, tho by Homer cook't" to demonstrate how seventeenth-century translators resisted reproducing culturally alien elements from classical texts.

Selective omissions and interventions must thus be situated within a broader historical continuum. Already in antiquity, Horace, in his *Ars Poetica*, had recommended judicious selectivity: *et quae desperat tractata nitescere posse relinquit* ("and leave out those facts which, if treated, may hopelessly sprout," *Art of Poetry*, vv. 149–150, cited by Dryden 1680). The translator's practice aligns with this long-standing tradition of adapting source texts to conform to cultural, religious, and aesthetic norms.

Ultimately, the three translations of *Entretiens* emerge as forms of rewriting that are both appreciative and critical. They appreciate Fontenelle's openness to scientific discovery yet resist his irreverent stance toward religion, adopting instead forms of self-censorship. As Ferguson (2008: 212) observes, "[Behn] feels free, as she does not with the Bible, openly to voice disagreement." Her omissions, therefore, constitute not mere suppressions but calculated manipulations that reveal her authorial independence. Within this interpretive framework, the manipulations stand as part of a deeply rooted lineage that extends from classical antiquity to the modern theorisation of translation as rewriting.

5.4.5 The Translator's Voice and Co-Authorship

The English translations of Fontenelle's *Entretiens* demonstrate that translators are not passive mediators but rather co-authors who shape texts in response to cultural, ideological, and political imperatives. Translation, as revealed by the works of Domville TT1, Glanvill TT2, and Behn TT3, is best understood as a form of co-authorship: an active negotiation between fidelity to the source, adaptation to the target audience, and self-protection in politically sensitive contexts. By reframing Fontenelle's ideas for English readers, these translators intervened in the philosophical and religious debates of their time, positioning themselves at the intersection of intellectual inquiry, cultural mediation, and censorship.

The concept of translatorial voice and visibility further illuminates this dynamic. As Venuti has argued, translation inevitably bears the imprint of the translator, whose presence is evident through lexical choices, stylistic preferences, and framing strategies. Domville's TT1 voice emerges in his cautious formality and deferential tone; Glanvill's TT2, by contrast, can be discerned in his anglicising substitutions, which reframe Fontenelle's thought in terms more familiar and acceptable to an

[9] Steiner (1975: 31) writes: "Few writers in the period mention Roscommon's *Essay*." (Emphasis added.)

English readership, while Behn's TT3 visibility manifests not only in her translation but also in her Preface, where she carefully distinguishes between the domains of science and religion.

Each translator thereby illustrates a distinctive mode of agency. Domville and Glanvill soften Fontenelle's irreverent tone, adjusting it to align with Protestant sensibilities and distancing themselves from his perceived "paganism." Their translations reflect the fraught religious and political atmosphere of late seventeenth-century England, where intellectual boldness had to be carefully balanced with rhetorical prudence. Behn, though equally attentive to these constraints, adopts a more assertive critical stance, enabling her translation to serve as both cultural mediation and intellectual commentary.

These translations underscore the fundamentally interventionist nature of translation. Far from being transparent conduits of meaning, translators emerge as co-authors whose decisions reveal their personal convictions, ideological positions, and responses to the socio-political conditions of their time. In this sense, translation must be regarded not only as an act of linguistic transfer but as an act of authorship in its own right, one that inscribes the translator's voice within the text and participates in shaping the intellectual history of the period.

5.4.6 Conclusive Remarks

The comparative analysis of the English translations by Domville (TT1), Glanvill (TT2), and Behn (TT3) demonstrates the interventionist nature of translation in the late seventeenth century. These translators were not passive intermediaries but active cultural agents who reshaped the reception of Fontenelle's *Entretiens* within the intellectual and ideological contexts of England and Ireland. In particular, these translators emerge as co-authors, situating their work at the intersection of literary creativity and cultural mediation. Their interventions, far from being neutral, reflect their intellectual involvement, religious beliefs, and cultural positioning.

As this case study illustrates, translation is inherently a negotiation with ideology, power, and knowledge. The translators indirectly participated in contemporary philosophical debates while simultaneously protecting themselves from political and religious risk. Their strategies reveal the extent to which translation history is also a history of intellectual struggle, negotiation, and authorship.

In this respect, Behn's Preface on translation, in particular, anticipates modern theories of manipulation, voice, and visibility. Her interventions are especially illuminating: they exemplify what Lefevere and the so-called "Manipulation School" later theorised as the universal dimension of translation, namely, rewriting shaped by ideology, poetics, and patronage. The techniques employed across these translations include omission, domestication, simplification, clarification, explicitation, and self-censorship, each applied in varying degrees.

A revealing example emerges in the transmission of Fontenelle's description of lunar topography, which reproduces scientific inaccuracies by conflating Riccioli's and Hevelius's incompatible selenographic systems. All three translators reproduce these inconsistencies without comment, thereby demonstrating a selective fidelity: they perpetuate scientific errors, yet show greater caution when dealing with politically or religiously sensitive material. Similarly, in Fontenelle's metaphor comparing lunar maps to city streets, Glanvill (TT2) domesticates the reference by replacing Paris with London, adapting the text to an English readership, whereas Domville (TT1) and Behn (TT3) preserve the original Parisian reference.

Domville and Glanvill frequently softened or domesticated references to align the text with English cultural expectations. Behn, by contrast, positioned herself more decisively within contemporary intellectual debates. She embraced Fontenelle's scientific rationalism but diverged from his perceived "paganism" (meaning atheism), which conflicted with her religious convictions. Her self-censorship is evident in the omission of Fontenelle's anti-clerical satire. Yet, she also demonstrates intellectual agency in her *Preface*, where she acknowledges the historical condemnation of Copernican theory as heretical but argues against its incompatibility with Scripture. Notably, her modest disclaimer, "as far as a woman's reasoning can go", simultaneously reflects the gendered constraints of her time and asserts her determination to claim a space for her intellectual commitment.

Taken together, Domville TT1, Glanvill TT2, and Behn TT3 represent three distinct but interrelated cases of translation as cultural intervention. Table 5.7 displays their comparative insights. Their work exemplifies the translator's dual role as mediator and author, reminding us that translation is never neutral. Ultimately, this

Table 5.7 Comparative insights of Domville TT1, Glanvill TT2 and Behn TT3

Aspect	Domville TT1 (1687)	Glanvill TT2 (1688)	Behn TT3 (1688)
Translator identity	Gentleman translator, little intellectual self-assertion; maintains anonymity of voice	Philosopher and theologian; positions himself as interpreter of science in harmony with faith	England's first professional woman writer; openly signs "Mrs. A. Behn," asserting personal intellectual authority
Preface	Minimal; presents the work as polite entertainment and conversational astronomy	Frames the text within orthodox Christianity; emphasizes harmony of natural philosophy with divine providence	Bold *Tanslator's preface*; addresses Copernican controversies, separates scripture from science, argues for fideism and intellectual openness
Theological position	Avoids theological issues, downplays potential heterodoxy	Cautious reconciliation: Science is legitimate but always under god's sovereignty	Negotiates tension embraces rationalism but insists the bible concerns salvation, not astronomy; challenges Jesuit anti-Copernican readings
Translation strategy	Literal, cautious, close to the French; limited interventions	Mix of fidelity and adaptation; clarifies passages for English readership, softens heterodox tones	Interventions through explicitation, corrections, and annotations; renders astronomy accessible and pedagogical

(continued)

Table 5.7 (continued)

Aspect	Domville TT1 (1687)	Glanvill TT2 (1688)	Behn TT3 (1688)
Audience orientation	General readers seeking amusement and fashionable knowledge; avoids controversy	Educated readership; appeals to philosophically minded but religiously cautious audience	Broad readership including women; encourages inquiry and debate, positions translation as cultural contribution
Historical context & role	First introduction of Fontenelle to English readers; establishes initial reception	Published amid glorious revolution; reflects desire to align new science with religious and social order	Proto-enlightenment intervention; asserts women's intellectual presence, mediates between reason and revelation at a crucial cultural moment
Cultural significance	Opens the path for later translations, but intellectually modest	Deepens English engagement with philosophy of science; stresses reconciliation with orthodoxy	Boldest and most innovative; integrates science, faith, and gendered authorship into enlightenment discourse

Source: Our original processing.

study highlights the historical significance of translation as both a literary form and a means of cultural mediation. It demonstrates how translations not only transmit texts but also actively contribute to the history of ideas, shaping intellectual and cultural discourses as profoundly as original works. Domville TT1 has the merit of establishing initial reception, Glanville TT2 softens the heterodox tones and stresses reconciliation with orthodoxy, and Behn TT3 distinguishes her Preface as an intellectual engagement and translation enriched with explicitation, corrections, and a pedagogical attitude.

References

Primary Sources

Behn, Aphra 1688. TT3: *A Discovery of New Worlds*. From French. Made English by Mrs. A. Behn. To which is prefixed a Preface, by way of essay on translated prose; wherein the arguments of Father Tacquet, and others, against the System of Coprnicus (as to the Motion of the Earth) are likewise considered, and answers: Wholly new. London, printers for William Canning, at his Shop in the Temple-Cloysters.

Domville, William. 1687. TT1: *A Discourse of the Plurality of Worlds*, written in French by the most ingenious Author of the *Dialogues of the Dead*, and translated into English by Sir W.D. Knight. Dublin: Printed by Andr. Crook and Sam. Helsham for William Norman bookbinder to His Grace the Duke of Ormond.

Fontenelle, Bernard le Bovier de Fontenelle. 1686. ST: *Entretiens sur la pluralité des mondes*. Paris: Veuve Blageart. Registered on Livre de la Communauté des Libraires & Imprimeurs de Paris, on 22 January 1686. Printed on 8 March 1686.

Glanvill, J. 1688. TT2: *A Plurality of Worlds*, written in French by the author of the *Dialogues of the dead*; translated into English by Mr. Glanvill. London: Printed for R. Bentley and S. Magnes.

Secondary Sources

Baker, Mona. 1993. Corpus Linguistics and Translation Studies. Implications and Applications. In *Text and Technology: In Honour of John Sinclair*, ed. Mona Baker, Gill Francis, and Elena Tognini-Bonelli, 233–252. Amsterdam: John Benjamins Publishing Company.

Baker, Mona. 2000. Towards a Methodology for Investigating the Style of a Literary Translator. *Target* 12 (2): 241–266.

Berman, Antoine. 1985. La traduction comme épreuve de l'étranger. *Texte* 4: 67–81 (English Translation Entitled "Translation and the Trial of the Foreign", by Lawrence Venuti published in Venuti, 2012: 240–253).

Boot, Peter. 2009. *Mesotext: Digitized Emblems, Modelled Annotations and Humanities Scholarship*. Amsterdam: Amsterdam University Press.

Borrelli, Alfonso. 1666. *Theoricae mediceorum planetarum ex causis physicis deductae.* [Theories of the Medici's Planets Derived from Physical Causes.] Florence: Typographia S.M.D.

Cipriani, Anna Maria. 2020. The Impact of Censorship on Translating and Publishing Virginia Woolf in Italy in the 1930s. *Translation Matters* 2 (2): 83–96.

Cipriani, Anna Maria. 2022. The Translator's Presence in (Re)translation of to the Lighthouse into Italian: A Corpus-driven Study. *Corpora* 17 (3): 423–448.

Cipriani, Anna Maria. 2023. *Literary Digital Stylistics in Translation Studies*. Singapore: Springer Nature.

Cottegnies, Line. 2003. The Translator as Critics: Aphra Behn's Translation of Fontenelle's *A Discovery of New Worlds* (1688). *Restoration: Studies in English Literary Culture, 1660–1700* 27 (1): 23–38.

Cottegnies, Line. 2004. Aphra Behn's French translations. In *The Cambridge Companion to Aphra Behn*, ed. Derek Hughes and Janet Todd, 221–234. Cambridge, UK: Cambridge University Press.

Cottegnies, Line. 2024. Aphra Behn's use of *translation*: Mediation, Adaptation, and Emulation in a Cross-Channel Perspective. *Sederi* 34 (2): 31–52.

Curry, Niall, and Tony McEnery. 2025. The Past, Present, and Future of Corpus and Translation Studies. In *Routledge Handbook of Corpus Translation Studies*, ed. Defeng Li and John Corbett. London: Routledge.

Dick, Steve. 1980. The Origins of the Extraterrestrial Life Debate and its Relation to the Scientific revolution. *Journal of the History of Ideas* 41 (1): 3–27.

Dryden, John (edited by). 1680. *Ovid's Epistles, Translated by Several Hands*. London: Jacob Tonson.

Even-Zohar, Itamar. 1978. The Position of Translated Literature with the Literary Polysystem. In *Literature and Translation: New Perspectives in Literary Studies with a Basic Bibliography of Books on Translation Studies*, ed. J. Holmes, J. Lambert, and R. van den Broek, 117–127. Leuven: ACCO. Reprinted in me. Even-Zohar (ed.), *Papers in Historical Poetics*, Tel Aviv: The Porter Institute, 21–27. Also, in Venuti (ed.) (2012: 162–167).

Ferguson, Margaret. 2008. "With All Due Reverence and Respect to the Word of God": Aphra Behn as Skeptical Reader of the Bible and Critical Translator of Fontenelle. In *Reading Women. Literacy, Authorship, and Culture in the Atlantic World, 1500–1800*, ed. H. Brayman Hackel and C. E. Kelly, 199–216. Philadelphia, PA: University of Pennsylvania Press.

Galilei, Galileo. 1632. *Dialogo sopra i due massimi sistemi del mondo tolemaico e copernicano*. Fiorenza [Florence]: Gio. Batista Landini. (1st Engl. trans. by Thomas Salusbury: *The Systeme of the World: in Four Dialogues. Wherein the Two Grand Systemes of Ptolomy and Copernicus are largely discoursed of.* London: William Leybourn, 1661. 2nd Engl. trans. by Stillman Drake. Berkeley, CA: University of California Press, 1953.)

Gill, Catie. 2020. The Bible and its Exegesis in Aphra Behn's "An Essay on Translated Prose" (1688)'. *Women's Writing* 27 (3): 310–324.

Hermans, Theo. 1985. Introducing: Translation Studies and a New Paradigm. In *The Manipulation of Literature: Studies in Literary Translation*, ed. T. Hermans, 7–15. London and Sidney: Croom Helm.
Hermans, Theo. 1996. The Translator's Voice in Translated Narrative. *Target* 8:23–48.
Hermans, Theo. 2007. Literary Translation. In *A Companion to Translation Studies*, ed. P. Kuhiwczak and K. Littau, 77–91. Clevedon: Multilingual Matters Ltd.
Hooykaas, R. 1972. *Religion and the Rise of Modern Science*. Edinburgh and London: Scottish Academic.
House, Juliane. 2015. *Translation Quality Assessment: Past and Present*. London/New York: Routledge.
House, Juliane. 2016. *Translation as Communication Across Languages and Cultures*. London and New York: Routledge.
Jockers, Mathew L. 2014. *Text Analysis with R for Students of Literature*. Heidelberg: Springer.
Jones, Francis R. 2020 [2009]. Literary Translation. In *Routledge Encyclopedia of Translation Studies*, ed. M. Baker and G. Saldanha, 3rd ed., 294–299. London: Routledge.
Kepler, Johannes. 1609. *Astronomia Nova*. Prague (Pragae) and Heidelberg: Gotthard Vögelin.
Klaudy, K. 1998. Explicitation. In *Encyclopedia of Translation Studies*, ed. M. Baker and G. Saldanha, 80–85. London: Routledge.
Laplace, Pierre-Simon. 1796. *Exposition du système du monde*. Paris: Cercle-Social.
Lefevere, André. 1985. Why waste out time on rewrites? The trouble of interpretation and the role of rewriting in an alternative paradigm. In *The Manipulation of Literature*, ed. Theo Hermans, 215–243. Abingdon/Oxon/New York: Routledge.
Lefevere, André. 1992. *Translation, Rewriting, and the Manipulation of Literary Fame*. London/New York: Routledge.
Lind, Sarah. 2007. Translation Universals (or Laws, or Tendencies, or Probabilities, or …?). *TIC Talk* 63: https://translation.bible/wp-content/uploads/2024/05/tt63.pdf.
Mellinger, Christopher D., and Thomas A. Hanson. 2017. *Quantitative Research Methods in Translation and Interpreting Studies*. London/New York: Routledge.
Mills, Amelia. 2025. Overcoming Barriers to Educated Discourse: A *Discovery of New Worlds* (1688), Translation, and Aphra Behn's "Passionate thirst of knowledge of the mind". *Women's Writing* 32 (2): 195–209.
Moretti, Franco. 2000. Conjectures on World Literature. *New Left Review* 1:54–68.
Moretti, Franco. 2013. *Distant Reading*. London: Verso Books.
Moretti, Franco. 2022. *Falso movimento. La svolta quantitativa nello studio della letteratura.* [*False Movement. The Quantitative Turn in the Study of Literature.*] Milan: Nottetempo.
Munday, Jeremy. 2016. *Introducing Translation Studies: Theories and Applications*. 4th ed. London/New York: Routledge.
Newton, Isaac. 1684. *De Motu Corporum*. London: Royal Society.
Newton, Isaac. 1687. *Philosophiae Naturalis Principia Mathematica*. Londinium [London]: Jussu Societatis Ragiae ac Typis Josephi Streater [by order of the Royal Society and the Printing House of Joseph Streater].
Ping, Yuan. 2024. Book Review: *Literary Digital Stylistics in Translation Studies* by Anna Maria Cipriani. *Digital Scholarship in the Humanities* 39 (2): 807–809.
Poisson, Siméon Denis. 1813. Remarques sur une équation qui se présente dans la théorie des attractions des sphéroïds. *Nouveau Bulletin de la Société Philomatique de Paris* 3 (75): 388–392.
Pym, Anthony. 1998. *Method in Translation History*. Manchester: S. Jerome Publishing.
Robinson, Douglas. 2002. *Western Translation Theory, from Herodotus to Nietzsche*. 2nd ed. Manchester: St. Jerome Publishing.
Saldanha, G. 2008. Explicitation revisited: Bringing the Reader into the Picture. *Trans-Kom* 1 (1): 20–35.
Schleiermacher, Friedrich. 1813. Ueber die verschiedenen Methden des Uebersetzens. In *Schriften und Entwürfe*, vol. 11., ed. M. Rössler with L. Emersleben. Reprinted in *Kritische*

Gesamtausgabe, ed. H. Fischer, U. Barth, K. Cramer, G. Meckenstock, K.-V. Selge, 67–93 Berlin: Walter de Gruyter, 2002. Translated by Susan Bernofsky: On the different methods of translating. In *The Translation Studies Reader,* by L. Venuti, 43–63. Routledge. 2012: London/ New York.

Schnell, Lisa. 2004. Aphra Behn, Fontenelle's *A Discovery of New Worlds* (1688). In *Reading Early Modern Women: An Anthology of Texts in Manuscript and Print, 1500–1700*, ed. H. Ostovich and E. Sauer, 350–351. New York: Routledge.

Schwahn, Walter, ed. (1994 [1928]) *Laurentii Vallee de Falso Credita et Ementita Constantini Donatione Declamatio*. Rome: Bibliotheca Scriptorum Graecorum et Romanorum Teubneriana.

Sprat, Thomas. 1667. *History of the Royal Society of London, for the Improving of Natural Knowledge.* London: J. Martin and J. Allestry.

Steiner, Thomas R. 1975. *English Translation Theory 1650–1800*. Assen: Van Gorcum.

Tahir, Gürcağlar. 2020 [2009] Retranslation. In *Routledge Encyclopedia of Translation Studies,* ed. M.B. Baker and G. Saldanha, 484–490. London: Routledge.

Thomas, Donald. 1969. *A Long Time Burning. The History of Literary Censorship in England.* London: Routledge & Kegan Paul.

Todd, Janet. 1993. *The Works of Aphra Behn*. Vol. 4. London: Pickering and Chatto.

Todd, Janet. 2000. *The Secret Life of Aphra Behn*. London/New York/ Sydney: Pandora.

Toury, Gideon. 1978. The Nature and Role of Norms in Translation. In *Literature and Translation*, ed. J. S. Holmes, J. Lambert, and R. van den Broek, 83–100. Leuven: ACCO. Reprinted in Lawrence Venuti (ed.), *The Translation Studies Reader*. Abingdon/Oxon: Routledge, 2012, 168–181.

Toury, Gideon. 2012 [1995]. *Descriptive Translation Studies – And Beyond*, 2nd ed. Amsterdam/ Philadelphia: John Benjamins.

Turnball, H. W., ed. 1960. *The Correspondence of Isaac Newton, Vol. II: 1676–1687*. Cambridge: Cambridge University Press.

Vanderauwera, Rita. 1985. *Dutch Novels Translated into English: The Transformation of a "Minority" Literature*. Amsterdam: Rodopi.

Venuti, Lawrence. 1998. *The Scandals of Translation. Towards an Ethic of Difference*. London. Routledge.

Venuti, Lawrence. 2008 [1995]. *The Translator's Invisibility. A History of Translation*. 2nd ed. London/New York: Routledge.

Venuti, Lawrence. 2012 [2000]. *The Translation Studies Reader*. 3rd ed. Abington/Oxon/New York: Routledge.

Vertesi, Janet. 2007. Picturing the Moon: Hevelius's and Riccioli's Visual Debate. *Studies in History and Philosophy of Science Part A* 38 (2): 401–421.

Whitaker, Ewen A. 2008. *Mapping and Naming the Moon*. Cambridge, UK: Cambridge University Press.

Whiteside, D. T. 1991. The Prehistory of the *Principia* from 1664 to 1686. *Notes and Records of the Royal Society of London* 45:11–61.

Wilkins, John. 1684 [1638]. *A Discovery of a New World*, 4th edition. London: John Gillibrand.

Xu, Han, and Yujie Huang. 2025. Corpus-based Translation and Interpreting Studies in the Age of AI: Innovations and Challenges. In *Translation Studies in the Age of Artificial Intelligence*, ed. S. Sun, K. Liu, and R. Moratto. London: Routledge.

Zhang, Xiaomin. 2025. Corpus-Based Studies of Explicitation. In *Routledge Handbook of Corpus Translation Studies*, ed. Defeng Li and John Corbett, 254–268. London: Routledge.

Zwischenberger, Cornelia. 2020. Norms. In *Routledge Encyclopedia of Translation Studies*, ed. M. Baker and G. Saldanha, 3rd ed., 375–380. London/New York: Routledge.

Zanettin, Federico. 2013. Corpus Methods for Descriptive Translation Studies. *Procedia - Social and Behavioral Sciences* 95: 20-32.

Zaixi, Tan. 2019. The Fuzzy Interface Between Censorship and Self-Censorship in Translation. *Translation and Interpretative Studies* 14 (1): 39–60.

References

Chapter 6
Conclusive Remarks

There are two opposing lines of reasoning surrounding everything.

Protagoras (486–411 BC)

6.1 Summing up

Generative Artificial Intelligence (GenAI) is redefining *Corpus Translation Studies* (CTS) and *Literary Digital Stylistics* (LDS) by extending automation beyond mechanical processing to interpretative annotation. Tasks once performed manually—such as identifying translation shifts, ideological manipulation, or stylistic transformations—can now be automatically generated, with GenAI providing explanatory metadata that justifies each annotation. This technology enables the large-scale analysis of multilingual corpora with unprecedented efficiency and interpretative depth.

Comparing outputs from multiple iterations or across systems—e.g., ChatGPT, Claude, and Gemini—facilitates cross-validation, increasing reliability and revealing potential biases embedded in individual models. In this context, fluctuation becomes an epistemic resource rather than a limitation. Nevertheless, automation alone cannot integrate textual evidence within the broader historical and cultural matrices that define translation practice; human interpretation remains indispensable.

The case study of the early English translations of Fontenelle's *Entretiens sur la pluralité des mondes* demonstrates these advantages. Combining computational pattern recognition with contextual human analysis yields both broader empirical coverage and more nuanced interpretation. Through this synergy, GenAI fosters a new methodological equilibrium that enhances efficiency without compromising

A. M. Cipriani, F. Milana, *AI-Powered Corpus Translation Studies at Work*,
New Frontiers in Translation Studies,
https://doi.org/10.1007/978-981-95-5933-6_6

scholarly rigour. Due to space constraints, only a selection of instances of universals has been presented to illustrate the effectiveness of the methodology.[1]

In the present study, we have focused solely on the descriptive comparisons of the main universals of literary translation, excluding other stylistic features of narrative literature, such as those discussed by Lefevere (1992a, b), Scholes et al. (2006), and Jones (2020).[2] Applied to Fontenelle's translations, GenAI produced extensive datasets of annotated shifts unattainable through manual means alone. These annotations, combined with expert contextualisation, illuminate both macro- and micro-level studies of stylistic strategies of translations. The integration of generative annotation and human interpretation allows a dual-scale reading—empirical and hermeneutic—linking linguistic data to ideological and historical meaning.

Future CTS and LDS workflows will likely evolve from linear to iterative models of collaboration. Instead of a sequential process where automation precedes interpretation, a cyclical machine-human exchange emerges: AI proposes provisional hypotheses, scholars validate and contextualise them, and refined insights inform subsequent computational stages. This feedback loop promotes conceptual precision and methodological transparency, ensuring that interpretative categories evolve alongside technological innovation.

The incorporation of GenAI into CTS and LDS marks a paradigmatic shift towards expansive, data-rich, and critically engaged scholarship. But genuine understanding remains anchored in human expertise. The Fontenelle's translation case study exemplifies how this integration reconfigures both the scale and depth of analysis, demonstrating how humanistic inquiry and computational intelligence can converge to advance translation studies in the present digital age.

6.2 Empirical Application

This study has analysed how Domville, Glanvill, and Behn reinterpreted Fontenelle's *Entretiens*, by systematically combining corpus quantitative techniques with qualitative close reading. The methodological design integrates type–token ratios, keyword and lexical examination, dispersion profiles, and word-cloud visualisation to identify distinctive stylistic tendencies across the three translations. The computational indicators were complemented with targeted micro-analysis of salient textual segments, thereby ensuring that patterns suggested by the macro-analysis were corroborated by textual scrutiny.

---

[1] All tagged results are available for download at http://fmilana.com along with all created materials online for further research.

[2] Part of those typical features are empirically inquired by Cipriani (2023) in translations of Virginia Woolf's *To the Lighthouse* using the LDS approach. The application of the AI-powered CTS to this last study could considerably upscale the results previously obtained with manual annotation.

Quantitative metrics reveal markedly differentiated translator profiles. Domville TT1 emerges as the most lexically constrained and stylistically restrained; his translation is characterised by limited variation and a predominantly functional vocabulary, suggesting a deliberate effort to reproduce the French text with minimal stylistic embellishment. Glanvill TT2 has a propensity to domesticate French conceptual structures for an English readership, signalling an intention to render the text rhetorically accessible and culturally aligned with Restoration discourse. Behn's translation, by contrast, demonstrates the highest lexical amplitude and is notably the most expansive in volume. Her version retains numerous French scientific terms and exhibits a sustained creative and foreignising orientation.

Macro-level metrics reinforce these distinctions. All three translations display an overall tendency toward simplification, consistent with seventeenth-century literary norms in the transfer of scientific prose. Yet the translators modulate simplification to differing degrees. Behn TT3, despite its elaboration, records the highest repetition rate, followed by Domville TT1 and Glanvill TT2, both of which show a lower rate of repeated words than Behn. This pattern suggests that the three translators pursued divergent balances between fidelity, rhetorical amplification, and stylistic fluency. Specialised corpus tools further detected significant lexical transitions—particularly between the "Second" and "Third Night"—coinciding with the growing conceptual density of the source text as it progresses toward cosmological speculation.

Micro-level investigation provides deeper insight into ideological and stylistic strategies. Domville TT1 adheres closely to the French original, maintaining its philosophical tone and preserving argumentative structure. Glanvill TT2, more ideologically cautious, softens or omits passages touching on theological and political sensitivities, thus aligning the text with post-Restoration orthodoxy and reinforcing cultural stabilisation following decades of upheaval. Behn TT3 adopts a distinctive literary stance: whilst practising selective self-censorship, she enriches the dialogue with moral reflection, rhetorical ornament, and heightened dramatic energy. This creative appropriation transforms Fontenelle's polite scientific conversation into a vividly imaginative text, traversing the boundaries between philosophical exposition and narrative entertainment.

In synthesis, these findings confirm that Domville TT1 embodies fidelity with minimal adaptation, Glanvill TT2 represents domestication and ideological mediation, and Behn TT3 exemplifies literary expansion with caution. The study demonstrates that integrating digital stylistic tools with hermeneutic analysis affords a more substantiated understanding of stylistic agency, ideological positioning, and the early English reception of scientific modernity. It is also worth noting that some of the historically enthusiastic reception of Behn's approach requires reassessment in light of systematic corpus evidence, which situates her intervention within a more nuanced and historically grounded perspective.

6.3 Different Heuristic Interpretations

Fontenelle's *Entretiens* emerged at a pivotal juncture in the Scientific Revolution, a period in which speculative cosmology coexisted with the gradual institutionalisation of empirical science. By drawing on the works of Copernicus, Kepler, Galileo, and especially Descartes, Fontenelle advanced a rational and imaginative exploration of the cosmos at a time when observational technologies and experimental protocols were still in their early stages of development. Institutions such as the Royal Society had only recently begun to formalise observational standards, which would progressively provide empirical scaffolding for hypotheses that initially relied on intellectual conjecture and theorising. In this respect, *Entretiens* epitomises the fertile tension between philosophical reasoning and emerging empirical culture.

Newton's *Principia* represented a decisive turning point by mathematically codifying universal gravitation, which had previously been conjectured by Copernicus, Kepler, and Galileo, while challenging Descartes's mechanical vortices. The coexistence of these competing explanatory frameworks generated profound debate throughout the late seventeenth and early eighteenth centuries. Yet interpretive hesitation persisted: even at the age of ninety-five, Fontenelle continued to question the unexplained nature of gravitational force within Newton's own *hypotheses non fingo*. As René Thom (1972: 8) famously remarked, Descartes "explained everything and calculated nothing," whereas Newton "calculated everything and explained nothing"—a juxtaposition that captures the era's epistemic tension only eased by Einstein's general relativity in the twentieth century.

Within this intellectual milieu, the *Entretiens* stands as a paradigmatic document that negotiates speculative audacity with epistemic humility. Through a refined dialogic form addressed to a broad readership—including women—Fontenelle popularised the plurality of worlds, championed rational inquiry over theological determinism, and articulated a forward-looking vision of Enlightenment progress. His conception of progress as the animating force of history, emphasised by Špelda (2024), underscores his enduring faith in reason as the engine of human advancement.

However, the three translators diverge significantly from Fontenelle's engagement with contemporary scientific controversy. None explicitly addresses the debate regarding celestial mechanics central to the original text. Behn, for instance, opts to maintain a conciliatory stance by reconciling the Copernican revolution with biblical interpretation, echoing John Wilkins's position—albeit without naming him. This reinterpretation stands in contrast to recent apologetic scholarship on Aphra Behn, which has tended to overlook her strategic alignment with religious literature.

6.4 New Problems

The integration of GenAI assistance into translation research introduces several methodological and epistemological considerations that require scrutiny. Human supervision of GenAI outputs, although indispensable, has inherent limitations and cannot entirely eliminate potential errors or biases. As a result, scholarly rigour demands that findings derived from AI-supported inquiry be subject to replication, critical review, and independent verification by other researchers. In this study, three separate AI systems (Chat GPT-4, Claude-3.7, and Gemini-2.5) were employed to cross-check, triangulate, and validate the results displayed in tables. Nevertheless, the involvement of a single research team underscores the need for collaborative research networks to enhance transparency, replicability, and accountability in AI-powered translation studies.

A further set of methodological concerns pertains to the subjectivity of historical and socio-cultural interpretation. Primary sources and scholarly traditions inevitably reflect established epistemic paradigms and ideological assumptions. As the familiar dictum reminds us, "history is always young, its youth preserved by fresh enquiry," yet historical narratives are shaped by the interpretative frameworks and biases of the sources that transmit them. This raises perennial questions regarding how inherited scholarly discourses mediate contemporary research and how such mediation influences our understanding of the past. Moreover, new archival discoveries and digital corpora are themselves embedded in ideological and epistemic contexts, reinforcing what may be termed the "multiple mediation problem." As discussed earlier, the optimal supervisory strategies for AI systems must therefore take into account the layered subjectivities of both historical sources and contemporary interpretation. The open-source data used in this study could, in principle, be re-processed in light of new evidence or future LLM training runs, further complicating questions of stability and reproducibility.

A further category of challenges concerns ideological influences, particularly gender-based interpretations of Aphra Behn's work. AI systems operate upon vast bodies of existing scholarship and may inadvertently reproduce dominant academic tendencies, including apologetic or celebratory narratives. Scholarship that foregrounds feminist or political readings of Behn must thus be contextualised within her specific historical milieu; as noted, her own intellectual and cultural standpoint may not align neatly with contemporary interpretative agendas. AI-assisted analysis provides an additional check by examining whether recent literature exhibits internal consistency or reflects ideological steering.

GenAI models often reflect the biases present in their training corpora, amplifying prevailing scholarly trends while overlooking critical counter-evidence. This risk parallels limitations within academic peer review, where narrow reviewer pools and dominant theoretical orthodoxies may inadvertently marginalise innovative or revisionist perspectives. Indeed, when evaluating Behn's translation of Fontenelle's *Entretiens*, GenAI systems initially reproduced prevailing positive assessments in the secondary literature, echoing apologetic academic literature and missing flaws.

Such instances illustrate the necessity of grounding AI-mediated interpretations in direct engagement with primary sources and the historical record.

Finally, philosophical debates concerning the nature of scientific reasoning intersect with these methodological concerns. The seventeenth-century intellectual division between Cartesian mechanism and Newtonian mathematical empiricism, as earlier recalled, shapes contemporary readings of Fontenelle's philosophical position and his steadfast attachment to Cartesianism. Behn's critique of Fontenelle's openness to the ignorant in natural philosophy further illuminates tensions between epistemic authority, gendered discourse, and emergent scientific rationality. This convergence of history, ideology, and philosophy reveals the layered complexity of AI-assisted research in humanities. It demonstrates that technological innovation does not mitigate but rather accentuates the need for critical, historically informed scholarly judgement.

6.5 Future Directions

This framework employs large language models (LLMs) to enhance corpus translation studies, moving the field beyond the constraints of exclusively manual analysis. While not definitive, the approach provides a methodological prototype and establishes a foundation for future developments. These include domain-specific fine-tuning, interactive machine learning, and heightened model transparency: three pillars that will shape the maturation of AI within translation studies and the broader digital humanities.

A primary direction for continued research is to improve performance and reliability systematically. Although current LLMs demonstrate notable flexibility, they still struggle with the subtle, historically contextual, and culturally sensitive interpretative judgments essential in CTS. Literary translation is fundamentally heuristic; it prioritises inference, nuance, and intertextual awareness rather than direct linguistic alignment. Consequently, while general-purpose models are valuable exploratory tools, they currently lack the precision required for specialised scholarly inquiry. Targeted fine-tuning of open-source LLMs on human-curated and discipline-specific corpora should therefore take priority. Such training must focus on phenomena central to translation scholarship, such as "simplification, explicitation, domestication, and self-censorship", and emphasise hermeneutic sensitivity.

The production of annotated corpora constitutes a distinctly scholarly contribution. Researchers should either generate these annotations or supervise their construction to ensure methodological coherence with the selected theoretical framework. This not only guarantees fidelity to scholarly priorities but also ensures that AI systems internalise the researcher's interpretive stance. Such a framework preserves critical agency and methodological integrity while providing the scalability needed to engage large textual datasets; an increasingly indispensable feature in humanities-oriented computational research.

Interactive machine learning (IML) presents another promising avenue. Unlike conventional supervised models, IML integrates iterative human feedback into the model refinement process, thereby enabling researchers to continuously adjust outputs, correct interpretative errors, and retrain models. Recent studies, including Milana (2025) and Milana et al. (2025), have demonstrated the effectiveness of IML in qualitative contexts, allowing scholars to tailor models to corpus-specific requirements. For CTS, this iterative feedback loop strengthens interpretive control, enhances transparency, and addresses limitations inherent in systems that might otherwise assign opaque categories to complex historical texts.

Improving explainability and transparency remains essential. Initial experiments with model-generated explanations signal progress, yet substantially more work is necessary before AI can command trust in specialised translation research. The integration of explainable AI (XAI) techniques, such as LIME, SHAP, and Integrated Gradients, which have already proven effective in other domains, can illuminate the internal logic of model decisions. Tools like token-level heat maps can visually identify linguistic forms influencing classifications, offering scholars an immediate and interpretable analytic interface.

XAI would enable scholars to scrutinise and, when necessary, dispute algorithmic interpretations, defending humanistic interpretive sovereignty. It would encourage more informed engagement with computational methods, narrowing the divide between traditional philological practice and algorithmic inference. Ultimately, implementing XAI in CTS would reinforce methodological robustness and promote a constructive dialogue between digital and classical scholarship, ensuring that computational innovation remains grounded in rigorous and critically reflective humanistic inquiry.

References

Cipriani, Anna Maria. 2023. *Literary Digital Stylistics in Translation Studies*. Singapore: Springer.

Jones, Francis R. 2020. Literary Translation. In *Routledge Encyclopedia of Translation Studies*, ed. M. Baker and G. Saldanha, 294–299. London/New York: Routledge.

Lefevere, André. 1992a. *Translating Literature: Practice and Theory in a Comparative Context*. New York: The Modern Language Association of America.

Lefevere, André. 1992b. *Translation, Rewriting, and the Manipulation of Literary Fame*. London/New York: Routledge.

Milana, Federico. 2025. *Evaluating Interaction with Machine Learning Text Classifiers and Interpretability Techniques*. PhD dissertation. London: University College London.

Milana, Federico, Enrico Costanza, Mirco Musolesi, and Amid Ayobi. 2025. Understanding interaction with machine learning through a thematic analysis coding assistant: A user study. *Proceedings of the ACM on Human-Computer Interaction* 9(2): 1-35.

Scholes, Robert, James Phelan, and Robert Kellogg. 2006. *The Nature of Narrative*. Oxford: Oxford University Press.

Špelda, Daniel. 2024. *The Origin of the Idea of Scientific Progress: Bernard de Fontenelle and His Contemporaries*. Cham: Springer.

Thom, René. 1972. *Stabilité structurelle et morphogénèse. Essay d'une théorie géneral des modèles*. Paris: InterEditions. Trans. D. H. Fowler, *Structural Stability and Morphogenesis: An Outline of a General Theory of Models*. Reading, MA: W.A. Benjamin, 1975.

Bibliography

Bode, Katerine, and Charlotte Bradley. 2025. Computational Literary Studies and AI. In *The Routledge Handbook of AI and Literature*, ed. W. Slocombe and G. Liveley, 235–243. Abingdon/Oxon/New York: Routledge.

Dick, Steve. 1980. The Origins of the Extraterrestrial Life Debate and its Relation to the Scientific revolution. *Journal of the History of Ideas* 41 (1): 3–27.

Dryden, John (edited by). 1680. *Ovid's Epistles, Translated by Several Hands*. London: Jacob Tonson.

Dubreuil, Laurent. 2025. *Humanities in the Time of AI*. Minneapolis: University of Minnesota Press.

Galilei, Galileo. 1632. *Dialogo sopra i due massimi sistemi del mondo tolemaico e copernicano*. Fiorenza [Florence]: Gio. Batista Landini. (1st Engl. trans. by Thomas Salusbury: *The Systeme of the World: in Four Dialogues. Wherein the Two Grand Systemes of Ptolomy and Copernicus are largely discoursed of*. London: William Leybourn, 1661. 2nd Engl. trans. by Stillman Drake. Berkeley, CA: University of California Press, 1953.)

Gavin, Dana J. 2025. *Generative AI and the Future of the Humanities*. Cham, Switzerland: Springer Nature.

Ghosal, Torsa. 2025. Towards Narrative AI Studies. In *The Routledge Handbook of AI and Literature*, ed. W. Slocombe and G. Liveley, 269–287. Abingdon/Oxon/New York: Routledge.

Gillings, Mathew, and Sylvia Jaworska. 2025. How Humans and Machines Identify Discourse Topics: A Methodological Triangulation. *Applied Corpus Linguistics* 5:100121.

Hooykaas, R. 1972. *Religion and the Rise of Modern Science*. Edinburgh and London: Scottish Academic.

House, Juliane. 2016. *Translation as Communication Across Languages and Cultures*. London and New York: Routledge.

Jain, Vishal, Archan Mitra, and Sanchita Paul. 2026. AI-Powered Literary Analysis: Redefining Themes, Symbolism, and Emotional Resonance in Contemporary Literature. In , ed. Role of AI in Producing, Evaluating, and Interpreting Literary Materials and A. Asrifan, 1–26. Hershey: IGI Global, Scientific Publishing. Forthcoming.

Kwok, Ho Ling, Yining Shi, Xu Han, Dechao Li, and Kanglong Liu. 2025. GenAI as a Translation Assistant? A Corpus-Based Study on Lexical and Syntactic Complexity of GPT-Post-Edited Learner Translation. *System* 130:103618.

Laplace, Pierre-Simon. 1796. *Exposition du système du monde*. Paris: Cercle-Social.

Liveley, Genevieve. 2025. Electricity and Alchemy: (Un)Explainable AI and (Un)Explainable Literature. In *The Routledge Handbook of AI and Literature*, ed. W. Slocombe and G. Liveley, 256–265. Abingdon/Oxon/New York: Routledge.

A. M. Cipriani, F. Milana, *AI-Powered Corpus Translation Studies at Work*,
New Frontiers in Translation Studies,
https://doi.org/10.1007/978-981-95-5933-6

Newton, Isaac. 1687. *Philosophiae Naturalis Principia Mathematica.* Londinium [London]: Jussu Societatis Ragiae ac Typis Josephi Streater [by order of the Royal Society and the Printing House of Joseph Streater].

Poisson, Siméon Denis. 1813. Remarques sur une équation qui se présente dans la théorie des attractions des sphéroïds. *Nouveau Bulletin de la Société Philomatique de Paris* 3 (75): 388–392.

Rapi, Muhammad. 2026. Interpreting Literature through an AI Lens: Cross-Cultural Dynamics and Insights. In , ed. Role of AI in Producing, Evaluating, and Interpreting Literary Materials and A. Asrifan, 97–122. Hershey: IGI Global, Scientific Publishing. Forthcoming.

Satpathy, Ipsecta. 2026. Artificial Intelligence in Cultural and Historical Literary Analysis. In *Role of AI in Producing, Evaluating, and Interpreting Literary Materials* ed. A. Asrifan, 205–224. Hershey: IGI Global, Scientific Publishing. Forthcoming.

Slocombe, Will. 2025. AIs Reading AI Narratives? In *The Routledge Handbook of AI and Literature*, ed. W. Slocombe and G. Liveley, 149–162. Abingdon/Oxon/New York: Routledge.

Slocombe, Will, and Genevieve Liveley. 2025. Introduction: Why AI and Literature? In *The Routledge Handbook of AI and Literature*, ed. W. Slocombe and G. Liveley, 3–16. Abingdon/Oxon/New York: Routledge.

Veale, Tony. 2025. What to Expect when You're Expecting: On the Creative Potential of Generative AI. In *The Routledge Handbook of AI and Literature*, ed. W. Slocombe and G. Liveley, 244–255. Abingdon/Oxon/New York: Routledge.

Venuti, Lawrence. 1998. *The Scandals of Translation. Towards an Ethic of Difference*. London. Routledge.

Wilkins, John. 1684 [1638]. *A Discovery of a New World*, 4th edition. London: John Gillibrand.

Zanettin, Federico. 2013. Corpus Methods for Descriptive Translation Studies. *Procedia - Social and Behavioral Sciences* 95: 20-32.

Zaixi, Tan. 2019. The Fuzzy Interface Between Censorship and Self-Censorship in Translation. *Translation and Interpretative Studies* 14 (1): 39–60.

Index

A. M. Cipriani, F. Milana, *AI-Powered Corpus Translation Studies at Work*,
New Frontiers in Translation Studies,
https://doi.org/10.1007/978-981-95-5933-6

MIX
Papier aus verantwortungsvollen Quellen
Paper from responsible sources
FSC® C105338
www.fsc.org

If you have any concerns about our products,
you can contact us on
ProductSafety@springernature.com

In case Publisher is established outside the EU,
the EU authorized representative is:
Springer Nature Customer Service Center GmbH
Europaplatz 3, 69115 Heidelberg, Germany

Printed by Libri Plureos GmbH
in Hamburg, Germany